MORE PRAISE FOR *RED MEAT REPUBLIC*

"Specht's evocation of specific places—from the plains and the varied sites of industrial labor to the shops where meat was bought and the tables at which it was eaten—persuasively grounds his story in American culture. This is an impressive and compelling book."

—HARRIET RITVO, author of *Noble Cows and Hybrid Zebras: Essays on Animals and History*

"Peeling the plastic wrap off the cut, Specht uncovers the political economy of modern meat, from violent dispossession to high-stakes struggles over labor and profits."

—KRISTIN L. HOGANSON, author of *The Heartland: An American History*

"Specht's wonderful and impressive research covers an enormous territory. *Red Meat Republic* will reshape historians' approach to this important topic."

—JOHN MACK FARAGHER, author of *Eternity Street: Violence and Justice in Frontier Los Angeles*

RED MEAT REPUBLIC

HISTORIES OF ECONOMIC LIFE

*Jeremy Adelman, Sunil Amrith, and
Emma Rothschild, Series Editors*

A list of titles in this series appears at the back of the book.

Red Meat Republic

A HOOF-TO-TABLE HISTORY OF HOW
BEEF CHANGED AMERICA

JOSHUA SPECHT

PRINCETON UNIVERSITY PRESS

PRINCETON & OXFORD

Published by Princeton University Press
41 William Street, Princeton, New Jersey 08540
6 Oxford Street, Woodstock, Oxfordshire OX20 1TR

press.princeton.edu

Library of Congress Control Number: 2018954992
ISBN 978-0-691-18231-5

British Library Cataloging-in-Publication Data is available

Editorial: Amanda Peery, Eric Crahan and Pamela Weidman
Production Editorial: Jenny Wolkowicki
Jacket design: Chris Ferrante
Jacket art: Alvin Davison, *The Human Body and Health*
    (New York: American Book Company, 1909) 38.
    Clipart, courtesy of FCIT
Production: Jacqueline Poirier
Publicity: Julia Haav and Kathryn Stevens
Copyeditor: Maia Vaswani

This book has been composed in Arno Pro

Printed on acid-free paper. ∞

Printed in the United States of America

10 9 8 7 6 5 4 3 2 1

For my parents

CONTENTS

ACKNOWLEDGMENTS

LIKE MANY ACADEMICS, I read the acknowledgments first. They give a sense of the author's intellectual world, revealing the connections that shaped his or her ideas and approaches. But more than that, acknowledgments provide a sense of the community that makes a book possible. To *Red Meat Republic,* the people below gave intellectual energy and support; to me, the people below gave the emotional strength to see the project through.

This project could not have been written without the help of people at archives across the United States and in Canada. The biggest thanks of all are due to the archivists at the Southwest Collection at Texas Tech University in Lubbock, Texas, and the Panhandle-Plains Historical Museum (PPHM) in Canyon, Texas. Thanks to Randy Vance at the Southwest Collection and Warren Stricker at the PPHM. Without the ranching sources in these archives, the broader story would not have come together. Then again, if these archives were not quite so organized about getting corporate ranching records from Scotland, I might have gotten a funded trip there as well. For the Chicago component of the project, the Newberry Library and the Chicago History Museum provided excellent support. A visit to the Library and Archives Canada in Ottawa made the section on the Grand Trunk Railway possible. The staff of Harvard Business School's Baker Library was invaluable when it came to research suggestions and helping me make sense of nineteenth-century trade cards. Finally, though I never physically visited the Kansas Historical Society, Lisa Keys and Teresa Coble were incredibly generous to a distant academic who always needed one more scan or photocopy.

Thanks also to the organizers and participants of the various conferences and workshops where I presented this material, such as the American Society for Legal History Conference; the "Scales of the Economy" workshop at Sydney University; the American Cultures Workshop at the United States Studies Centre in Sydney; the American Society for Environmental History Conference; the Business History Conference; the Society for Range Management annual meeting; the Massachusetts Historical Society; and the Workshop for the History of the Environment, Agriculture, Technology, and Science. Finally, I did much of the revision of this manuscript as a Ciriacy-Wantrup Postdoctoral Fellow at the University of California, Berkeley. Thanks to everyone I met in the College of Natural Resources' Department of Environmental Policy, Science, and Management, particularly Kathryn De Master, who helped me navigate Berkeley, and Lynn Huntsinger, who recruited me for the Society for Range Management Conference.

Thanks as well to everyone at Princeton University Press. When I first approached Princeton, I had a set of interesting (though rough) chapters and a mostly terrible introduction. Amanda Peery recognized that there was something to the project and helped me turn the introduction into a piece of writing that makes people take notice (or so I hope). Later, she did the same for the full manuscript. I had heard you don't get editing like this anymore, so I consider myself lucky. Thank you to Brigitta van Rheinberg for her advice and good company when we met in Melbourne. Maia Vaswani has been a thorough and thoughtful copy editor. Thanks to her for putting up with my poor understanding of capitalization and general sloppiness. Eric Crahan and Jenny Wolkowicki helped tremendously in the production phase.

This project began at Harvard. My supervisor, Walter Johnson, signed my dissertation acceptance with an exclamation mark, and this was ample encouragement to turn it into a book. I've always been amazed by his ability to distill a set of convoluted ideas to their important core, and thankfully he shared some of that ability with me. Thanks, too, to Emma Rothschild, who believed in the project from the start and has often stepped in with crucial support. Jill Lepore, who rounded out my committee, taught me to think like a reader and that there's nothing more difficult, or rewarding, than writing well.

Thanks also to my friends at Harvard who helped me develop the ideas that would become *Red Meat Republic*. In particular, Philippa Hetherington, Ross Mulcare, Ben Siegel, and Jeremy Zallen were important interlocutors and friends. Thanks as well to Greg Afinogenov, Mou Banerjee, Jessica Barnard, Rhae Lynn Barnes, Rudi Batzell, Eva Bitran, Shane Bobrycki, Rebecca Chang, Eli Cook, Rowan Dorin, Josh Ehrlich, Emily Gauthier, Tina Groeger, Carla Heelan, Philipp Lehmann, Aline-Florence Manent, Jamie Martin, Jamie McSpadden, Yael Merkin, Erin Quinn, Mircea Raianu, David Singerman, Liat Spiro, and Jenny Zallen.

I completed the manuscript at Monash University in Melbourne. Charlotte Greenhalgh was revising her own manuscript as I worked on mine and her support and insight kept me from climbing out of my office window. Clare Corbould not only provided intellectual insight and career advice, but she and her family made me feel welcome in Melbourne. Meanwhile, Adam Clulow is a model of a charitable and engaged colleague, providing me with encouragement and advice about book revision. Thanks also to Bain Attwood (who helpfully read the whole manuscript), Andrew Connor, Ian Copland, Daniella Doron, Jane Drakard, David Garrioch, Heather Graybehl, Michael Hau, Peter Howard, Carolyn James, Julie Kalman, Ernest Koh, Paula Michaels, Ruth Morgan, Kate Murphy, Kathleen Neal, Seamus O'Hanlon, Susie Protschky, Noah Shenker, Agnieszka Sobocinska, Taylor Spence, Alistair Thomson, Christina Twomey, and Tim Verhoeven.

Thanks as well to the other friends, professional and personal, that I made along the way. James Sherow got in touch after reading one of my articles and has become a mentor and friend. He read the entire manuscript and provided thorough comments. Thanks also to Dan Birken, Dani Botsman, Katlyn Carter, Brian Delay, Phil Deloria, Crystal Feimster, Korey Garibaldi, Steve Howard, Jonathan Kenny, Nikhil Menon, Scott Nelson, Emily Remus, Trevor Seret, David Sievers, Elliott West, Bob Wilcox, and Rebecca Woods.

This book would not have been possible without the support of my family. My sisters, Amanda Norris and Rachel Specht, are two of my biggest fans and patient supporters. For the fact that I'm rooting for labor over capital, here and in the outside world, I can thank my dad, Larry Specht. Judith Podell taught me the hard work that goes into writing and editing. Both she and my dad read and commented on the entire manuscript. My stepfather, Jim Murphy, taught me that being an intellectual is about more than working at a university. Conversations with him are always a reminder of the beauty of ideas. My mother, Genie Murphy, has been a constant source of advice, emotional support, and insight. When this project was still a vague idea, she and Jim, armed with an easel, paper, and Sharpies, helped me create an elaborate project plan that got me to the finish line. Mom, I'll be seeing you soon about my second project. Thanks as well to my grandmother, who I barely knew, but sacrificed so much to give my mother, and by extension me, a better life.

Finally, I want to thank Sarah Shortall. At the start of this project Sarah was my best friend. At the end of the project, she's my wife. Sarah supported me emotionally and intellectually through the entire process, which has included a long-distance relationship stretching first from Australia to the United Kingdom and now from Australia to the United States. Though we spend too much time too far apart, she is always in my heart.

RED MEAT REPUBLIC

Introduction

JONATHAN OGDEN ARMOUR could not abide socialist agitators. It was 1906, and Upton Sinclair had just published *The Jungle*, his explosive novel about the American meatpacking industry. Based on two years of research and six weeks of undercover reporting, Sinclair's book was the arresting tale of an immigrant family's toil in Chicago's slaughterhouses.[1] Unfortunately for Armour, *The Jungle* was not his only concern. A year before, muck-raking journalist Charles Edward Russell's *The Greatest Trust in the World* attacked a packing industry that comes to the American dining table "three times a day . . . and extorts its tribute."[2] In response to these attacks, Armour, head of the enormous meatpacking firm Armour & Company, took to the *Saturday Evening Post* to defend himself and his industry. Where critics saw filth, corruption, and exploitation, Armour saw cleanliness, fairness, and efficiency. If not for "the professional agitators of the country," the nation would be free to enjoy an abundance of delicious and affordable meat.[3]

Armour and his critics could agree on this much: they lived in a world unimaginable fifty years before. In 1860, most cattle lived, died, and were consumed within a few hundred miles' radius. By 1906, an animal could be born in Texas, slaughtered

1

in Chicago, and eaten in New York. Americans rich and poor could expect beef for dinner. The key aspects of modern beef production—highly centralized, meatpacker dominated, and low cost—were all pioneered during the period.

America made modern beef at the same time that beef made America modern. What emerged in the late nineteenth century was truly a red meat *republic*; beef production and distribution were tightly linked to the development of the federal state and the expansion of American power west of the Mississippi. During the 1870s, small-scale cattle ranchers supported as well as instigated and justified wars against the Plains Indians. In Wyoming and Montana, wealthy ranchers dominated state and territorial governments, shaping their early histories. Meanwhile, the emergence of the regulatory state was closely connected to beef production. Key federal bureaucracies, such as the Department of Agriculture, the Bureau of Animal Industry, and the Bureau of Corporations were in large part outgrowths of state attempts to regulate beef production and distribution. In Chicago, the "Big Four" meatpacking houses were some of the first large, integrated corporations, pioneering the assembly line, managing global distribution, maintaining complex supply chains, and growing into the largest private employers of their day.

For Jonathan Ogden Armour, cheap beef and a thriving centralized meatpacking industry were the consequence of emerging technologies such as the railroad and refrigeration, coupled with the business acumen of a set of honest and hardworking men like his father, Philip Danforth Armour. According to critics, however, a capitalist cabal was exploiting technological change and government corruption to bankrupt traditional butchers, sell diseased meat, and impoverish the worker. Ultimately, both views were in some sense correct. The national market for fresh beef was the culmination of a technological revolution, but it was also the result of collusion and predatory pricing. The modern slaughterhouse was a triumph of human ingenuity as well as a site of brutal labor exploitation. Industrial beef production, with all its troubling costs and undeniable benefits, reflected seemingly contradictory realities. This book explains the origins and ongoing resilience of a beef production system that was at once revolutionary and exploitative. To do so, this story puts people and social conflict at its center. Technological advances and innovative management techniques made cheap beef possible, but they did little to determine who would benefit most from this new regime (meatpackers and investors) or bear its heaviest costs (workers, small ranchers, and American Indians). This new beef production system was the product of thousands of struggles, large and small, in places like the Texas Panhandle, the West's burgeoning stockyards, and butchers' shops nationwide. The story of modern beef, then, is fundamentally political.

By looking closely at conflicts between workers, industrialists, bureaucrats, and consumers, this book highlights the individuals and conflicts that shaped food industrialization. Its conflict-centered approach builds on the work of others who have explored agricultural production and capitalist transformation, most notably William Cronon in *Nature's Metropolis*.[4] At times, however, these works lose sight of the people and the struggle at the center of economic shifts, making processes like centralization and commodification appear predestined, when they were anything but. This book demonstrates that what might seem like structural features of the beef industry, such as the invisibility and brutality of slaughterhouse labor, were actually the outcome of individual choices and hard-fought policies. This view allows us to see possibilities when they were foreclosed—could today's struggling ranchers have dominated a system the meatpackers now control? In exploring the contingent reasons why meatpacker-dominated, low-cost beef production won out, this book explains the ongoing resilience of a system that has remained in key ways unchanged since *The Jungle*'s publication.

This approach requires a wide lens, one that captures New York meat riots as well as Texas cattle deals. Consequently, this book is the first hoof-to-table history of industrialized beef production. The sheer scope of this analysis demands a broader conception of industrial beef, motivating my use of "cattle-beef complex," a term denoting the set of institutions and practices keeping beef on the dinner table.[5] The emergence of this complex was as much a question of land as business, as much a question of taste as labor.

Making Beef Modern

The transformations that remade beef production between the end of the Civil War in 1865 and the passage of the Federal Meat Inspection Act in 1906 stretched from the Great Plains to the kitchen table.[6] These changes began with cattle ranching. Antebellum ranching had been local and regional. Beyond the few Mexican holdings that survived the Mexican-American War, the people who managed cattle out west were the same people who owned them. In the East, disconnected and relatively small farms produced beef and other agricultural products largely for regional markets. Then, in the 1870s and 1880s, improved transport, bloody victories over the Plains Indians, and the US West's integration into global capital markets meant investors as far away as Scotland funneled money into massive operations like the three-million acre XIT ranch. Ranchers large and small soon participated in an international network of cattle and capital.

Meanwhile, Chicago meatpackers pioneered centralized food processing. Before the Civil War, small slaughterers around the nation's cities worked seasonally. The largest early nineteenth-century packers, centered around Cincinnati—known then as "Porkopolis"—employed only a fraction of the people that the big houses would eventually control. Starting around the time of the Civil War, a group of Chicago companies capitalized on sizable government contracts to dominate the beef and pork industries. Through an innovative system of refrigerator cars and distribution centers, these companies sold fresh beef nationwide. Millions of cattle were soon passing through Chicago's slaughterhouses each year.[7] These companies did not want to replace local retailers, but aggressively and often coercively sought partnerships that bankrupted retailers' local wholesale supplier. By 1890, the Big Four meatpacking companies—Armour & Company, Swift & Company, Morris & Company, and Hammond & Company—directly or indirectly controlled the majority of the nation's beef and pork.

These changes in production accompanied a far-reaching democratization of beef consumption.[8] Despite the efforts of reformers, debates over industrial change and the growing concentration of capital were quite distant from consumers, for whom the real story was a bigger steak at a cheaper price. Nineteenth-century dietary information is limited, but evidence suggests meat consumption rose dramatically.[9] Immigrants celebrated the abundance of beef in the United States. Butchers lamented that "common laborers" demanded fine cuts of meat. When customers faced price spikes, they would even occasionally riot, breaking windows and seizing cuts of meat.[10] Americans would come to see cheap and sanitary beef as a necessity.

Industrial beef emerged at the nexus of opportunity and policy. Abundant land, the potential to link distant places, and swelling urban cities provided the opportunity, while politicians and bureaucrats gradually accepted the idea that mass production in the interests of low prices and, later, sanitary food was the highest policy priority. This is not to say that industrial food production emerged according to some overarching plan. Ranchers, meatpackers, politicians, and bureaucrats all sought to channel policy decisions to advance their own interests or undermine rivals' efforts.

These actors all framed their interests in a way that made them palatable to a wider audience. Often, the strategy was to portray industrialized food as inevitable. This way of framing changes in food production helped transform centralized, industrial food from strange and artificial to familiar and natural. Starting with the meatpackers' own accounts of the rise of their industry and appearing in the first histories of the business—the first historian of modern meatpacking, Rudolf Clemen, also happened to be an Armour employee—it was argued that the industry's rise was the inevitable consequence of technological change.[11] In response to his critics, Jonathan Ogden Armour characterized unfettered private control of meat, vegetable, and fruit shipping as "not only natural but inevitable."[12] According to this logic, it was better for regulators to accept centralized meatpacking, despite the cries of traditional butchers and populist ranchers, than try to stop the march of economic progress.

Meanwhile, ranchers developed their own arguments. Ideas about progress and improvement justified their expropriation of American Indian land. Later, ranchers in the 1890s defended their industry as family centered, nonindustrial, and authentically American, a perspective that still informs public perception of the business. Where meatpacking had Rudolf Clemen, ranching had Joseph McCoy. A businessman and town booster (promoter) for Abilene, Kansas, McCoy built one of the most iconic cattle towns of the period and was ranching's great participant-historian. His book, *Historic Sketches of the Cattle Trade of the West and Southwest*, is widely considered one of the most influential books about the industry's history, despite McCoy's clear romanticization of ranching and relentless attacks on his chief enemy, the railroads.[13] Men like McCoy developed the romantic image of ranchers and cowboys that moved cattlemen to the center of western mythology. These images provided consumers wary of industrial slaughter with an acceptable—even heroic—face for the new food regime. Even today, in a massively centralized, thoroughly capitalized, and highly subsidized industry, producers still advertise with craggy-faced men riding lonesome prairies.

How Beef Transformed America

The cattle-beef complex was national in scale and revolutionary in effect. In the American West, its emergence was a story of ecological changes with profound political implications. In a matter of decades, an ecosystem founded on the relationship between ranchers and cattle displaced a system of nomadic peoples and bison. Cattle ranching not only justified the expropriation of American Indian land, but it was also part of the material process of doing so; ranchers and cowboys supplied the US Army, occasionally accompanied the military on raids or reconnaissance missions, and even at times organized their own expeditions. Further, the profitability of ranching encouraged the rapid settling of the American West. Though pastoralism would eventually give way to farming, US power in the American West had its roots in cattle raising.

However, the changes were not merely ecological. Beef production promoted a continent-spanning standardization of the built environment. As ranches, stockyards, and butchers' shops participated in expanding networks of commodities and capital, they adapted themselves to appeal to distant customers. Ranchers wooing far-away investors and cattle towns looking for new visitors appealed to each by mimicking what was already familiar to these actors, whether uniform cattle pens or railroad cars.[14] This standardization of spaces meant that people who worked in the industry could move quickly from place to place. At the same time as this built a thriving national market, it exposed specific places to the vagaries of that market. A cattle town might overtake a rival by appealing to ranchers with familiar amenities—livestock exchanges, clean stockyards, etc.—but when every aspiring cattle town took this approach, one town became the same as any other. As business and capital came and went, towns like Abilene, Kansas, or regions like the Texas Panhandle were subject to a nineteenth-century form of deindustrialization.

This remaking of land and space also contributed to a remaking of American institutions. The American regulatory state grew as it struggled to deal with the consequences of a new way of producing beef. Business concentration was at the heart of the landmark Sherman Antitrust Act, and its chief initial focus was on the power of the railroads. However, the shipment of refrigerated beef was deeply connected to this story. Railroad attempts to manage traffic often focused on the relative rates for shipping live cattle and refrigerated beef. The Chicago meatpackers fought for more than a decade against these attempts to fix shipping costs. This fight actually ended in the meatpackers' victory; eventually the mighty railroads would ask regulators for protection from the ruinous demands of Chicago's Big Four.

Early attempts to protect and encourage consumers also placed beef at the heart of the expansion of federal power. An act of Congress ordered the Bureau of Corporations, the forerunner to the Federal Trade Commission, to make one of its first investigations an inquiry into "the unusually large margins between the price of beef cattle and the selling prices of fresh beef, and whether the said conditions have resulted in whole or in part from any contract, combination, in the form of trust or otherwise, or conspiracy, in restraint of commerce."[15] The same day in 1906 that Teddy Roosevelt signed the Pure Food and Drug Act, he also signed the Federal Meat Inspection Act, empowering an army of Department of Agriculture bureaucrats to inspect the nation's meat supply.

On the business end, the Chicago meatpackers drove far-reaching changes in the nature of American agriculture. Fresh fruit distribution began with the rise of the meatpackers' refrigerator cars, which they rented to fruit and vegetable growers. Production of wheat, perhaps the United States' greatest food crop, bore the mark of the meatpackers. In order to manage animal feed costs, Armour & Company and Swift & Company invested heavily in wheat futures and controlled some of the country's largest grain elevators.[16] In the early twentieth century, an Armour & Company promotional map announced, "the greatness of the United States is founded on agriculture," and depicted the agricultural products of each American state, many of which moved through Armour facilities.[17]

Beef was a paradigmatic industry for the rise of modern industrial agriculture, known as "agribusiness."[18] As much as a story of science or technology, modern agriculture is a compromise between the unpredictability of nature and the rationality of capital. This was a lurching, violent process central to the cattle-beef complex as meatpackers displaced the risks of blizzards, drought, disease, and overproduction onto cattle ranchers. Today's agricultural system works similarly. In poultry, processors like Purdue and Tyson use an elaborate system of contracts and required equipment and feed purchases to maximize their own profits while displacing the business's risk onto contract farmers.[19] This is true with crop production as well. As with nineteenth-century meatpacking, relatively small actors conduct the actual growing and production, while companies like Monsanto and Cargill control agricultural inputs and market access.

The cattle-beef complex was enormously resilient. The meatpacker-controlled system of cheap refrigerated beef survived rancher protest, labor unrest, railroad opposition, and regulatory reform. This resilience was rooted in two factors: the first in the realm of production, the second in consumption. In production, policy favored a flexible and stable food system above all else. Standardization was key here. Since disparate places were increasingly well connected and functionally identical, disruptions in, say, Illinois, could be smoothed out with changes in Colorado. This made meat production bigger than any particular geographic place, whether Texas, the Plains, or even Chicago. Further, the agribusiness model, which displaced economic and environmental risks onto ranchers and small producers, meant that packing-industry profits, as well as the system as a whole, thrived even in the most difficult times.

The cattle-beef complex's resilience also depended on beef's supreme importance to consumers. Because industrial production provided ever-cheaper beef, critics of the system in 1890, as today, faced—often rightfully—charges of elitism. When butchers sought regulation curtailing the Chicago meatpackers' power, they had to acknowledge to lawmakers that industry decentralization would increase prices. Lawmakers would ultimately side with industrial production. In contrast, charges that beef was not sanitary—such as during the US Army beef

scandal of 1898—spurred rapid consumer mobilization and state action. But once the Chicago packers resolved these sanitation issues, it merely strengthened their grip. While consumers' concerns about prices and sanitation seem self-evident, we have to understand the logic of consumers who demanded beef more than any other food, and were at times willing to riot for cheap beef rather than eat fish or chicken.

Beyond the United States

Though the rise of industrial beef is an American story, it is one with global influences and consequences. Cattle are global organisms; their DNA reflects the intermingling of subspecies from two distinct periods of domestication in South Asia and the Middle East.[20] Further, cattle from the Americas exhibit adaptations made to survive in the aftermath of the Columbian exchange.[21] As these animals adapted to arid and nutrient-poor climates, they developed a rapid reproductive cycle, which explains both their abundance and their popularity with ranchers. However, these changes were not all desirable. Adaptations that made them hardier also meant the breeds were lean and slow to gain weight, making them, according to one account, as juicy as "a boiled grand piano."[22] The final—and most consumer friendly—adaptation of American cattle only came with the infusion of northern European stock like the Hereford and Angus in the late nineteenth century, constituting yet another stage in the globalization of cattle bodies.

As with cattle themselves, American cattle raising reflected a blend of imported traditions. Spanish ranching, with its emphasis on horses and animal roping, shaped ranching in the West and Southwest, while northern European traditions of cattle fattening and hands-on care would underpin cattle raising in the corn belt and Midwest.[23] Similarly, recent work has shown that African traditions were important to the development of American ranching.[24] To the extent any distinctly American cattle-raising tradition exists, it is the product of a slow blending of a variety of influences.

Meanwhile, ranching as a highly capitalized enterprise had its roots in transnational flows of capital and people that reached the American ranching industry in the 1880s. Abundant American land became a target for British capital, which soon leveraged the Scottish and English cattle-raising tradition. "Land and cattle companies" began buying cattle across the American West to amass herds with as many as a hundred thousand animals. This infusion of foreign capital, paired with the subsequent importation of ranching expertise in the form of itinerant European ranch managers, turned western ranching into big business. These operations began supplying Chicago meatpacking markets as well as corn-belt cattle fatteners, creating an integrated cattle-raising system. Ultimately, the land and cattle business would turn out to be a land and cattle bubble, but in the process European capital helped create the perfect conditions for the emerging Chicago meatpacking houses: abundant supplies of cattle with financially desperate owners.

Meanwhile, the global consequences of American ranching and meatpacking were profound. Some of the same Scottish pioneers of American ranching would travel to South America to start ranches there. French investors sent Murdo Mackenzie, the Scottish-born manager of the American Matador ranch, to South America to help organize the Brazil Land, Cattle and Packing Company. In the early twentieth century, the Chicago meatpackers took over the Latin American beef processing industry, opening facilities in Brazil, Argentina, and elsewhere.

Swift & Company purchased an Argentinian food distribution company in 1907 and developed a rivalry with several other Chicago houses for control of the country's beef trade.[25] Local competitors would learn from and even improve on the Chicago model; in 2007, the Brazilian company JBS purchased Swift & Company, making JBS the largest meat processor in the world.

The cattle-beef complex would also shape global foodways. The transatlantic meat trade would contribute to the democratization of meat consumption in Great Britain. The export of live cattle and, later, refrigerated beef from the United States to Great Britain was a thriving—and contentious—trade. Starting in the 1870s this trade expanded rapidly, and in 1901 more than three hundred million pounds of dressed beef crossed the Atlantic. South American beef would come to dominate the British market in the next couple years, but the Chicago meatpackers directly and indirectly controlled much of that trade as well.[26]

On the lower end of the quality scale, canned beef would become a vital product for militaries in the age of imperialism. Few people willingly ate canned meat during the nineteenth century, but soldiers could be compelled to do so. The German, French, and British militaries all purchased millions of pounds of Chicago canned beef and used it to keep their armies supplied. This was particularly important in tropical places, where other foods spoiled quickly.

One of the key contradictions of global agriculture is the way that farming and animal husbandry remain inescapably local—a plot of land or a herd of cattle—yet are subject to distant networks of capital, commodities, and people. This means that accounts of their origins must be sensitive to the specificity of these processes as well as their global element. In the case of the cattle-beef complex, this means exploring a distinctly American story with global origins and consequences.

A Steer's-Eye View of the History of American Capitalism

To tell the story of the rise of industrialized beef in America I use novel sources, as well as asking new questions of traditional archives. Scholars of industrial meat production have long faced the particular challenge of the dearth of business records for meatpacking's key period, the late nineteenth century. These records are spotty, missing, or otherwise inaccessible. To get around the missing records, I turned to a variety of sources, and this has allowed me to better understand the cattle-beef complex as a whole.

The records of late nineteenth-century ranching corporations are traditionally used in narrower histories of Texas and western ranching, but when used to examine the rise of industrialized meat they have bigger implications. They can help us rethink the history of food and American capitalism. Ranches like the Matador, Swan, XIT, and others coordinated efforts of investors in Europe, ranch managers across the West, and buyers and agents in Chicago and in the East. Messages between ranch managers and agents in Kansas City, Chicago, and elsewhere provide a window into their participation in the national beef distribution system and their attitudes about the emerging giants of the late nineteenth century: the Chicago meatpackers. These sources portray attempts to remake western environments, and frictions between the needs of investment capital and millennia-old agricultural processes. Meanwhile, I use cowboy songs, trade cards, and recipe books to explore the cultural meanings of ranching and beef, as well as how these meanings shaped the nineteenth-century economy.

Building outward from these sources, this book draws wider conclusions about the beef industry and advances arguments about the nature of American business development. It shows how the changing relationships between nature and capital were key to the United States' broader economic history. New technologies like the railroad and financial innovations like futures contracts have rightfully been placed center stage in the history of American capitalism. Yet, western railroads were profitable to the extent that they could move agricultural bounty, and futures contracts were, at least initially, about managing ecological risk. Animal husbandry and agriculture inspired institutional and regulatory developments at the heart of the nineteenth-century economy. American industrialization has natural roots.[27]

Further, this book argues that even if markets are deeply political, the cultural history of consumption is closely tied to how and why markets are regulated. Consumer tastes had profound effects on the beef industry; the pervasive preference for fresh, rather than cured, beef is in part what made beef production a highly capitalized and centralized industry. Keeping meat chilled all the way from Chicago to New York was difficult prior to electrification. It is important to understand why the industry was so aggressively regulated around sanitation as opposed to, say, labor, and such an understanding should come before debates over whether industry effectively captured regulation like the Pure Food and Drug Act.

Finally, this history of the American beef industry shows that mobility was vital to the emergence of national markets.[28] It was the desire to move goods over long distances that sparked the standardization mentioned earlier. The fact that stockyards began to look similar across the country or butchers' shops carried similar cuts of meat was a consequence of businesses moving goods nationally and, later, globally. The expansion of the federal regulatory state was an attempt to manage this process. For instance, the patchwork of state laws regulating the movement of cattle became inadequate once animals were being shipped nationally or even across the Atlantic, promoting calls from both business and consumers for federal regulators to referee the process. Still, this emergence of a national market was a product of conflict and competition; standardization and regulation were processes born of individual attempts to profit from the beef trade.

This analysis will help explain the nature and strength of agribusiness today. Though this was not always the case, spatial flexibility and the close relationship between the centralized regulatory state and big business mean that centralized food production is here to stay. Industry critics must consider this reality before advocating practices like locavorism or decentralization. Similarly, the history of the cattle-beef complex reveals the limits of consumer politics and the long history of the fixation on low prices. Questions about how to reform food production—or whether it even needs reform—must start from questions of political economy, rather than the all-too-popular resort to consumer choice.[29]

While looking at what the beef industry can tell us about industrialization, regulation, and business practices, we should not forget that at the center of this story is the relationship, usually economic but at times emotional, between cattle and people. The domestication of cattle stretches back ten thousand years, and scientists and archaeologists still debate its origin and time line.[30] The centrality of grazing animals to human society goes back even farther. Some of humanity's earliest known works of art—in the Lascaux caves in France—feature aurochs (cattle's precursor), horses, and other game. From earliest domestication, a variety of cattle breeds, ranging from those almost entirely independent to those requiring near-constant supervision, have accompanied most African and Eurasian societies as creatures of economic, social, and spiritual importance.[31]

Cattle are not sacks of flour. Cattle fought with one another and with their owners. They wandered off. When their young died on the trail they straggled at the back of the herd, trying to turn back. It was their ability to feed themselves on the range that was the origin of much of their value, meaning they were even performing a kind of labor. Though it is impossible to understand what the cattle-beef complex meant to them, it is important to recognize that the very possibility of this system depended on the fact that these animals were capable of moving, working, and, in small ways, resisting.

Book Overview

This book follows beef from hoof to table. Turning a particular animal or cut of meat into an abstraction—beef—is an ongoing process, whether on a ranch, in a slaughterhouse, or on a stove top. Cultural systems and values as diverse as kosher dietary laws and the mythology of the cowboy inform each step of this process. Specific moments can threaten a commodity, such as when food contamination turns a steak from delicacy to poison or when a lightning strike turns a herd of cattle from an asset to a stampeding mess. Commodities are abstractions that must be understood through the particular.

The first chapter, "War," explores western cattle ranching's origins in Indian land expropriation. Western ranching was about scattering cattle far and wide on marginal land, and this required remaking the Great Plains as an ecosystem as well as a political space. Through analysis of conflicts like the 1874–75 Red River War and the stories of ranching pioneers like Susan Newcomb, I argue that the cattle-beef complex depended on land expropriation through both deliberate government policy and independent rancher effort. This expropriation was part of a wrenching process of transforming the Great Plains ecosystem from a grass-bison-nomad system to a grass-cattle-rancher one. The violence of Indian War—romanticized and reimagined as the against-all-odds struggles of early ranchers—created the cattle-beef complex's foundational myths.

Chapter 2, "Range," traces the origins of large-scale ranching to a speculative bubble that funneled investment capital to the US West from back east and as far away as Scotland. Investors created a multitude of large, highly capitalized, corporate ranches that made cattle raising big business, but also spurred speculation, overproduction, and poor management. This system eventually collapsed as blizzards and mismanagement collided to bankrupt or cripple the majority of the large ranches. Ranching would thereafter be conducted on a smaller—and less profitable— scale. The rise and fall of corporate ranching is a tale of alternate possibility—food production today could look quite different if not for the collapse of these ranches at the same moment the Chicago meatpackers were gaining power. This chapter argues that far from being inevitable, the way ranching looks today—small-scale and largely privately run—is a result of a mix of chance, policy, mania, and ecological limitation.

Chapter 3, "Market," takes a bird's-eye view of cattle raising. At its core, the cattle-beef complex was about mobility—the ability to move commodities farther and faster than ever before. This depended on a kind of flexibility in production that was a consequence of deliberate policy and historical accident. A

study of the cattle disease Texas fever and the story of the cattle
town of Ellsworth, Kansas, reveal that this complex began in
particular places, but soon outgrew them as a consequence of
the emergence of standardized spaces, whether stockyards,
railcars, or feedlots. Mobility also depended on trust, and this
was a consequence of state regulation of animal diseases and
business practices. Ranchers and meatpackers, in concert with
local, state, and national politicians, shaped this system as they
sought to turn a profit in the cattle business.

Though the cattle-beef complex was a national and global
system, the first three chapters of this book focus heavily on the
US West. There were more beef cattle east of the Mississippi than
west at the time, so this focus might seem odd. But understanding western ranching is essential because it helps us to understand ranching culture, as well as enables us to consider alternate
possibilities. The way consumers, businesspeople, ranchers, and
lawmakers understood ranching helped justify and defend the
system. Large-scale corporate ranching was also tried out west at
a time when eastern production was overwhelmingly small-scale
and family oriented. Though corporate ranching was a failure,
attention to its rise and fall suggests it was not inevitable that the
Chicago meatpackers would dominate this system. The classic
image of cattle ranching is a western one, and it is there that
ranching was woven into the country's DNA.

Chapter 4, "Slaughterhouse," explores how a small number
of companies headquartered in Chicago came to dominate the
cattle-beef complex. The Chicago packinghouses fought with
railroads, laborers, and traditional butchers to secure shipment
of centrally slaughtered "dressed beef" and, in the process,
became some of the largest and most profitable companies in
the United States. In regulating these new, massive companies,
bureaucrats and lawmakers embraced a consumerist mentality

that prioritized cheap beef over concerns about price fixing, worker exploitation, and butcher displacement. Because the Chicago companies aligned consumer interests with their own, they came to dominate the beef production system.

The final chapter, "Table," examines beef's culinary importance to understand why and how consumers mobilize around political issues, particularly of price and sanitation. A consumer protest over rising beef prices—a "meat riot" according to New York's papers—will reveal what cheap beef meant to hungry consumers. This chapter also studies a core tension in consumer perspectives on food production: acceptance of mass production's inevitability, despite abstract concern about its effects. Overall, the chapter develops a theory of food as a commodity to understand how consumers' relationships with their food influence food production.

The cattle-beef complex was the product of thousands of small debates, struggles, and fights over keeping one's job, protecting a home, or making a dollar. Ultimately, these were contests over what our food system should look like and how our society should be organized. Low prices and sanitary meat at the expense of all else won out. It was a system predicated on land dispossession, low wages, animal abuse, rancher impoverishment, and environmental degradation. But it also democratized beef; hungry consumers could eat what they wanted, and it tasted good. Railroads, refrigeration, and capital made this system possible, but politics and struggle determined its contours. Food production and consumption are not a transparent reflection of our stage of economic development, but rather an ongoing, and at times violent, contest over how we should and should not produce our food.

1

War

FOR TWO HUNDRED YEARS, societies organized around
horses and buffalo ruled the Great Plains. But by 1876, this
world was unraveling. Few felt this more acutely than the Kiowa
artist Wo-Haw. US soldiers had captured Wo-Haw during fighting between bison hunters and the US military on one side and
an alliance of Indian polities on the other, over control of the
Texas Panhandle. While imprisoned in Fort Marion, Florida,
Wo-Haw created *Between Two Worlds*. At the center of the piece,
the subject is caught between bison and bull, torn between the
worlds each represents.[1] The bison stands alongside tipi and
camp; the bull towers over farmhouse and fields. The subject
warily faces the bull, pipe extended.[2]

This chapter puts words to Wo-Haw's art. It is the story
of the origin of what was then known as the "Cattle Kingdom,"
the destruction of the Plains bison herds, and the fracturing of
the societies that lived off their hunt. Cattle ranchers and bison
hunters, supported by the US military, fundamentally reshaped
the Great Plains, expelling American Indians from western
lands and appropriating that land for use by white settlers and
ranchers.[3] Without this process, beef's move to the center of the
American diet might not have been possible.

FIGURE 1. *Between Two Worlds* drawing by Kiowa artist Wo-Haw, 1877.
There is a relationship between the image's subject and the artist's
name: wohaw is a Plains Indian word for "beef cattle." Reproduced
by permission from Missouri History Museum, St. Louis.

During the American Civil War, the Great Plains and parts of
Texas and the Southwest were thrown into chaos. But the end
of hostilities brought the expansion of settlement, the spread of
railroads, and the rise of the commercial bison hunt, transforming simmering conflict between settlers and the Plains Indians
into formal warfare. Armed with the logistics strategies and
warfare techniques pioneered during the Civil War, generals
like William Tecumseh Sherman and Philip Sheridan confined
the Plains Indians to reservations.[4] By the end of this process,
vast expanses of newly available grazing land would be immor-
talized as the "open range." Ranchers would spread hundreds of
thousands of cattle over seemingly limitless grassland. The open

range is often romanticized as untouched by human hands or industry; in reality, it was produced by the violent exclusion of people and bison.

Ranchers were not merely beneficiaries of this process. They were often agents of conquest. Cowboys and small ranchers fought American Indians and organized raids to recapture stolen cattle or simply exact revenge. In many places, commercial bison hunting and land seizures reduced Indian peoples to near starvation, prompting livestock thefts that white settlers would use to justify brutally disproportionate violence. In California, this process culminated in what historian Benjamin Madley has called a genocide of the Yuki people. Settlers allegedly killed as many as fifteen people for every animal the Yuki slaughtered or stole.[5] Meanwhile, cattle continued to spread far and wide, crowding buffalo and roaming onto Indian land.

Ranching also enabled conquest in another, less tangible way. Americans had once deemed much of the trans-Mississippi West the Great American Desert, a place devoid of agricultural possibility.[6] But early cattle-raising experiments inspired Americans who hoped to occupy the plains. Ranchers could put the Great American Desert to use. Their distinction between this productive use and the allegedly backward practices of the societies that previously occupied the Plains would provide a kind of justification for the violence on which the cattle-beef complex rested. The stories ranchers and hunters told themselves and others were as much a tool of conquest as their rifles.

Cattle raising was a central part of remaking the West and a foundation of US power there. Treasury Department official Joseph Nimmo observed in 1885 that the "range-cattle business has also been perhaps the most efficient instrumentality in solving the Indian problem. . . . By this means a vast area, which, but a few years ago, was apparently a barren waste, has been converted into a scene of enterprise and of thrift."[7] From Texas to Montana, the cattle-beef complex and the American state were coevolving.

The story of ranching and the Indian War did not end with the initial wave of conquest and land expropriation; the US government's solution to what it considered the ongoing problem of Indian peoples—namely, the reservation system—would prove an enormous boon for ranchers. The US government's method of Indian pacification, through a conscious targeting of the means of subsistence—the bison—as well as by confining American Indians to reservations, created a population dependent on government-supplied rations. Ranchers found contracts to provide these rations extremely lucrative, and at times used them as an outlet for otherwise unsalable meat.

For bureaucrats and the public, the sight of impoverished American Indians accepting government-issued cattle and then slaughtering the animals—a "brutal and brutalizing spectacle" according to one contemporary newspaper—confirmed their view that Indian social and political collapse was a consequence of degenerate culture.[8] Cultural explanations for what was then known as the "Indian question" relied on characterizations of American Indians as either criminals or children. Descriptions of beef handouts, with their emphasis on both savagery and abjection, supported both views.

Beyond eliding US responsibility for Indian poverty, these accounts justified a heavy-handed paternalism.[9] As a result, solutions to the "Indian question" often took the shape of forcibly managing land on behalf of Indian polities, or the American government ignoring treaty terms because the agreements were not in what officials deemed the Indians' best interests. It was no coincidence that these measures often favored cattle ranchers.

Bureaucrat Joseph Nimmo advocated shrinking reservations to not only "put [residents] in the way of becoming civilized," but also because "nearly all the area which will thus be thrown open to white settlement consists of good grazing land."[10] The claim that measures like this were win-win only encouraged further exploitation.

Just as cultural narratives of Indian social and political decline justified paternalism, cattle ranchers' part in the Indian Wars of the 1870s helped justify the emerging ranching system by binding the Cattle Kingdom to the myth of the frontier. This myth, which casts frontier areas as places of individualism and justifiable, if at times regrettable, violence in the interests of civilization, has been a potent force throughout American history.[11] The tale of ranchers taming the West fits neatly into this larger narrative, as the "cowboy and Indian" trope in film, music, and literature attests. Advertisements and promotional materials for the beef industry still trade on this imagery, whether through expansive images of western plains or stylized depictions of cowboys and the old West.

Accounts of the late nineteenth-century US West have rightfully emphasized the role of formal military conquest in pacifying and dispossessing the Plains Indians. Yet, small-scale conflicts over cattle movement and bison hunting were equally important.[12] Threats to ranchers or cattle often provided the pretext for military intervention. On the northern Plains, the first Sioux War had its origin in a botched military attempt to arrest a Lakota man for killing a wayward ox.[13] Ranchers and hunters, often the very same people, materially supported the military, providing supplies or local knowledge about Indian supply routes. Organized and well armed, in some places ranchers even acted as paramilitaries. It was not merely that the military swept the Great Plains clear during the decades after the

Civil War, and that ranching arose in place of the bison hunt. Rather, cattle ranchers and bison hunters precipitated conflict with American Indians and agitated for government intervention.[14] They also worked with the military to achieve their collective aim: the expropriation of native land.

This story unfolded on the northern, central, and southern Plains. Texas is often the focus here, in part because Texas was the key state for creating the Cattle Kingdom in reality and idea. Nevertheless, the processes discussed in this chapter spanned the entire American West. Where the southern Plains saw the violence of the Red River War, the northern Plains had the Sioux Wars of 1876–77. Rationing contracts were as corrupt in Kansas as they were in Montana.

The chapter begins with the spread of horses and cattle across North America; the former sparked the golden age of Plains Indian nomads and the latter would be its undoing. A discussion of Texas frontier life leading up to the Red River War of 1874–75 shows how bison hunting, land dispossession, cattle ranching, and war were deeply related. An analysis of the reservation system follows, revealing how the system subsidized ranchers and justified ongoing land dispossession. At every turn, there were ranchers, seeking green pastures and even greener government contracts.

The Golden Age of the Plains Nomads: Buffalo and the Spread of Horses across the Plains

A stretch of dry, flat, and mostly treeless land between the Mississippi River and the Rockies extends from Texas to Canada.[15] Before the Civil War, General John Pope referred to it as "barren country" that was "not susceptible of cultivation or settlement."[16] Today this "barren country" encompasses parts of Texas; all of Oklahoma, Kansas, Nebraska, Wyoming, and Montana; and much of the Dakotas. All of these states have booming agricultural industries. Why did some of today's most productive land look that way to Pope? The answer was as much about the region's inhabitants as it was about the climate.

Seeing abundance required eyes capable of grasping the possibilities this seemingly limitless land held for grazing animals and mobile humans. This was how the Comanche, Cheyenne, Sioux, and Kiowa saw the Plains. But it had not always been that way. Once they had lived on the fringes of the Plains, combining small-scale hunting with shifting cultivation agriculture.[17] This all changed with the arrival of horses in North America. From the back of a horse, the once elusive Plains bison could be hunted in endless quantities. The Great American Desert was actually a land of plenty.[18]

To understand how horses revolutionized this world, one must first understand the Plains ecosystem. The Plains are arid. Mean annual rainfall for the entire region is under sixteen inches.[19] On the eastern Plains rainfall is closer to forty inches, enabling larger tallgrasses to dominate, whereas in the rain shadow of the Rocky Mountains, on the High Plains, only shortgrasses can survive. In between, the two grasses intermingle, depending on local conditions and long-term weather trends.

But these rainfall totals are only averages. Year to year, precipitation varies dramatically, with decades of abundance following or preceding equally long stretches of drought. As a result, bison populations could swell rapidly in rainier periods and collapse spectacularly in times of drought. This harsh reality for the Plains nomads would also be a problem for cattle ranchers; their fortunes were equally dependent on the climate. But this was far from anyone's mind in the mid-nineteenth century.

An unusually wet period from 1750 to 1850 that had spurred large increases in the bison population and correspondingly increased the power and wealth of the Plains Indians.[20]

Before horses, the bison reigned supreme. Though the pre-Columbian bison population is a matter of debate, current research places their number at roughly thirty million in North America as of 1700.[21] A foot taller than most cattle and significantly heavier—bulls weighing as much as sixteen hundred pounds—angry or frightened bison could easily trample hunters on foot. Before horses, the bison hunt depended on the combined effort of many people and hunting dogs to drive the beasts to jumps where they would fall to their death or fatal injury. But this complicated process was only feasible in the summer when bison gathered to mate. The rest of the year the animals were too dispersed to be hunted efficiently.[22]

Not so after the spread of horses. When the Spanish first reached North America, they maintained careful control over the horse herds that underpinned their might. Yet these herds grew rapidly, and the 1680 revolt of the Pueblo people against Spanish rule led to the capture of several herds.[23] Though the Spanish soon regained control of the Pueblo, horses entered the vast intercontinental Amerindian trade network, spreading northward rapidly.

Entire peoples reorganized their societies around the bison hunt, throwing the Great Plains into turmoil. Bison meat, bones, and hides provided almost every need. The essentials that the hunt could not provide, like horses, could be acquired through raiding or trade.[24] Societies that had existed on the fringes of the Plains relocated to them year-round, embracing a completely nomadic lifestyle. These shifts sparked vicious fighting for access to prime hunting grounds. Warriors quickly discovered a truism of Eurasian warfare: men on horseback were far more powerful than men on foot. The Comanche eventually grew into an empire more powerful than their sedentary Amerindian and European rivals.[25]

What resulted was not a stable social and political order in harmony with nature.[26] This system of hunting, raiding, and trade was in constant flux, which actually kept bison populations healthy.[27] What was bad for people—constant warfare—was good for the bison. Areas no entity could control were ones in which no one could reliably hunt. Here, bison thrived.[28]

During the nineteenth century, however, the political upheaval ended. The Lakota, Cheyenne, Kiowa, and Comanche reached agreements about territory and hunting grounds. Their hunters could now meet the surging demand from the eastern United States for bison hides, popularly known as "buffalo robes," which were as warm as they were fashionable. Though the total collapse of the bison herds did not occur until the arrival of American hunters, herds were already entering a gradual decline.[29]

Though many white Americans initially failed to appreciate the Plains' possibilities, they could not miss the herds of bison that stretched to the horizon. Imaginative (or greedy) men recognized that this apparent desert held great potential. Man and horse would still reign supreme, but the ecological and economic foundation of their power would be cattle, not bison. As E. V. Smalley of Saint Paul, Minnesota, explained, this dream rested "upon a theory . . . that the native grasses of the plains and valleys which had formerly supported vast herds of buffalos would support vast herds of cattle . . . and that as the wild animal had managed to exist through the severe winters in the dry herbage, the domestic steer would learn the same method of self-preservation."[30] It was this dream, of the Cattle Kingdom, that transformed the Great Plains from a place European people wanted to cross into one they wanted to occupy.[31]

Though perceived similarities between cattle and bison inspired white Americans to seek Plains riches, beliefs about the differences between the two animals justified the buffalo's extermination. While early ranchers romanticized cattle, bison were monstrous.[32] Surveying the Texas countryside, one settler described the "big ugly buffalo that fairly blacken the valleys and hill sides."[33] And at least in Fort Davis, Texas, there were many incidents of cruelty to bison, whether tying up the animals and cutting them, or watching as packs of dogs killed and devoured them.[34] When a group of settlers caught one "monster," they tied it up and cut off its tail. After they chased the animal around for a while, "the boys concluded that they had seen enough sport from our buffalo so they shot him dead."[35] Whereas cattle represented the first signs of civilization, bison were wild beasts. It was a short step from here to the view that the people living off their hunt were not putting the land to its highest use. Creating the Cattle Kingdom would require dealing with the people and the bison that were said to "infest" the Plains.

"A Helping Hand over This Wild and Destitute Country": Life on the Texas Frontier and the Red River War

Susan Newcomb turned eighteen on the plains of West Texas, a place she hated. She had moved there with her husband, Samuel Newcomb, six years earlier and despite her wishes—"if I had wings to fly I would abandon it forever"—she persevered.[36] Samuel insisted they stay; the promise of free land and cheap cattle was greater than his fear of enemies "continually depredating on the people, killing, stealing, and driving off our cattle."[37] The Newcombs were foot soldiers in a relentless and bloody war to remake the West.

Susan and Samuel Newcomb had moved to West Texas, just outside Fort Davis, during the 1860s. The region was in chaos, necessitating an almost martial lifestyle. On July 30, 1865, Samuel wrote that "the country is without law or protection, the frontier people must now do something themselves."[38] On one roundup a year earlier, or as Newcomb called it, a cow hunt, his party gave chase to seven Indians driving about ninety head of horses. When the Indians fled, the party kept the horses as well as a saddle and several other items. Newcomb claims they rode back to a nearby settlement to find the horses' owners, but makes no mention of the animals' fate.[39] In Susan Newcomb's diary, settlers are described selling unclaimed animals they had recovered (or perhaps stolen) in a raid.[40] In another entry, she describes men preparing to go on an "Indian hunt."[41] Even the Newcombs' language is militaristic. Samuel Newcomb describes his lists of the participants in cow hunts or buffalo hunts as "muster rolls."[42]

When not seeking safety in forts, ranchers spread very thin, making their ranches the ultimate outposts of western expansion. In a lonely diary entry written while her husband was on a cattle drive, Susan Newcomb observed that "the time passes slow and lonsome with me while he is gone, one reason is we live so far from any one eighteen miles from a living being I get very lonsome sometimes when I think about being so far from any one in an Indian country."[43] These settlers had few welcome guests, and mostly Newcomb worried about unwanted Indian visitors who "shoot us when ever they get a chance, and take our horses where ever they find them without even giving us a quartermaster's-receipt for them."[44] At great personal risk, Susan Newcomb was building the Cattle Kingdom.[45]

Susan and Samuel Newcomb were just the kind of people who would transform the Cattle Kingdom from aspiration to reality. They persevered in the face of violence, loneliness, and poverty. On her eighteenth birthday, Susan Newcomb reflected on the fact that she "[had] been graciously spared by the wise providence of God," and went on to "hope that he will stretch forth a helping hand over this wild and destitute county."[46] That helping hand would take the form of the US military, but Newcomb and her husband deserved more of the credit than they likely realized.

The Newcombs' arrival in Texas during the early 1860s was well timed, as it was a period of transition for the region. Cattle ranching in Texas (and in the American Southwest more broadly) stretched back well before the Mexican-American War, when the area was Mexico's far north. For as long as a century, settlements across Mexico's far north farmed and traded slaves and goods with the Plains Indians. During the early nineteenth century, this arrangement broke down, owing in part to declining bison herds, and the Plains Indians increasingly waged war on northern Mexico, spiraling the region into violence and chaos.[47] Quite literally, the southern Plains' shifting ecological foundations were shaping its political ones. The Mexican state weakened, and Anglo settlers became increasingly committed to the idea that Texas could be made theirs through occupation and Indian pacification.

The Anglo-American population swelled during the first half of the nineteenth century.[48] Tens of thousands of settlers now coexisted uneasily with the area's Mexican and Indian inhabitants. These Anglo-Americans had little respect for the Mexican government and soon declared independence, forming the Republic of Texas in 1836. This sparked a Civil War, plunging the region into a decade of fighting.[49]

This violence culminated in what is popularly known as the Mexican-American War. Recent scholarship has emphasized the centrality of Indian polities to this struggle, and though either "Mexican-American War" or, perhaps more appropriately, the "US-Mexican War" are convenient names, it really was a war among three powers: Mexico; the United States; and a coalition of Comanche, Kiowa, and other nomadic polities.[50] The United States would win the war on paper, and the 1848 Treaty of Guadalupe Hidalgo ceded nearly a third of Mexico to the United States. But it was more complicated than that, as revealed by the treaty's article 11, which obligated the United States to control and pacify the "savage tribes" that inhabited the region.[51] In practice this meant that the treaty was little more than a promise that the land could belong to the United States, should the Indians be pacified. In the 1830s and 1840s, the Comanche were firmly in control of large swaths of the region, but the treaty had created a belief in Americans that they had a legitimate claim to the land.

Immediately following the treaty of Guadalupe Hidalgo, the United States made great strides in pacifying the region. As Gary Anderson has argued, this was about seizing Indian land and violently creating an Anglo-American polity through a kind of ethnic cleansing.[52] But this process saw major reversals during the Civil War, as was the case with US power across the West. During the war, white American authority—both Union and Confederate—waned as the collapse of the region's traditional beef markets meant cattle populations boomed.

Following the war, ranchers and the military cooperated to reestablish control of the southern Plains. Ranchers provided intelligence and, at times, supplies. The military, in turn, helped recover stolen livestock. When one cavalry lieutenant performed a search for stolen cattle, he brought along the animals' owners. The owners' collaboration with the military was so close that when two of the cattlemen's horses gave out, the cavalry company even gave the ranchers fresh mounts so they could relay a message to headquarters. Other cattle owners continued with the unit to lead the detachment to an Indian trail and spring the cattlemen had found.[53]

In 1871, when the commanding officer of Fort Concho, Texas, dispatched men to investigate cattle thefts in the area, he sent for Richard Francklyn Tankersley, a local stockman, as well as two other ranchers, presumably to provide intelligence.[54] Tankersley was one of the richest men in the area, and his efforts were specially commended by the military officer he accompanied, who noted that Tankersley joined the expedition "simply because he wishes to assist in punishing the Indians," who had stolen another rancher's cattle.[55] Beyond help from ranchers, cattle themselves proved a crucial supply for military outfits on the Plains. Cattle on the hoof functioned as a ration and supply train in one, since the cattle could walk along with the regiment. Military orders often indicated that fresh beef would be driven with the command.[56]

Key to building support for rancher efforts was military acceptance of ranchers' understanding of property and theft. In ranchers' eyes, a simple mark—or, in the case of Mexican cattle brands, an enormously complicated mark—burned on an animal's side made it property, no matter how far the animal wandered from the ranch house.[57] This conceptual understanding of branded cattle as mobile property, coupled with the standard practice of grazing cattle on unfenced land, ensured conflict. Ranchers cared little whether their cattle wandered onto land occupied or used by southern Plains Indians, but they cared a great deal if these cattle were stolen or killed. Complaints to military authorities about "depredations"—to use the word from the time—were less often about raids on cattle that ranchers were actively driving than about the theft of cattle grazing far out of sight.

Conflict over cattle grazing and theft simmered in Texas for roughly a decade after the Civil War. Settlers were growing more and more committed to a life on the Plains at the same time that they were growing more and more angry about conflict with Indians. Settlers believed they had a right to occupy the southern Plains, and that the military had an obligation to support them. Though the military's leadership was wary of this position, it sympathized with the settlers. Armed with the military's sympathy, a relatively small number of cattle owners could control large swaths of land. For if their cattle remained property as far as they wandered, the cattle could act as mobile colonizers, turning disputed land into valuable beef and threats to their grazing—real and alleged—into an acceptable pretext for military intervention.[58]

When the US Army's initial piecemeal attempts to resolve minor conflicts over land and cattle failed, its leadership concluded that peaceful coexistence with American Indians was impossible. Instead, the army embraced total military conquest as necessary for the reservation system's success. On the southern Plains, the chief conflict was the Red River War, in which the US military defeated an alliance of Kiowa, Comanche, and Cheyenne who had violently opposed the movement of white bison hunters in the region.

The Red River War, like most Indian Wars of the late nineteenth century, was the result of private greed, federal incompetence, and cultural misunderstanding. The war had its origins in a set of 1867 agreements, known collectively as the Medicine Lodge Treaty, that were intended to stop just the kind of constant low-level conflict highlighted above.[59] The Kiowa,

Comanche, Plains Apache, Cheyenne, and Arapaho agreed to move to reservations in exchange for the guarantee that the land would be "set apart for [their] absolute and undisturbed use and occupation."[60] The federal government also promised to build various utility buildings on the reservation and provide a yearly ration of clothing, agricultural implements, and other goods.[61] In exchange, the polities gave up claims to the land outside the reservation areas (with one large exception to be addressed shortly) and pledged that "they will not, in future, object to the construction of railroads, wagon-roads, mail-stations, or other works of utility or necessity which may be ordered or permitted by the laws of the United States."[62] This guarantee extended to infrastructure on reservation lands, though the government promised compensation for these improvements. From the federal perspective this infrastructural point was key, as one of the central members of the Treaty Commission, William Tecumseh Sherman, once told his subordinate Philip Sheridan that the railroad "will help to bring the Indian problem to a final solution."[63] Sherman's view would ultimately prove correct.

There was, however, one clause of the Medicine Lodge Treaty that was sure to lead to trouble. According to article 11, the Kiowa and Comanche would withdraw to reservations, but "reserve the right to hunt on any lands south of the Arkansas [River] so long as the buffalo may range thereon in such numbers as to justify the chase."[64] Though the Kiowa and Comanche viewed this land as a protected hunting ground, US negotiators believed the land would be a temporary hunting region until the inevitable decline of the bison made hunting unsustainable and the land went to the United States. Whether the result of malice or foolishness, article 11 was almost sure to lead to violence.

Though the bison herds on the southern Plains were now somewhat protected, the central Plains became a killing field.

Hunters made fortunes killing bison and skinning them for their magnificent pelts.[65] A new leather tanning process developed in the early 1870s allowed bison hides, already prized for their warmth, to be easily converted into leather, opening up a range of industrial uses in the United States and abroad.[66] The bonanza did not last long. After more than a million robes, tens of millions of pounds of bison bones, and other by-products had passed through western rail depots, the central Plains herds were decimated. At the start of hunting season in 1874, hunters looked on the northern side of the Arkansas River and saw slim pickings, and on the southern side, abundance.[67]

A group of hunters and a merchant decided they would make the dangerous move south of the Arkansas River, founding the settlement of Adobe Walls. The Comanche (and their allies) viewed this group as the vanguard of an invading horde. Indians as well as American soldiers and hunters all knew that the bison was the foundation of Plains Indian political and military power. Furthermore, the entry of hunters into the area was a clear display of aggression. White hunters of bison were heavily armed and willing to exact retribution on those who resisted their efforts. When the Kiowa and Comanche saw the US military failing to stop the hunters, they concluded that article 11 of the Medicine Lodge Treaty was disingenuous. Under the leadership of Comanche chief Quanah Parker and the teachings of Isa-tai—a medicine man who spoke of divine intervention to unite the Comanche, Kiowa, Cheyenne, and others in a righteous battle against the buffalo hunters and the treaty-breaking Americans—an alliance of roughly five thousand Indians formed to drive the hunters from the southern Plains.[68]

Parker and Isa-tai's alliance chose the trading post of Adobe Walls as its first target. Merchants formed the core of the Adobe Walls settlement, supplying hunters as well as buying hides.

Bison hunters would also use these establishments as a kind of home base between hunts. Though many of Adobe Walls' merchants and hunters found out about the alliance's planning during the week before the attack and withdrew, a core of especially bold (or greedy) hunters and merchants remained.[69]

During the morning of June 27, 1874, the alliance attacked. The warriors were confident, since during a preraid ceremony Isa-tai had announced that their victory was prophecy and that he would arm the warriors with bullet-proofing medicine. The hunters and merchants hastily retreated into three buildings that, according to G. Derek West, operated as "three miniature 'forts,' which, being situated in the open ground, gave them a good field of fire and some mutual support."[70] The men built crude defenses using sacks of flour and wheat, and dug in for the battle. The next few hours saw a lengthy firefight, but the better-armed hunters eventually won the day. Crucially, hunter Billy Dixon shot and seriously injured leader Quanah Parker, disheartening the alliance, members of which began to doubt Isa-tai's prophecy.

The Adobe Walls fight left the hunters even more determined. In a letter a few weeks after the battle, a local hunter wrote of the battle that "the Indians got a more severe punishment than they received any time during the war of 67, 68, + 69 from the soldiers. . . . Every one here is in hopes that this will bring on a general Indian War."[71] It did.

The attack on Adobe Walls provided the US military with a convenient pretext for a decisive campaign on the southern Plains. Previously, Indian raiding parties had successfully used guerrilla tactics to evade the slower US Army. This time, five columns of cavalry and infantry would converge on the Texas Panhandle, surrounding the Indian alliance and eventually crushing it. This victory would pave the way for the longer-term strategy: destroying Indian subsistence through the extermination of the bison. Military leaders Sherman and Sheridan had learned during the Civil War that the key to victory was the elimination of supply lines and enemy subsistence. Just as the Confederacy had railroads and plantations, the Plains nomads had buffalo. In a letter to Sherman, Sheridan wrote that "the best way for the government is to now make them poor by the destruction of their stock, and then settle them on the lands allotted to them."[72] And so a policy of turning a blind eye would become one of deliberate support: troops would protect the hunters.

Over the course of many small skirmishes, Quanah Parker's alliance was encircled and driven into the Palo Duro Canyon, site of the war's decisive battle on September 28, 1874.[73] Casualties were low, but troops captured the alliance's horses. Though the notation in the US Army's regimental returns was perfunctory—the commanding officer merely noted "captured horses were shot"—the event was of monumental importance to the future of the Comanche, Kiowa, and Cheyenne.[74] Without horses, the bison hunt and therefore the ability to survive on the Plains was gone. Scattered bands of the alliance held out for the following winter and spring, but in June 1875, the last, now ragged, bands surrendered. They agreed to withdraw to reservations in Indian Country (present-day Oklahoma) and relinquish their claim to the Panhandle as a hunting ground. The alliance's leadership was sent to join Wo-Haw and others at a military prison at Fort Marion, Florida.

The Kiowa and Comanche who gave up the fight and settled permanently on the reservation understood what the collapse of the buffalo population meant to their society. They had hoped they could survive on a combination of rations and limited hunting, but by January 1878, the hunts were failing and the US government official in charge of the reservation, known as the Indian agent, was asking his superiors to expand ration issues. In February, Kiowa chiefs requested a meeting so that the agent would "write down and send to the Washington Father the talks they were going to make." According to the agent, in his five years at the agency he had "never seen them or heard them talk with more anxiety than on this subject, not a defiant threatening talk or manner, but as one asking for succor from what he regarded as a terrible fate."[75]

In their remarks, the chiefs explained "we consider ourselves passing away, as our buffalo are passing away." Though this should be read to some extent as hyperbole, the chiefs went on to explain the spiritual significance of the buffalo, to which they considered themselves "kindred." In a particularly grim passage, Kiowa leader Crow Lance observed that "the dark night of the Kiowas is coming on," and asked that his words be passed on to their compatriots imprisoned in Florida, so they "may know their time is close at hand." Once the chiefs were done with their message, the agent provided his thoughts, which appear pitifully inadequate to address the men's concerns. Following their remarks, the agent "addressed them briefly on the example set them by the white man in trusting to his labor and energies in pushing aside the difficulties of life." The agent did not record the Kiowa reaction.[76]

Despite these protests, nothing stopped the commercial bison hunt. With the Kiowa and Comanche crushed, the way was paved for mass buffalo hunting on the southern Plains. Hunters like John R. Cook had only fleeting sympathy for Quanah Parker and his people. In his memoir of his time as a commercial hunter, Cook explained that "It is simply a case of the survival of the fittest. Too late to stop and moralize now. And sentiment must have no part in our thoughts from this time on. We must have these 3361 hides that this region is to and did furnish us inside of three months, within a radius of eight miles from this main camp. So at it we went."[77] It would only take a short time to complete their work. By 1877, roughly five thousand hunters stalked the southern Plains.[78] Within a few short years, the southern Plains herds were nearly gone.

Large ranches opened in the wake of this violence. In 1876, Charles Goodnight, the "father of the Texas Panhandle," founded what would become the famous JA ranch in the Palo Duro Canyon. The site of the decisive battle of the Red River War, breathtaking in its beauty—Georgia O'Keeffe would later describe the canyon as a "burning, seething cauldron, filled with dramatic light and color"[79]—was also perfect cattle country. In his account of the founding, Goodnight makes no mention of the battle that had happened nearby just two years before. From our perspective, this paints a more flattering picture: Goodnight was moving cattle into a largely unoccupied area and he makes no admission of cattle ranchers' complicity in the violence of the Indian Wars. Yet Goodnight likely left out the details of the battle of Palo Duro Canyon and his role in land expropriation not because they were unflattering, but because they were unremarkable. A rancher was putting land to its highest use, and those who would threaten his roaming cattle were simply failing to recognize his rights as a property owner.

This violence on the southern Plains had its analogues in the North. Though some of the specifics varied, with the notable difference being additional conflicts over mining, many of the central themes were evident. For instance, while the key conflict during the Sioux War was over the Black Hills, the routing of the Northern Pacific Railroad through one of the last remaining bison hunting grounds on the northern Plains played a major role in increasing tensions between the United States and the Lakota and Cheyenne. Furthermore, much of the military's leadership participated in conflicts across the Plains, which helped explain the similarities in strategies employed. Ranald Mackenzie, commanding officer at the Battle of Palo Duro Canyon, led a decisive victory in Wyoming Territory at the Dull Knife Fight, helping end the Great Sioux War.[80]

As on the southern Plains, low-level violence precipitated formal military conflict. Much of this conflict revolved around cattle thefts and threats to ranchers. Wealthy ranchers, who held much political clout in places like Wyoming and Colorado, agitated for military intervention. Writing in the wake of both the Sioux War and the Ute War of 1879—in which the Utes of southwestern Colorado killed the local Indian agent, precipitating military intervention that culminated in Ute removal to Utah and the opening of millions of acres of Ute land to ranching and farming—wealthy Wyoming rancher Thomas Sturgis wrote two pamphlets advocating a heavy-handed military policy.[81] Sharply critical of the reservation system and President Grant's reformist "peace policy," Sturgis argued that rather than being a benign ward, "the Indian . . . [is] a lunatic, whose impulse is dangerous, and who must be restrained."[82] He hoped for expanded military intervention on the Plains and cited the constant conflict between settlers and Indians— framed in terms of settlers' suffering at the hands of Indian criminals—as the central problem of life in the West. Though it's unclear how much of an audience Sturgis received for his pamphlet, his underlying assumptions—namely, that Indians were a threat to private property and that harsh military measures were needed to protect white settlers—were the same as those on the southern Plains.

One of the most famous first-hand accounts of the commercial bison hunt, John R. Cook's *The Border and the Buffalo* contains a story that while likely apocryphal, reflects white attitudes toward the relationship between the bison hunt, Indian conquest, and western development. According to Cook's story, during the mid-1880s, at the height of the cattle boom and more than a decade after the southern Plains Indians had been confined to reservations, the Texas legislature considered a bill to protect the few remaining bison. In an address to the legislature, Philip Sheridan, one of the chief architects of Indian conquest in the West, delivered a speech celebrating the buffalo hunters as central to the success of the Indian Wars. He explained that hunters:

> have done [more] in the last two years and will do more in the next year, to settle the vexed Indian question, than the entire regular army has done in the last thirty years. They are destroying the Indians' commissary, and it is a well-known fact that an army losing its base of supplies is placed at a great disadvantage. Send them powder and lead, if you will; but for the sake of a lasting peace, let them kill, skin, and sell until the buffaloes are exterminated. Then your prairies can be covered with speckled cattle, and the festive cowboy, who follows the hunter as a second forerunner of an advanced civilization.[83]

Though tragically accurate, this assessment was wrong on one count: the cowboy was more the buffalo hunter's accomplice than the second forerunner of civilization. One settler might ranch as well as hunt, while another might view the bison hunt as a means to financing a cattle herd of his own. In an 1879 letter to his mother, famed hunter John Wesley Mooar lamented the failing buffalo hunt, but spoke greedily of his "little bunch of cattle."[84] Through a combination of formal military support and the individual decisions of thousands of ranchers and bison hunters, white Americans had violently remade the ecological foundations of Plains power from a nomad and bison system to a rancher and cattle one.

Beef Handouts and the Reservation System

FIGURE 2. 1891 photograph of a government beef issue on
the Pine Ridge Reservation. Library of Congress.

One or two hundred white Americans gathered outside the
walls of Fort Bennett, South Dakota, on October 29, 1889, to
watch "Uncle Sam" distribute an "Indian free lunch." A herd of
cattle was weighed, slaughtered, and distributed to hundreds
of Cheyenne. A young lady lost her appetite as she watched an
"old buck smack his lips over a 'dainty' morsel." The *Aberdeen
Daily News* reporter covering the scene was less squeamish, rev-
eling in how "Indians were seen eating the meat while it was
yet warm with the life blood, and quivered as it was cut off in
chunks by their knives." The reporter explained to distant readers that "when you behold [the Indian's] eagerness to devour
that which you would throw to the dogs; when you see his ava-
ricious appetite for meat dripping with blood . . . all the poetry

your mind has ever evolved about the noble red man of the prairies is knocked into everlasting oblivion."[85]

This was only one of many such scenes recounted in contemporary newspapers. An even more popular trope than that of the hungry "old buck" was the ravenous squaw. Trail driver C. C. French claimed that "it was no uncommon sight to see a squaw at one end of an entrail and a dog at the other end, both eating ravenously."[86] Another symbol could be found in Indian appearance. A story from the *Bismarck Daily Tribune* described a group of Sioux with lurid fascination: "Eagles' feathers and like ornaments frequently adorned their persons, but their principal clothing consisted of cast off garments of civilization, covered in nearly every case by a dirty government blanket." Perhaps most importantly, the reporter's account suggests the Sioux's outward appearance reflected their inner depravity, for "when a poor steer was struck in some spot that was not vital a grunt of satisfaction and pleasure arose from 1,000 Indian throats at the wounded animal's suffering."[87] Reporters seemed oblivious to

UNCLE SAM FEEDING "POOR LO" AND FAMILY.

FIGURE 3. Illustration from Joseph McCoy's *Historic Sketches*.

the irony of the joy they (and presumably their readers) took in their painstaking descriptions of these moments.

For white Americans these scenes were not only entertainment, they were also vindication. They were proof not only that American Indians could not support themselves, but also that land dispossession was part of a broader march of progress across the American West. After the end of the Indian Wars of the 1870s, the spectacle of the beef ration became a major way that readers and western tourists made sense of interaction between whites and American Indians. These accounts began with an observed cultural difference—say, a Sioux preference for raw meat—and exaggerated or fabricated aspects of the incident to reinforce views of Indian savagery. This contributed to a narrative of Indian cultural failure underpinning their social and economic collapse—rather than violence and land dispossession.[88] This simultaneously effaced US responsibility for what was then known as the "Indian question" (or "Indian problem") and justified further exploitative and paternalist measures.

Policy documents drew on these tropes as well. In his essay "The Indian Question," former US Commissioner of Indian Affairs Francis Amasa Walker stressed the precipitous decline of the Indian from one who "shook the infant colonies in terror." Now, the Indian is "represented upon the annuity or feeding-lists of the United States by a few score of diseased wretches, who hang about the settlements, begging and stealing where they can, and quarreling like dogs over the entrails of the beeves that are slaughtered for them."[89]

The "Indian question" was founded on a set of assumptions about American Indians' place in society that underpinned a range of contradictory approaches. Both the advocates of a gentler reformist policy—adopted by President Grant and his Quaker Indian commissioners as the "Peace Policy"—and hard-liners like Thomas Sturgis shared the assumption that Indian culture was to blame for their lack of economic advancement.[90] Policy debates often cited struggling Indian farmers and ranchers as an example of personal and cultural failure, despite the fact that the 1870s and 1880s were a time when the vast majority of white farmers could not turn a profit.[91]

The debate over whether to encourage Indians to farm or ranch illustrated these assumptions. In the Senate Indian policy hearings of the 1880s, the question of occupations was of central interest. When Senator Henry Dawes asked Indian agent William Swan for his opinion, Swan replied that "an Indian will naturally take to herding."[92] Infantry lieutenant Alfred Meyer agreed that it was crucial to play into the Indian's "natural" affinities, but this was exactly the aspect that worried those who advocated for farming. James McLaughlin, agent for the Standing Rock Agency, believed that it was exactly because "the pastoral life is the one nearest their hearts" that incentives to herd could not bring about genuine reform.[93] Colonel Charles C. Gilbert, who commanded a fort near Standing Rock, agreed that herding would just encourage the Indian to continue to keep ponies and encourage his troublesome "natural instincts."[94] For another military leader, General Alfred H. Terry, it was less about natural instincts than the general framework of civilizational advance; he argued that farming advocates made "the error of passing over, or rather of attempting to pass over, one of the natural steps [herding] in the progress of civilization."[95] According to Terry, ranching was the first step on a civilizing journey.

Both sides of this debate started with the same underlying assumption that culture was what mattered, not the quality or quantity of reservation lands. Further, comparably little consideration was given to differences in Indian societies or modes of political organization. The absurdity of the debate is especially apparent when one considers the extent to which Euro-American settlers endlessly debated whether their own land would be more profitable if used as pasture or farm. Many combined both depending on their circumstances and land quality. Here, questions of culture were not important.

Yet discussions about Indian ranching or farming were not abstract debates—they guided actual policy. Though more insidious examples appear below, a short example of how an Indian agent addressed the theft of nineteen horses from Otterbelt, a Comanche man, will illustrate the effect of these ideas. In accordance with a treaty agreement, the government undertook to compensate Comanche for thefts committed by white settlers. Yet in a document outlining his advice for how to handle Otterbelt's case, Agency Superintendent William Nicholson decided that the case could be used as a "means of teaching the Indians." Though Otterbelt could be compensated in money, or perhaps replacement horses, the superintendent recommended providing restitution in the form of cattle, because ranching "should be encouraged to the utmost extent. It is the readiest way to their self support and cattle are far less liable to be stolen than ponies."[96] Otterbelt's desires are not even noted. Though the more sinister effects of this kind of paternalism are explored below, the resolution of Otterbelt's claim is a small example of the effect of the pervasive mind-set that Indian affairs should be managed in the "interests" of Indians.

Further, these debates and assumptions would have far-reaching implications for the cattle-beef complex. The reservation system benefited cattle ranchers in two key ways: (1) by providing a favorable market for cattle, and (2) by creating circumstances that allowed for the low-cost leasing and later purchase of Indian lands for grazing. These factors not only supported ranchers, but also undermined reservation life. According to historian William Hagan, cattlemen's role as "exploiters of Indian lands and meddlers in tribal politics" contributed strongly to the failure of the reservation system.[97] Cattle were at the heart of a cycle of immiseration and policy justification.

American cattle ranchers secured lucrative government contracts to supply reservations with beef.[98] These contracts provided good rates for the entire supply period (often six months or a year), safeguarding ranchers against short-term fluctuations in cattle prices. Furthermore, these contracts were often more profitable than direct sale in Chicago markets. For example, an 1883 contract to supply roughly 6.5 million pounds of beef to the Rosebud Agency in South Dakota compensated suppliers $3.93 per hundred pound weight of cattle (on the hoof) at a time when prices in Chicago ranged by quality from $3.50 to about $6.00. As contemporary critics observed, ranchers used these contracts as outlets for their lowest quality cattle, which in Chicago would have almost certainly gone for about $3.50, making ration contracts lucrative agreements.[99]

These contracts were at times an outlet for diseased or rejected cattle. In a letter to A. G. Boyce, ranch manager of the XIT ranch, Abner Taylor, head of the ranch's Chicago office, warned him to stop shipping "big jawed" steers to Chicago. A swollen jaw was a symptom of either actinomycosis or actino-bacillosis (thought to be the same disease at the time), meaning it was illegal for the animal to be sold for human consumption and it would not be bought by the Chicago meatpackers. These cattle were a problem for ranchers, since they could not be sold in formal cattle markets. But Taylor had learned of a solution from a friend whose "advice is that we try + get a small gov't contract next year—and if we can do so he says we can clean up the ranch by putting in all the drags + big jaws we have."[100] Generally, these contracts were to supply beef to reservations.

It was no secret at the time that ranchers secured high prices for substandard beef through a combination of government corruption and incompetence. Contemporary newspapers and ranchers railed against the "Indian Ring," a nefarious circle of Indian Affairs officials and suppliers who used corrupt contracts and bribery to fleece the US government. As Montana rancher Granville Stuart has suggested, "everything brought from the East shrinks most awfully in this dry altitude."[101] Some cattlemen even went to the length of manipulating the scales used to weigh their animals prior to sale.[102]

Scrupulous Indian agents knew about rampant corruption and tried (usually unsuccessfully) to prevent it. When John M. Thayer became suspicious of a herd being taken to the Upper Missouri, he proposed using "men to inspect these cattle [that would] be incorruptible, for efforts will be made to buy them up, men who are strangers to the contractors, and who are unapproachable should be sent out to receive the cattle."[103] It is unclear what ultimately happened with the herd.

Even when corruption was not an issue, government agents were inexperienced buyers, and inadvertently provided ranchers extremely favorable terms. Many contracts allowed ranchers to supply cattle in the late fall, when it would become the government's responsibility to care for them in the winter, the season during which cattle lost the most weight and in which stock owners carried the highest risk of loss. By the time the Sioux received their ration—the size of which was based on the animals' weight at the time of sale—the animals had lost a significant mount of weight.[104] Ranchers used these contracts to minimize their risk and shift the burden onto government bureaucrats.[105]

Cattle contracts supplied rations at immense cost to the public and in grossly insufficient quantities to keep recipients fed. This was hardest on men like White Thunder, a Lakota who had to listen to public criticism of wasteful Indians, when he believed that if men in Washington would just "go around among my people, and see how our houses are put up; and when you see the miserable condition of the people you will cry."[106] For ranchers and cattle marketers, this misery was good business.

Grazing cattle on reservation lands, whether illegally or with dubiously acquired leases, was another way that ranchers profited from the reservation system. When it came to leasing, ranchers both benefited from and contributed to American Indian political instability. In some places, ranchers secured leases through bribery, while in others the fact that reservation authorities were unwilling or unable to keep ranchers out led communities to embrace leasing as a way to realize some profit on land that otherwise would be illegally occupied.

Illegal grazing was common across the West. According to most treaty terms, it fell to the US government to protect property rights on reservations, and any attempt on the part of tribal government to forcibly enforce these rights risked military intervention. But government officials showed little interest in enforcing such property rights. When Lakota Chief Red Cloud complained to Senate investigators about squatters grazing cattle illegally on his reservation, Committee Chairman Henry Dawes changed the subject.[107] Elsewhere, John Scott, Indian agent for the Ponca, Pawnee, and Otoe Agency, observed that before formalized leasing, "cattle [were] running everywhere."[108] At the Rosebud Reservation on the northern Plains, there were so many trespassing cattle—as many as 2,500—that residents used grass fires to try to prevent illegal grazing.[109] At least some of those cattle belonged to George Edward Lemmon, who was a respected local businessman, prompting him and his associates to go to the lengths of setting up a kind of shell company to conceal their involvement in illegal grazing.[110] The local Indian agent, Valentine T. McGillycuddy, was largely indifferent to the practice, simply returning trespassing cattle to their owners.

In light of these violations, it was easier for Indian agents to push their wards to embrace formalized leasing rather than actually enforce their property rights by policing reservation lands.[111] Agents, cattlemen, and tribal governments negotiated informal leases. Often, the push for these leases came from the same men who had been grazing illegally, as was the case with George Lemmon on the Sioux Reservation.[112] Agreements set prices for use of grazing land and were to an extent enforceable, but also existed in a legal gray area as actual control over leasing of reservation land was reserved to the federal government. Secretary of the Interior H. M. Teller grudgingly tolerated the system, though avoided taking a clear stand on the practice.[113]

The land policy on the Cherokee Strip, a stretch of largely unused prime grazing land in the Indian Territory, illustrates this reality.[114] Initially, the Cherokee government tried to institute a tax to charge nearby ranchers to use the Strip. Though conscientious ranchers paid the tax, many avoided the tax collectors by alternately moving their cattle on and off the land. This upset scrupulous ranchers and Cherokee alike, spurring both to embrace informal leasing as a means of curbing the practice.

The parties involved consulted directly with Secretary of the Interior Teller. The exact content of the approval proved extremely controversial once the leases became the subject of congressional scrutiny, but some form of government sanction was clear. Rancher R. D. Hunter explained that "[the Secretary] did not consider that he had the power to approve the lease, but he did not see any reason, if the Indians were agreeable and we could make the leases with these Indians, why there should be any obstacle."[115] Other cattlemen reported similar replies. Following a close vote on the leasing arrangement in the Cherokee assembly, roughly nine ranching entities (individual and corporate) leased between five and six million acres of land for a period of ten years for ten cents an acre.

Making the best of a bad situation—renting land that would otherwise be illegally occupied—was the stated aim of Indian agents and the Cherokee leadership, though this may have been a pretext for widespread corruption. The leasing rates were extremely low; rents immediately to the north in Kansas and south in Texas were almost twice as high.[116] Upon scrutiny, vague claims of bribery emerged, though ranchers and agents alike denied any wrongdoing. In an investigation into the leases, Cherokee witnesses were uneasy naming names, but A. E. Ivey, a former newspaper editor, related stories of cattlemen complaining about the high costs of securing leases, referring not to the stated cost but to "the price paid outside of the $100,000 rental." Ivey also claimed to know a man who began to support the lease proposal only after receiving a $400 bribe.[117]

The attitude of Cherokee supporters of the leases seemed to be that shady tactics were justified because the arrangement was for the good of the Cherokee Nation.[118] Furthermore, the view appeared to be to let sleeping dogs lie. Cherokee chief Dennis Bushyhead discouraged Ivey from cooperating with investigators since their snooping would hurt the nation.[119] Lawyer and Cherokee delegate to the US Congress, Richard Wolfe condemned the entire investigation, arguing it was using corruption claims as a cover for an attempt to co-opt leasing rights and take away something that "we claim the right to do ourselves as a nation."[120]

Nevertheless, the leases came at a high cost to individual people. A leasing agreement thwarted the ranching efforts of a Cheyenne woman identified only as Mrs. Belinti. When she and her husband prepared to ranch a stretch of land along the Washita River, the Cheyenne Indian agent angrily evicted them. After relocating two more times, she wrote a desperate letter to the Department of the Interior, explaining that "one Bickford, a white man from Leavenworth, who had a large herd of cattle there evidently with the agent's and his son-in-law's consent, told us that we could not stay there, but had to move, because he, Bickford, had a better right to that part of the reservation."[121] Bickford was a leaseholder, and after going through even more struggles with ranchers and her Indian agent, Belinti gave up and left the area.

Belinti's story suggests that corrupt Indian agents were behind much of the leasing conflict. Though firm evidence is difficult to find—one sympathizes with the attempts of the Department of the Interior's leadership in Washington to root out corruption when every charge turned on conflicting eyewitness accounts—there were certainly cases of leasing agents abruptly leaving their posts to begin lucrative ranching careers. Furthermore, many Indians reported that agents often threatened them into signing leases. In Montana, Crow Indians reported that a Major Armstrong had told them that those refusing to sign a lease would no longer receive rations.[122] Armstrong denied the charges, but did resign.[123]

This type of corruption was especially dangerous since Indian agents had the first opportunity to frame reservation conflicts for their superiors. In March 1884, Cheyenne and Arapaho Agent John Miles reported that a band of Kiowa were slaughtering and stealing cattle on the reservation.[124] Though Miles viewed the Kiowa actions as a criminal act, they were likely protesting leasing policy. About a month before the thefts, a group of Kiowa wrote letters to Washington complaining about illegally grazing cattle and voicing the Kiowa men's opposition to the leasing measures. The men were concerned that "the white men's cattle will soon be here so thick that there will be no room for the Indians who have small bunches of stock."[125] The Kiowa shared their reservation with the Comanche, and the aggrieved ranchers had bribed a group of Comanche into granting leases for the reservation as a whole, without the consent of all affected parties.[126] When the Kiowa resisted, the ranchers, likely with the help of the local Indian agent, tried to brand them criminals and dupe the US military into enforcing their corrupt contract.

This story also reflected the popular strategy of securing a lease by bribing anyone willing to sign a piece of paper. Because agents in Washington had a poor understanding of local politics, they could not determine whether a group of people was able to speak for a reservation's desires as a whole. Local agents alleviated this problem, but they too often had difficulty determining the meaning of lease signatures. Names were forged on leases to add the appearance of broad support for, or opposition to, a measure.[127] These practices contributed to systematic corruption within Indian political systems, which in turn would support white claims that Indians were incapable of self-governance.

Leasing arrangements varied widely owing to the enormous variety of local conditions and views. In some cases, most of a reservation supported leasing as a legitimate source of profit. In others, white ranchers crowded out Indian ranching operations. Yet in most if not all of these cases, ranchers worked behind the scenes to advance their own interests and subvert Indian politics in the process. Furthermore, ranchers spread misinformation to bureaucrats in Washington, who, even when well intentioned, ignored local Indian politics in favor of making decisions based on their theories about racial progress and the eventual resolution of the Indian question. The general effect was that Indians were usually blamed for any problems or conflict.

Leasing agreements, like lucrative government contracts, were the principal way in which ranchers benefited from the reservation system. In the case of leases, the Cherokee and other nations may have received payment, but it was almost certainly less than if a fairer property regime had existed. Similarly, these agreements made for vast tracts of land in which large ranching corporations crowded out small-scale Indian ranchers, further limiting their subsistence options. Some Indian polities did indeed have valuable rangeland, especially once the other land in the West was overgrazed, but because they did not have the capital to start their own operations, they had no better option than to lease. Leases made the best of an exploitative situation, even as they strengthened the reservation system's grip.

Lurking behind government approval for leases was the belief that reservations were too large. This view came from ranchers, bureaucrats, and the general public. Joseph Nimmo captured this view most clearly when he observed that since "the buffalo has been driven off, a nomadic mode of life within that region is no longer possible; therefore reservations far beyond the needs of the Indians are to them a curse rather than a blessing."[128] This assumption had enabled the kind of paternalist policies that led to favorable leasing agreements and lucrative contracts, but, surprisingly, the culmination of its logic, the 1887 Dawes Severalty Act, was one many ranchers opposed.

First passed in 1887 and amended in 1891, 1898, and 1906, the Dawes Act led to a decline in Indian-controlled land of almost seventy-five percent. Underpinning the act was a claim that dividing common lands into individual parcels would help Indians break their apparent dependency on the federal government.[129] Beyond the problematic assumptions embedded in this view, it also amounted to a land grab. Perhaps the most blatant example being the eventual creation of the state of Oklahoma from what had previously been set aside and known as Indian Territory.[130]

Ranchers had a conflicted relationship with the act. Severalty threatened the extremely lucrative system of large-scale leases ranchers in Oklahoma and elsewhere had managed to create. Ranchers fought the implementation of the severalty plans aggressively, delaying their implementation in certain areas until lengthy leasing agreements had expired.[131] Nevertheless, by the time the leases went out of effect, the ranchers had already benefited greatly. Furthermore, the fact that ranchers opposed these measures in no way diminished their role in promoting the circumstances and ideas that contributed to the Dawes Act. It was a historical irony; a set of assumptions about Indian poverty and land use that both had benefited ranchers and they had done a good deal to promote became enmeshed in broader debates that worked against rancher interests.

The belief that Indian behavior explained Indian poverty drove reservation policy.[132] Indians were either lazy or ignorant and had to be taught self-sufficiency, or they were criminal, and should be violently punished by the US military. These assumptions allowed ranchers to manipulate Indian policy to their benefit, whether in the form of profitable leases or generous beef contracts. Just as the story of the development of western ranching cannot be understood outside the context of land expropriation and the reservation system, the evolution of federal Indian policy cannot be understood outside the context of contests for control of the Plains' most valuable commodity: cattle.

From War to Criminality: Retelling the Story

In 1893, Charles Goodnight sued the Comanche Nation.[133] His claim: nearly thirty years before, Comanche raiders had stolen ten thousand of his cattle. The raiders then drove the herd to the Mexican-Comanche trading post of Quitaque and sold the cattle to Mexican merchants, who resold the animals in New Mexico and Colorado. Goodnight would win his case and receive a payment from the US Treasury, which settled the cases on behalf of the Comanche.

Goodnight's lawsuit was one of many legal disputes between settlers and Indians stretching back to the early national period. In 1796, the federal government had created an indemnity system meant to promote peace by allowing settlers and American Indians means to seek compensation for property crimes committed by either party. In reality, though, the enormously corrupt system was all but closed to Indians and did little to preserve the peace. Goodnight's suit was one of a spate of cases in the 1890s because the federal government, hoping to eliminate a wasteful and ineffective system, had announced that it would no longer accept claims after the spring of 1894.[134] Though Congress or the Department of the Interior had resolved claims directly during most of the nineteenth century, rampant corruption motivated Congress in 1891 to pass an act granting the United States Court of Claims jurisdiction over these claims, known as depredation cases.[135]

In a formal sense, Goodnight's claim was valid. Several Mexican stock dealers testified to seeing Comanche raiders selling cattle with Goodnight's brand. Though the fact that his case relied on eyewitness testimony almost thirty years after the fact makes it slightly suspect, there was ample evidence from many sources that a group of Comanche did in fact take his cattle and sell them to traders.[136]

Nevertheless, the claims system was rotten at its core. Suits were predicated on flawed assumptions surrounding evidence, cattle ownership, and the political situation in Texas at the time. The cases presupposed that the 1860s and 1870s were a time of relatively unproblematic US sovereignty over Texas, and Indian raids were isolated criminal acts as opposed to acts of war. This self-serving narrative reimagined the history of West Texas in a way that both criminalized the Comanche and legitimated rancher and buffalo-hunter encroachments. In paying ranchers out of previously negotiated annuity funds created for American Indian polities, the depredation cases were simultaneously material subsidy to ranchers and conceptual ammunition for those who would justify land expropriation and heavy-handed federal Indian policy. Goodnight's case was emblematic; the man known as the "father of the Texas Panhandle," who had founded a ranch not far from the decisive battle of the Red River War, was now receiving compensation for what were allegedly Comanche thefts.

Fundamentally, these suits were predicated on the legal acceptance of a cattle brand creating an inherent property right. Cattle were rarely stolen from a rancher's direct control, but rather seized as the animals wandered far from the ranch house. Goodnight's cattle were "running in Jack, Palo Pinto, Young, and Throckmorton Counties."[137] The Coggin brothers lost nearly 3,900 cattle "on the open range," as did the claimants in many other related suits.

The criminalization of Indian theft was an outgrowth of the requirement that to bring a case, the United States and the tribe to which the thieves belonged had to be currently at peace, or, to use the language at the time, the Indians had to be "in amity with the United States."[138] If a state of war existed, the cattle taking was an act of war; if there was a broader state of amity, it was a criminal act. Claimants initially tried to base their claims on any treaty that declared perpetual peace, but in *Marks & Wollenberg v. The Piute and Bannock Indians*, the court held that the existence of a treaty declaring peace was not enough proof, since treaties could be unilaterally broken. Instead, the courts attempted a complicated weighing of the facts of the case, their political context, and a host of other factors. Eventually the Justice Department began circulating a memo that listed dates of formal conflict with Indian nations, and announcing that claims within these dates would not be accepted.[139]

Yet in Goodnight's case—to take one example of many—this process assumed a stable political system to which all Comanche were bound. However, this was a projection of American or European forms of government onto Indian political organization. Individual Indians were often willing to negotiate and the federal government was willing to listen, but this did not necessarily mean the US government was negotiating with anyone particularly important. Moreover, just because a few or even most Comanche had agreed to reside on reservations and give up their claims to Southwestern land did not mean that a state of peace existed for all Comanche (or Cheyenne or Kiowa). There may have been peace between the United States and the Comanche according to some narrowly bounded definition, but as the diaries of Susan and Samuel Newcomb attest, Texas in 1865 was not a peaceful place.

Claimants were aware of the difficulty establishing questions of amity and framed their suits to exploit this situation. Chicago lawyer Isaac Hitt told a client that "proving the friendly condition of the Tribe no matter what kind of nor how much mischief its individual members were doing" was of critical importance. Claimants should choose their words carefully. If a careless claimant used phrases like "the Indians were on the war path," it could undermine the case by implying the tribe as a whole was at war. Claimants should instead stress that "individual Indians or squads of Indians" committed the depredation, "while the tribe as a tribe was at peace."[140] Based on Hitt's advice, the cases were explicitly framed in order to portray depredations as criminal, rather than political, acts.

Just as the very basis of these cases depended on a flawed understanding of Indian political organization, the standards of evidence were similarly problematic. Because cattle were generally stolen out of sight, the evidence that they were stolen by Indians—and not whites—was nearly all circumstantial. In their 1880s suit, Samuel and Moses Coggin claimed that they knew Comanche were responsible for 1870 cattle thefts because "the Indians generally understood to be of the Comanche tribe were raiding though that section of Country." Or, as claimant Frank Collinson elaborated, that Indians were then raiding was "an established fact and well known at the time."[141] Nevertheless, such claimants continued to emphasize that these were not acts of war, because a state of amity existed with the relevant polity.

To provide specific evidence, ranchers described signs of Indian activity. In Goodnight's case, they never actually spotted the thieves, but while trailing them the men found horses with "the marks and indications of what we knew at the time as Comanche ponies"—specifically, sores from being ridden bareback and split ears, used as a Comanche ownership mark.[142] In the Coggin case, the men found moccasin tracks and cattle that had been killed with arrows.[143]

Claimants cited years of frontier experience to make their interpretation of the evidence credible. To explain how he knew the thieves were Indians and not Mexican, Goodnight explained that "I have been on the frontier since I was 16 years of age. . . . I speak the Mexican language and am thoroughly acquainted with their manners, ways, and customs, and from my 30 years experience on the frontier and in the cattle business, I can say unhesitatingly it was Indians that drove my cattle off."[144] Similarly, cattle trader Manuel Gonzalez used his knowledge of the Texas frontier during the 1860s to justify his assertion that the men who stole Goodnight's cattle were Indian because, "no white men dared travel across Texas from that point into New Mexico in the direction in which these cattle were being driven, because the Indians were so thick that they would have been killed and scalped before they had gone 50 miles, and nobody dared to travel across that country without a strong military escort."[145] In another case, Henry Sisk explained that he knew Comanche had stolen cattle because "I had been on the frontier since 1856; I had fought them before, and had seen other Indian tribes, and saw arrows left on the ground which I knew to be Comanche arrows."[146] For these men, their time on the frontier not only established expertise, it also bolstered credibility.

The depredation case law did allow the accused to present their perspective, though this appears to have been more a formality than an actual process. Rather than making the proceedings fairer, this provision lent them a false air of objectivity. When a claim was filed, the local Indian agent was instructed to organize a council, announce the charges, and see if "the Indians in council recognized, remembered, and admitted the depredation charge."[147] Nevertheless, few court decisions mention the Indian perspective. Even when agents made an effort to allow a response, it merely underscored the absurdity of the process. In April 1890 Indian Agent Charles Adams organized a meeting at the Kiowa, Comanche, and Wichita Agency to ask about seven depredation cases spanning several decades. It was unclear if anyone involved in the cases was even in the room. The answer for all the charges was either denial or "both tribes claim to have no knowledge of this crime."[148]

The depredation cases had the trappings of impartiality: seemingly high standards of evidence and great concern for the legitimacy of claims. Judges went to great lengths to fairly consider what constituted amity, whether an entire people could be held accountable for isolated actions, or whether a claim was fraudulent. Furthermore, the Justice Department did reject many dubious claims. As lawyer Isaac Hitt told a client, "a claim must be fully and equitably proven before a judgment will be rendered for its payment."[149] Yet the ultimate effect of the depredation cases' emphasis on fair procedure was to legitimate a system that took US authority and Indian criminality as a starting point.

At the broadest level, the depredation cases rewrite the narrative of the Indian Wars of the period.[150] The courts did recognize periods when nations were at war and therefore not liable, but in giving priority to this generally large-scale and formal violence—similar to understanding land expropriation as a series of large-scale military conflicts—over the constant low-level conflict on both sides that characterized the period, most Indian resistance is criminalized. In bracketing off particular periods of war as well, the government is effectively claiming total authority over the area during the times it claims are peaceful, when these regions (like the southern Plains) were much more areas of contention than of US domination. This framing of Indian-white conflict was more than a bureaucratic story, it was part of a broader process that justified the Department of the Interior's paternalistic stance toward leases, rationing, and severalty.

The cash settlements in these cases were yet another small but not entirely insignificant subsidy to ranchers. The government recognized that many claims were inflated, and only paid out a fraction of the amount requested, but this was still a substantial amount.[151] At a time when cattle prices had hit rock bottom—the early 1890s through 1910s—cattlemen could receive compensation for cattle at their old ballooned values. It also seems an unlikely coincidence that in many of the depredation cases the cattle were "graded up to some extent and were a better class of stock than the general run of Texas cattle," to use the Coggin brothers' description.[152] In their simultaneous subsidy of ranchers and marginalization of American Indian resistance, the depredation cases were emblematic of the linkages between material factors and the ideas—about property, American Indian culture, ranching, etc.—that shaped the cattle-beef complex.

Conclusion

The rise of industrial beef might seem to be one primarily of slaughterhouses and stockyards, or capital and corporations. But without the violence and dispossession explored in this chapter, the story told in the remainder of this book would not have been possible. Beef's move to the center of the American diet depended on bison hunters' and ranchers' ecological remaking of western lands with the support of the US military.[153] Further, this process produced a set of narratives that not only justified seizing American Indian lands but also placed ranching at the heart of the story of the American West.

Fighting with American Indians over control of the Plains also shaped Westerners' relationship with the American state.

In cattle ranchers' ongoing demand for government support as well as perpetual dissatisfaction with the help they did receive, we see the origins of an American mind-set that celebrates independence even as it remains largely blind to the pervasiveness of the federal government in the West.[154] Susan Newcomb may have settled in a "wild and destitute country" at great personal risk, but it was no coincidence that she and her husband did so in the shadow of Fort Davis.[155]

Through the efforts of people like Samuel and Susan Newcomb, the history of the cattle-beef complex braided with a national myth of the frontier.[156] This myth traced the origins of what it meant to be American to the process of westward expansion and the idea of Manifest Destiny. As Wyoming rancher Thomas Sturgis suggested, westerners viewed the violent settling of the West as a national project, for not only did "every town in every county, every county in every state, [have] its sons in the army," many westerners were only a generation or less removed from life back east.[157]

War, the destruction of the bison, and the piecemeal creation of a reservation system were processes fundamental to ranching in the United States. Pacification of the southern Plains Indians freed the way for the mass trailing of cattle out of Texas and onto northern ranges, also violently cleared of people and bison. Yet accompanying this incredible dispossession and conquest was a process of historical forgetting that culminated in the idea of the West as the "open range," a wide-open land looking for inhabitants, human and animal alike. This idea absolved cattle ranchers of complicity in the violence on which their profitability rested.[158]

The open range was most famously commemorated in what would become the state song of Kansas: "Home on the Range." The song is a lengthy celebration of a cloudless land "with diamond sand" where the "deer and the antelope play." In the initial version of the song, there is no mention of the land's past human inhabitants, as if this wonderful place were merely awaiting its rightful occupants. There is a version of the song that mentions the fighting on the Plains in passing. A 1910 version collapses decades of violent struggle into the words, "The red man was pressed from this part of the West / He's likely no more to return."[159]

The open range was more imagined than real, but the idea's power helped make western violence and land dispossession a reality. Not just a land waiting to be occupied, it was an ideal that had to be created. The land and its inhabitants had to be pacified, the canvas cleared, for the coming of the Cattle Kingdom.

2

Range

WITH ABUNDANT land and high cattle prices, the early 1880s were good times for optimists and hucksters alike. Walter Baron von Richthofen was both. Born to an aristocratic family in Silesia, von Richthofen moved to Denver, where he became a civic leader working to promote investment in Denver and across the West. His 1885 book *Cattle-Raising on the Plains of North America* "treats the subject of cattle-raising in the West fully and systematically," though that does not preclude a healthy dose of boosterism; he deems the industry "the El Dorado of the day."[1]

The argument for a bovine El Dorado began with a Malthusian belief in endless demand. Von Richthofen explained that "there is constantly increasing tendency to over population, while the food-producing capacity has about reached its limit in most of the European countries."[2] The equally enthusiastic James Brisbin, author of *The Beef Bonanza*, agreed that "the beef business cannot be overdone," in large part because "the number of people are increasing much faster than the number of cattle."[3] Better yet, people loved the taste of beef.

Von Richthofen's analysis relies on colorful anecdotes and rosy math. There was the story of the Irish servant girl who received back wages in the form of cattle and in a few short years

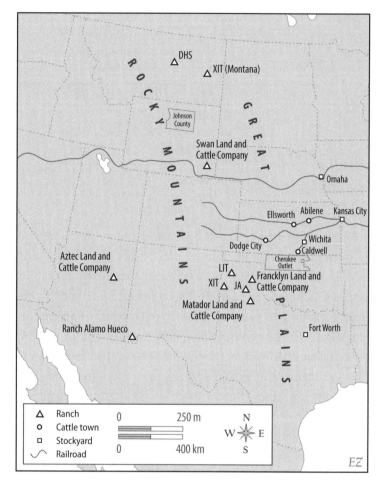

MAP 1. This map shows some of the key ranches and locations
discussed in this chapter. Map by Ezra Zeitler.

turned $150 into $25,000. Mr. Day of Wolf Creek, Indian Territory, bought $15,000 worth of Texas cattle in 1875 and six years
later sold his herd for $450,000.[4] The key was reproduction.
Von Richthofen generously estimated that "natural increase"
was at eighty percent of the number of cows (with roughly half

the offspring female). By this calculation, 100 cows would, in ten years, produce 1,428 heifers (young female cows) and an equal number of males, for a total of nearly 3,000 cattle. Deaths from all causes would only amount to two to three percent a year, an estimate that cattle ranching's reality would prove ridiculous, but one that would allow an extremely detailed and precise-seeming chapter of von Richthofen's book to show how an investment could be doubled in only five years—even by a tenderfoot.

Alongside absurd estimates of the returns to be made raising cattle,[5] von Richthofen pushed a vision of a corporatized industry. He explicitly compared the future of cattle ranching to the railroad or telegraph industries, explaining that investors had to get in early and become the large capitalists, before someone else did. Act fast, for "opportunities for wealth and high returns for one's money will have passed away, and industries, like the cattle business and land ownership, may become monopolies."[6] Booster James Brisbin imagined similar corporate possibilities, arguing that a large ranch, "conducted on strictly business principles, would realize a far larger profit on the money invested than if put into mining, lumber, iron, manufacturing, or land companies."[7] For a time, these predictions were correct.

Following the violent expropriation of Indian land during the 1870s and the growth of transportation networks that enabled the rapid distribution of beef and cattle, investors across the United States and as far away as Scotland funneled capital into places like the Texas Panhandle and southern Wyoming. Dreaming of Plains riches, these investors believed the optimistic math peppered throughout von Richthofen's and Brisbin's guides. Rich young men from the East would head west armed with some seed money and the connections back home to secure investment.[8] For instance, Harvard classmates

Frederic deBillier and Hubert Teschemacher moved to Wyoming in 1879 and amassed a large herd, in part with money from Teschemacher's father.[9] In addition to eastern wealth, British capital was a crucial source of funding. According to historian Herbert Brayer, British investors organized roughly thirty-seven UK-based cattle companies with more than $34 million in capital between 1879 and 1900. All but one was organized before 1886, when the investment craze ended.[10] Within a decade, large cattle-ranching operations covered the Plains.

The collapse of corporate cattle ranching would be as spectacular as its rise. Blizzards decimated the industry during the late 1880s. Tens of thousands of cattle froze to death on the range, and even the survivors were too thin to sell. As vulnerable ranches went bankrupt, they flooded markets with their stock, willing to sell at any price to placate investors and bondholders. Even well-managed operations were sucked into the maelstrom. Large midwestern operations felt the pinch as well, since they were now competing in cattle markets with panicked western ranchers.

This disaster had long-term repercussions: on the other end of ranchers' desperate cattle deals were buyers for the Chicago meatpacking houses. In fact, the panic came at almost the same moment that the Chicago houses were beginning to gain market power, and the abundance of cheap cattle accelerated this process. Though it had initially looked as though large corporate ranches could dominate the beef supply chain, by the time the ranching industry pulled out of this crisis in the 1890s, the meatpackers were far too powerful. A rancher-centered meat-production system would never again be a serious alternative to a meatpacker-dominated cattle-beef complex.

Contemporary observers explained the collapse of the ranching boom as a consequence of the overstocking of western ranges, rooted in laziness and corporate greed.[11] An 1888 article in the British publication the *Economist* on why American ranching had been so "unremunerative" cited poor management and waste, noting that men who should have been working were instead hunting and fishing and squandering investors' money on servants dressed in "red livery."[12] Forest Service official Will Barnes condemned ranchers' "fancied opulence" and desire to make a quick profit. Barnes titled a description of the disaster "The Inevitable Happens—Overgrazing and Disaster."[13] In these accounts, the winters of the late 1880s were particularly devastating because greedy ranchers had forced many more cattle onto the Plains than the ecosystem could support.

Although hard winters caused very real damage, this explanation is a little too convenient. Regarding overstocking, there was little precise information on how many cattle were actually scattered across the West at the time, and no clear idea of how many cattle the Plains could actually support. Yet the overstocking account was emphasized for political reasons; it allowed later ranchers, often working with family members or in small-scale partnerships, to dismiss corporate ranching as an unfortunate chapter in the history of cattle raising, superseded by men who lived closer to the land and used principles that went beyond pure corporate greed. Some sources have even argued that ranchers used overblown overgrazing claims to deter would-be rivals.[14]

Yet academic accounts of late nineteenth-century ranching and the rise of western industry broadly echo this account. Business and environmental historians have overemphasized business's ability (or inability) to rationalize nature. In the business account, disaster stems from poor business practices, irrational exuberance, or a lack of technical knowledge. For environmental historians, disaster is a consequence of transforming a landscape all too well. As an area is integrated into commodity markets, environmental destruction and catastrophe follow.[15]

The collapse of corporate ranching was not merely the consequence of overstocking. Rather, it was the result of an interplay between natural and economic forces that cut to the heart of ranching as a nineteenth-century enterprise. Ranching's risks and rewards stemmed from a cattle ranch's existence as a for-profit ecosystem. Profit depended on harnessing profitable ecological processes—grazing and reproduction—and eradicating unprofitable ones—fire, predators, and starvation. Herd growth, or "natural increase," was key, but only up to a point. For instance, eradicating wolves entirely could cost tens of thousands of dollars; better to simply keep their populations in check and accept the occasional lost calf as a cost of doing business.

As this example suggests, profitability ultimately depended on finding the cheapest means of allowing cattle to care for themselves. Range grasses were free, but they were not as nutrient-dense as a feed like corn, so cattle had to scatter far and wide to stay fed. Ranchers had to spread their stock farther than the animals could be actively monitored. This created great risk as few ranches had a precise idea of how many animals they owned, despite the seemingly precise numbers local managers provided far-away investors.

The central fact of nineteenth-century ranching was that instability and profitability grew from the same soil. The ranching disaster was not a consequence of business's inability to tame nature, but rather because in the nineteenth century, profitable ranching was predicated on not doing so. Competition only exacerbated this tendency; ranches that took the most risks could offer the lowest prices, forcing more conservative rivals to follow suit.

This system worked well for a time, but even the slightest disturbance—or fear of one—could topple it. Keeping careful track of a ranch's many cattle herds was prohibitively expensive, but this was exactly what anxious investors and corporate managers demanded. Capital wanted precision but profit required uncertainty.[16] The harsh winters of the late 1880s were so destructive because they exposed this contradiction. When anxious investors and managers surveyed their herds in the aftermath of these winters, the mismatch between what was on the books and what was on the ground erased profits and sparked panic. This story, then, is one about contradiction and scale. The microlevel practices of ranching—scattering cattle far and wide, allowing cattle to care for themselves—collided with the macrolevel needs of capital for precise business practices.

Especially when landscapes are first integrated into an economic system, the slippage between the rationality of business and the unpredictability of nature is a tremendous source of profit. This may help explain the boom and bust nature of economic development in the American West, especially in agriculture. That large profits require substantial risk is a truism of financial capitalism, and the natural world's unpredictability only exacerbates this tendency. The same precipitation that as snow could sweep away an entire season's profits—to paraphrase the *Economist*—could, if a few degrees warmer, promote the growth of abundant grass and profits.

Though this fundamental feature of nineteenth-century ranching—that profitability and instability were at its core—was a disaster for individual ranchers, it was extremely productive for the broader system. Because ranching was a perennially risky but also profitable endeavor, there were always people looking to make a profit raising cattle. Walter Baron von Richthofen was not alone in his optimism. There was a tendency toward overproduction in cattle, ensuring the meatpackers always had desperate suppliers.

Similarly, in the aftermath of corporate ranching's failure, ranchers' self-understandings, forged in critiques of corporate ranching, encouraged individual participation in a risky and in many ways financially exploitative ranching system—small-scale producers taking most of the risk as they sell to food processors. Here is a key part of the cattle-beef complex's eventual resilience: ranchers shoulder the risk, and the meatpackers have cattle in good times and bad. This also explains why the meatpacking industry can be so centralized and heavily corporatized, while ranching presents itself as authentic, family oriented, and noncapitalist.

Understanding this story requires focusing on western ranching and corporate ranching, two subjects that some critics have argued are overemphasized in the history of American beef. While corporate ranches only controlled roughly fifteen percent of beef cattle in the United States,[17] their story would generate some of ranching's core myths. Similarly, examining the operation of the largest ranches magnifies and highlights contradictions that were present even in the smallest ones.[18] This chapter emphasizes western ranching over midwestern or eastern ranching because the West was where corporate ranching emerged as an alternate possibility to the meatpacker-dominated system that prevailed. Nevertheless, cattle raising outside the West was vitally important to this system as a whole, and it will be examined at length in the next chapter.

Understanding ranching in the 1880s is crucial for understanding the rise of the broader cattle-beef complex for three reasons: (1) the boom, built on paper dreams, brought investment to western communities, (2) the collapse of corporate ranching as the Chicago meatpackers were gaining power explains the disappearance of an alternate rancher-dominated system of industrial agriculture, and (3) the morality play around corporate ranching's failure reinforced the mythology of the cattle-beef complex.

Though ranching comes down to pasturing cattle on quality land until fat enough to sell, the specifics are a bit more complicated. Calves had to be branded, fences maintained, prairie dogs poisoned, and more. If the rise and fall of corporate ranching can be found in the interplay between the practices of ranching and the economic forces of cattle marketing and investing, then understanding how a ranch actually worked is vital. A discussion of the founding of ranches and their cattle, land, and labor needs follows this introduction. The cowboy labor section closes with a discussion of the cowboy's cultural significance and how it was perpetuated through trail and ranch songs. The chapter then returns to the overarching story: the collapse of corporate ranching. The conclusion connects the collapse of corporate ranching to the broader story of the cattle-beef complex.

"As Large as All Yorkshire": Buying, Counting, and Managing Cattle

Large corporate ranches arrived in the American West in the late 1870s. In 1879, the Anglo-American Cattle Company became the first British ranching enterprise in the West, purchasing herds in Wyoming and Dakota territory.[19] Within two years of its founding in 1880, the Edinburgh-based Prairie Cattle Company went from an investment pamphlet to an operation with roughly one hundred thousand cattle in Colorado and the

Texas Panhandle. Meanwhile, east-coast transplants leveraged connections back home to secure money from places like New York and Boston.[20] Though a bit late to the party, a group of Boston-based businessmen and investors organized the Aztec Land & Cattle Company in 1884, which for a time owned large herds in the Southwest.

Generally, these large companies would buy out local ranchers or partner with them. One of the Prairie Cattle Company's important early acquisitions was the LIT ranch, which had belonged to George Littlefield, one of the Texas Panhandle's pioneering cattlemen. That same year, the Dundee-based Matador Land & Cattle Company bought Texan Henry Campbell's Panhandle cattle herds and made him the ranch's superintendent. The XIT, perhaps the largest ranch of the 1880s, began as a three-million-acre grant given to Chicago-based investors and builders in exchange for building the Texas statehouse. It became a ranch after John Farwell went to England and secured investment in the Capitol Freehold Land & Investment Company, which would finance the XIT. Similarly, the legendary JA ranch combined famed cattleman Charles Goodnight's knowhow with Scotch-Irish businessman John Adair's capital.

In addition to large ranching operations, there were many small-scale, privately held ranches. Many, many cattle belonged to people who might only have had a few dozen animals scattered over a ragged stretch of land that barely qualified as a pasture. Nevertheless, the corporate boom was a turning point for the industry. If you were not working for or part of a corporate ranch, you were competing with them in the cattle markets or for range land. While frustrating for small-time ranchers, there was a silver lining: experienced cattlemen were always watching for an opportunity to sell their herd at an inflated price to the newest ill-informed venture.

For a new ranch, the first order of business was amassing a cattle herd. It was in this process that one can find seeds of the industry's collapse. Large ventures, usually with more money than expertise, would move in and buy out many small ranchers in order to build one giant herd. Grift was common. Few, if any, sellers knew exactly how many cattle they owned, and all parties involved in a purchase had incentive to inflate the number of cattle concerned as well as their fecundity. The seller would overrepresent to inflate profits, and the purchasers did not mind, since large herd sizes, even if only on paper, attracted investors.

Even honest negotiators found it difficult to keep accurate count of a herd. Land was the West's great resource, and given enough space, cattle could turn it into salable flesh. But this required grazing animals across vast distances, and far from cowboys' watchful eyes. This meant that few knew exactly how many cattle were scattered on an individual range, and nobody knew exactly how many cattle were across the entire West.

When it came time to buy or sell cattle en masse, the practice of spreading cattle far and wide led to serious problems.[21] Because a thorough count was prohibitively expensive, transactions were done using an estimate known as a book tally. Ranchers used the numbers from their last thorough count—often several years out of date—and made allowances for estimated losses and gains. An even fuzzier method was "to multiply the [number of] calf brandings of the season in which the estimate is made by four, which is held to give a fairly near approximate to the number of the whole cattle on the range."[22] Once the involved parties reached an agreeable number, ownership was simply transferred without a direct count, in what was known as a "range delivery." From the moment of purchase, the strategy of natural increase—releasing cattle onto the range and checking on them a season later—collided with the necessity of making the ranges legible to investment capital.

Unfortunately for ranchers, there was no better solution. As one manager explained to suspicious investors, "when you consider that our range for instance is as large as all Yorkshire, some idea of the difficulty of collecting all its cattle on a thousand hills may be surmised." Book tallies and range delivery were necessary evils, despite the fact that, as the same manager explained, "there is no doubt that under this era of Company promoting, and buying not what is seen on a range, but what Ranche Books state are there, an immense deal of fraud is lying in wait for the investing public."[23] Though this practice was manageable in calmer times, the investment bonanza of the early 1880s attenuated the already faint links between marks in a herd book and actual animals on the range. Yet this reality was also what enabled ranching to be as profitable as it was; range delivery created risk, but scattering animals far and wide made high profits possible.

Once a herd was acquired, investor demands amplified problematic counts. Investors wanted returns, and the best way to show them—especially when cattle prices were slumping— was with generous herd growth. One trick was to count herd growth as revenue. As a herd grew, there were more animals, and if prices remained the same that meant a more valuable herd. But this required using an estimated (and potentially out-of-date) price. Critics argued it was better to base revenue on actual sales, and not venture an estimate. And yet this alternative also came in for criticism, since sales were largely seasonal and investors demanded more up-to-date calculations. Counting herd growth as revenue was common practice, but one that inspired sharp dispute, with critics alleging it was used to mask slumping prices and suspicious math.[24]

Though the inaccuracy of herd size estimates is difficult to quantify, evidence suggests inflated numbers were widespread. Examples abound of managers clarifying estimates, quietly acknowledging over-counts, or making dramatic corrections. When the Prairie Cattle Company went into decline because of alleged mismanagement, an outside investigator concluded that the actual herd size was dramatically lower than the stated one. Not only had the ranch inadvertently over-counted by a thousand animals, but a manager had "neglected to make any deduction for two years' mortality among the cattle."[25] In 1886, the *Economist* cited yet another ranch as short nearly seventeen thousand cattle, a substantial portion of their claimed herd size.[26]

Even well-run operations struggled with herd counts. Correcting the book count was part of daily business. Tiny deductions and additions around the margin, trying to bring paper counts in line with reality, were common. When Matador manager William Sommerville discovered that the ranch's herd book had overstated the number of two- and three-year-old steers, he used rough estimates to correct: "I think therefore that a deduction should be made of all the remaining threes, and half of the twos on the books."[27] Though ranchers worked to align estimated and actual numbers, the frequency of this work hints at a chronic divergence between book counts and reality. The Matador, for instance, needed a massive revision of its herd statements in the early 1890s. Between 1883 and 1890, the Matador herd crept up from 77,200 head to 97,781. In 1890, the office herd-size statement read "not declared"; the following year the count was down to 70,200, and the year after that the herd was at 58,016. In both 1891 and 1892 the number of cattle sold was lower than in previous years, suggesting the revision was not the result of sales. Rather, the revisions suggest a process of bringing the herd estimate in line with reality, to account for the twin forces of overestimated natural increase and underestimated mortality.

The brand book, a ranch's "official record," was the chief means by which distant investors tried to understand the reality of ranges and cattle herds in rural Texas.[28] The tallies in this book were used to plan yearly sales, calculate profits, and track performance. Though investors and managers often treated it as truth, it was at best an outdated—and at worst a deeply flawed—representation of what was actually going on.

At times, however, shareholders and reporters became suspicious of the numbers stated in the brand book. This was evident in a public debate in the *Economist*, which, due to the amount of British capital headed to the American West, reported on American ranching. An 1883 letter in the *Economist* compared the Prairie Cattle Company's original herd-size statement with a newly published one and concluded that the size increase was impossibly large. In a response letter, the company's chairman, J. Guthrie Smith, claimed that the current numbers were accurate and that the problem was with the original herd count, which was off by fifteen thousand animals. This was because the original count "did not include the calves which were branded between the provisional purchases of certain herds by our agents and delivery to the company."[29] In a follow-up, the original critic, identified only as *Vaquero* (Spanish for "cowboy"), expressed further shock at this explanation. If the company knew the original numbers were in fact too low, then the company had been lying for years about the herd's overall rate of increase. If the original herd size was actually 118,500 rather than the originally claimed 104,000, yearly reports of the growth of the herd must have been exaggerated. *Vaquero* explains that in light of the discrepancy, "the herd has not increased then, from

104,500 to 140,000 since its acquisition . . . but from 118,500 to 139,000," or fifteen percent less than claimed.[30] Even if there was no fraud, *Vaquero* argued the company was a mess, since "it is a most extraordinary acknowledgement for a director to make, that such an asset as 14,000 calves should not have been included in the reports of the company in one form or another."[31]

This kind of fuzzy accounting was endemic to nineteenth-century ranching and would pose enormous problems in the wake of the devastating winters of the mid- to late 1880s. It also poses great challenges in evaluating the claim that the ranges were overstocked. As cattleman John Clay would observe about book counts, "tis safe to say that in many cases not half the number of cattle represented on the books were in actual existence."[32] Yet the efforts of scrupulous managers to correct these problems indicate that uncertainty in ranching was not simply a question of fraud or manipulation. Duplicity was there, in abundance, but the story of ranching was not a simple tale of greed and dishonesty. Rather, indeterminacy was part of nineteenth-century ranching's DNA. Careful counts were pro-hibitively expensive, making widespread risk and uncertainty unavoidable. Fraud merely exacerbated this tendency.

Land: Private and Public

Imaginary herd increases required the stroke of a pen; actual increases required good land. But it was not as simple as finding a quiet spot. Ranges had to be secured from other people and their cattle. Even following the Indian Wars of the 1870s, remak-ing the Plains was not a smooth process, but rather a violently contested one that pitted large ranchers against small oppo-sition, whether herder or farmer. Keeping out rivals required fences, law suits, angry letters, and, at times, Winchester rifles. Meanwhile, the Plains' ecosystem had to be remade into one conducive to cattle raising. Cattle could take care of themselves, as long as there were not too many wolves, fires, or thieves. Nature had to be remade to allow nature to take its course. Furthermore, this all had to be achieved at the lowest cost possible.

The first step was finding some good land. Armed with vague reports or their own memory, cattlemen would ride a territory to survey its potential. To partners and investors, local disadvantages—such as vulnerability to blizzards or a lack of water—were minimized. Often, accounts of the process read less like a sober account of a business decision and more like a mythical origin story. One group of men " 'prospecting' for cattle ranges" had nearly given up "when a camp of hunting Indians told us that if we crossed the range we should find . . . the Powder River Valley, the old winter home of the Red Cloud Sioux." The land was perfect, for the range could "fairly claim . . . a local exemption from snow storms," due to the valley's favorable geography.[33] Elsewhere, Granville Stuart and his colleagues found a "magnificent body of hay land with cold springs all through it" that was beautiful and "well grassed, well watered, and good shelter." Apparently on this range "it does not snow deep and it cannot lay on the ground because there is too much wind."[34] It would become the site of Stuart's first cattle operation, the DHS ranch.

Despite these types of claims, land was only potentially good. Some animal populations had to be kept in check, while others had to be excluded entirely. Water access had to be secured. Wildfire prevention was a must. Even the cattle's life cycle was regulated in the interest of getting stock to market efficiently.

Wolves were a serious threat to calves.[35] Through a combination of hunting and "liberal use of poison,"[36] ranchers worked to eliminate them. George Tyng, whose thousand-square-mile range was home to several packs of wolves, estimated that even a small pack killed roughly one animal per day. Opting for a plan of aggressive hunting, Tyng decided he would not suffer the same fate as more complacent ranchers who had endured considerable losses.[37] Cowboys for the Prairie Cattle Company, for example, told managers that during the late 1880s their calf crop was short owing to the prevalence of the wolves that stalked the company's hillside pastures.[38]

Less violent, but no less disruptive, were gophers and prairie dogs, whose burrows tore up ranges, injuring cattle and horses alike. Texas rancher George Loving was particularly upset about their effects. In a report to government bureaucrats studying American ranges, he argued that prairie dogs consumed and destroyed more range than cattle did, and "if the dogs were destroyed that part of the state would furnish grazing to twice as many cattle as it ever can do as long as the dogs are permitted to remain." He praised Texas's Staked Plains, a land "almost entirely free from prairie dogs," as a bovine Garden of Eden.[39] In two subsequent letters, Loving expressed further dismay about the "increased supply of prairie dogs" in western Texas.[40] Elsewhere, ranchers debated the cheapest and most effective prairie dog poisons in letters. When one writer asked industry journal the *Breeder's Gazette* if castor beans would kill prairie dogs, the journal explained that the beans would more likely attract more of the critters.[41]

Because cattle cannot graze farther than six or seven miles from a water source, access to water was a major concern across the arid West.[42] Even in relatively wet areas, the West's extreme rainfall fluctuations meant that few ranches were free of concern. During particularly bad droughts, watering holes turned to mud and even grasses began to dry out and die.[43] In some areas, ranchers dug artesian wells. The Hansfield Cattle

Company had a particularly elaborate operation in which windmills pumped water into massive holding tanks.[44]

Fires were a real threat, as cowboy work songs suggest. "The Cowman's Prayer" pleads, "Prairie Fires, won't you please stop? / Let thunder roll and water drop / It frightens me to see the smoke / unless it's stopped / I'll go dead broke."[45] These fears were not unreasonable. In the winter of 1885–86 the XIT failed to make fire guards, and after a wildfire, "this loss of the grass . . . followed by a winter of unusual severity caused great anxiety," and in the end considerable loss.[46] Some ranches used controlled burns and built firebreaks to avoid what happened to the XIT. Though fire prevention was critical to protect investments, fires—human caused or otherwise—had long been an important part of the Plains ecology.[47] Fire prevention would later cause long-term problems, though this was little known at the time.

Remaking the land went hand in hand with remaking cattle. Across the world, cattle biology was bound up with the surrounding farming system; in a place like England, where cattle were primarily raised on farms and actively managed, the most dominant cattle breeds were much more dependent on farmer intervention and were more valuable, but also more labor-intensive. In the US West, ranchers initially relied on the hardy and independent Texas longhorn to fit their hands-off ranching model.[48] Yet these cattle also matured more slowly and produced less salable meat, so ranchers were often thinking about how to improve their animals.

Over time, American ranchers began to experiment with less hardy European breeds. But cost was always a concern and maximizing profit required balancing cattle's ability to gain weight rapidly with their ability to survive on their own. One manager emphasized how hard it was "to secure well bred animals of good individual merit without losing sight of that most important quality, hardiness, or what is known on the range as 'rustling qualities.'"[49] Others were suspicious of any attempt to improve range cattle. A. S. Mercer observed that "a striking peculiarity of the range-raised cattle is that if you destroy the perfect liberty of action, they at once become dependent—lose their will power and rustling qualities."[50] One far-sighted rancher argued that reliance on "rustling qualities" was actually a problem because it encouraged the use of less labor-intensive—and less profitable—breeds. He hoped the system would change because "cattle graded too highly will not be as prolific with the present system."[51] In the short term, however, few ranchers could afford to go against the dominant trend.

Approaches to cattle breeding also related to another ranching practice, that of regulating the herd's reproductive cycle. Though cattle production remained seasonal, it was important to ensure animals would not be born too early in the year. Calves born in February or March could be susceptible to an unexpected late-winter storm.[52] Even the animal's life cycle reflected the same logic of the ranch—profit came from slightly realigning what were otherwise natural-seeming processes.

In some ways, remaking the Plains ecosystem was the easy part; keeping out rival ranchers and settlers was more difficult. To do so, ranchers embraced legal, extralegal, and outright illegal measures. Now-standard practices like branding, fencing, and private land ownership require a widespread acceptance of their legitimacy, which, initially at least, was not present. Stealing cattle or cutting fences was a common form of resistance, and at times sparked large-scale violence.

Although the earliest operations found simply grazing cattle on publicly available land enormously profitable, it eventually became necessary to find a cheap means of securing the best land for oneself. This became especially acute in the early 1880s, with the sheer number of settlers and small-scale ranchers moving onto ranges across the West making it difficult even for powerful ranchers and cattlemen's associations to keep them out. For instance, the Francklyn Land & Cattle Company found that the company's ranges were "squatted-upon by actual settlers who let fires get into the grass; by accidents; or purposely, to drive away the cattle from their unfenced or weakly fenced crops."[53] The only solution appeared to be formal ownership of the land they wished to use.

Because buying all the land one wanted to use would reduce profits, ranch managers employed a range of creative strategies. Buying an area's water access gave no direct right to the broader pasture, but effectively controlled the surrounding area.[54] A related strategy was to buy an overwhelming percentage of land on a pasture, knowing that rivals would not find it profitable to own small, scattered patches.

Nevertheless, these approaches had risks. As the Matador's managers discovered, if ranches were not careful to own the entirety of their range, they risked an aggressive speculator buying land out from under them. In 1882, the ranch's managers found that a rival had purchased "86,000 acres of land right in the heart of the Matador." The purchaser had little use for the land and the Matador's operators believed it was an "attempt to blackmail." They had no choice but to negotiate with the owner, who likely made a nice profit. Though the Matador escaped with little actual damage, a manager observed that the incident "shows the necessity of a concern like ours abroad establishing on a permanent basis putting itself on an impregnable position on the land question."[55] He was adamant that land purchases were necessary to protect against "land speculators," and the Matador soon expanded its holdings.[56]

Relationships with established neighbors could also be tense. The Matador initially had an informal relationship with the Espuela ranch by which they would share water access and occasionally cross each other's land. However, this happy state of affairs would prove short-lived. When the Espuela ran short of grass, managers surreptitiously grazed their cattle on Matador land. Angry about the intrusion, one Matador employee grumbled that "the least thing they might have done would have been to ask our permission first."[57] While relatively benign, the incident illustrated that even amicable relations could sour over land issues.

For some ventures, ranching was secondary to a longer-term goal of land investment. The XIT, which operated on a massive grant given to the firm that built the Texas State Capitol, was intended as a way to use the land before its eventual sale. During a shareholder meeting, a manager explained that "our Company is emphatically a land investment company, its primary and main object being to dispose of its land, when the proper time comes, at remunerative prices, to emigrants and settlers."[58] The Aztec Land & Cattle Company's statement of incorporation outlined the company's goal to first buy the Atlantic & Pacific Railroad's alternating land grant section in Arizona, then acquire the rest of the checkerboard and hold on to the enormous parcel. They proposed "combining with home and European immigration and colonization societies and transportation companies, with whom highly advantageous arrangements for locating settlers on these lands can be made."[59] Managers were confident that in only a few years the value of the Aztec's land would "far exceed" the one dollar per acre they had paid for it.[60] For operations like the XIT and the Aztec Land & Cattle Company, a cattle ranch was a profitable innovation on an older land company model of simply holding

unoccupied property until westward expansion made parceliza-
tion and sale profitable.

For these companies as well as traditional ranches, property
rights were more complicated than simply holding a deed; they
had to be enforced. The struggles of the Prairie Cattle Company's managers to control their range illustrate the limits of
formal property rights. Shepherds were surreptitiously using the
Prairie's ranges.[61] The managers proposed expanding cowboy
efforts to patrol the range for trespassers and thieves, but this
was only so effective; the need to protect property rights always
conflicted with the necessity of keeping labor costs low. One
company employee thought these costly attempts to exclude
trespassers constituted an attempt to "dominate the whole
range to the exclusion of every one else—a thing impossible."[62]
Beyond costs, ranchers had to balance their desire to secure
their ranges with concerns about angering local residents, who
could break fences, destroy cattle gates, or start fires."[63] Ranchers seemed to be fighting a losing battle.

Furthermore, even formal property rights were far from
absolute. Fences could not impede established trailing routes,
and this was the cause of heated and, at times, violent confron-
tation.[64] The desire to block popular trails was understandable.
Trail herds could spread disease, and if the paths went through
especially nice land, the cowboys would linger and graze their
herd at the owner's expense.

An agent of the Spur ranch initially tried accommodating
men trailing cattle, but was quickly driven to extreme measures.
He had allowed herds to travel almost thirty miles across his
land, but "there seems to be no limit to the number coming, and
as each one that gets through encourages others to follow, I have
been compelled to issue orders to permit none to go through
unless at the place and by the route that inconveniences us the

least."[65] The manager eventually grew so frustrated that he part-
nered with nearby ranchers to create and promote a minimally
disruptive trail, drafting an advertisement outlining the trail
and explaining that the ranches involved "now beg respectfully
to invite your cooperation."[66] The attempt had mixed success.
One cattleman was pleased with the new route, while another
threatened to sue for damages for blocking the old route.[67]
Meanwhile, on the XIT, Abner Taylor grew so frustrated with
herds passing through his pastures that instead of promoting an
alternate route, he ordered his men to stop the trailing by any
means, even "if you have to do so with Winchester [rifles]."[68]

These issues of land access and land rights were inseparable from a larger conflict between large and small ranchers. Big
ranchers, corporate or otherwise, fought endlessly with men
who maintained herds of only ten or twenty cattle. They often
accused these smaller operations of stealing unbranded calves
from their herds, a charge that, while sometimes true, was just
as often a pretext for measures to exclude small ranchers. Meanwhile, small ranchers claimed that larger outfits illegally fenced
good land and tried to intimidate them into leaving. These
small ranchers framed their opposition in terms of equality and
access over monopoly. As one supporter of curtailing the power
of large ranches complained, "no one seeks to abridge the range
industry, but the whole nation will join hands to prevent the
range from being monopolized."[69] Though much as been made
of the open range and cattle raising in commons versus fenced
areas, ultimately the real fight was between ranchers and ranching corporations that counted their cattle in the thousands and
the family that might only have a few dozen animals. The open
range was actually compatible with either system, and at different times and in different places, both groups embraced or
rejected direct property ownership.

In response to some of these fights, wealthy cattlemen began to organize and dominate "cattlemen's associations." Ostensibly to protect ranchers' collective interests, they were often intended to exclude poorer competitors through exclusionary range laws. For instance, restrictions on moving cattle favored ranchers with the resources to follow complicated branding laws and requirements. North Texas ranchers supported a measure requiring that cattlemen notify neighbors before moving a herd. This ensured time for careful inspection of the herd's brands to ensure there had been no intermingling with nearby stock, or accidental theft.[70] Yet the law was designed for large operations that moved thousands of cattle seasonally, rather than for the kind of highly mobile pasturing practices of people who only owned ten or twenty cattle. When these men tried to move cattle without the requisite notice, they could be accused of theft.

One of the key developments in the struggle between elite ranchers and poorer rivals was the spread of barbed wire fencing. Several designs for wire fencing received patents in the early 1870s, but credit for barbed wire usually goes to Joseph Glidden of De Kalb, Illinois, who received his patent in 1874. Because the Plains were relatively treeless, barbed wire was a cheap alternative to prohibitively expensive wooden fences. Barbed wire spread rapidly throughout the West in the 1870s and 1880s; production rose from ten thousand pounds of the fencing material in 1874 to more than eighty million pounds just six years later.[71] According to economic historians, this was a key moment in the history of western development, since wire fencing provided a crucial means of controlling cattle and enforcing property rights.[72] But there was more to this process than a new technology, for wire fencing precipitated a violent struggle over western land use. Fences could control animals, but people were a different story.

The *Breeder's Gazette* covered a range of fencing disputes during the mid-1880s, many of which were over access to water. Small ranchers argued that fencers were monopolizing water access and that fence cutting was necessary to save their herds.[73] In Montana, one rancher complained that there was so much fence that "cattle are 'worn out' going long distances for water." The author argued that in light of an ongoing drought, fences blocking access to water should be "thrown down."[74] Whether seeing their herd struggling against a fence for water just out of reach or finding a mile-long fence blocking their traditional trailing route, small ranchers harbored a hatred for wire fencing.[75] Initially at least, many ranchers and settlers embraced fence cutting to resist barbed wire's spread. Whether this was illegal was, and still is, unclear. In a time of dubious land ownership and property rights, appropriate fence locations were as much a question of custom as formal law. Cutting a specific fence could be completely justified to some and outrageously illegal to others. Fence cutters ultimately caused millions of dollars in property damage. Landowners responded with their own measures, organizing cattlemen's associations and "law and order" associations to patrol for fence cutters.[76]

Fencing quickly became a political issue. One small-scale rancher, in an attitude reflective of a widespread belief, connected fencing to the perils of corporate ranching, arguing that "one thing is certain—no country can improve or settle up that is fenced in for miles and owned by large corporations."[77] The *Mobeetie (TX) Panhandle* advocated the opposite position, complaining in 1883 about insufficiently harsh penalties and explaining that "men should and must be protected in their rights of property, else government is useless."[78] Meanwhile, the Texas Greenback Party explicitly opposed mass fencing.[79] In Texas, fence cutting became a felony in 1884, but only after an acrimonious debate in the state legislature. Up in Wyoming, ten large ranches were cited in 1886 for illegal fencing, and the state's territorial governor was ousted following a fencing scandal.[80] Not coincidentally, the ousted Governor George Baxter was a manager of the Western Union Beef Company, which would later be implicated in the violence of the Johnson County War, which will be discussed shortly.[81] Even the secretary of the interior had to weigh in following a spate of letters. Secretary Henry Teller suggested ranchers and farmers should cut illegal fences themselves.[82]

While this remained a tense issue, fence cutting did eventually peter out as a result of successful enforcement and eventual acceptance of a new western property regime. The Texas Rangers in particular were associated with curbing fence cutting, with one member supposedly advocating buried dynamite as a deterrent.[83] Persistence also helped—barbed wire's low cost meant fences could be strung and restrung. However, enemies of fencing did have some success; protests and sabotage likely curbed some of the most egregious examples of illegal fencing.

Small ranchers, shepherds, and farmers used fence cutting as a means of opposing what they saw as the illegal or unfair occupation of range lands. The dispute illustrates that the rise of a property regime and certain patterns of land holding in the West were as much about political and social conflict as a new fencing technology. Barbed wire only became an effective tool of land ownership through a combination of monitoring on the part of cowboys and the support of a legal regime that embraced the interests of large landowners. Barbed wire helped end the open range, but only in concert with a struggle between landowners and small-scale ranchers.

While the fight over barbed wire was widespread but diffuse, the fighting in Johnson County, Wyoming, was acute and violent. Central to the mythology of the West, the Johnson County War of 1891–92 was also important to the history of the cattle-beef complex.[84] The violence between stockholders large and small—and, in later tellings, between honest, hardworking men and corrupt elites—helped produce stories about ranching and western life that would resonate in the postcorporate ranching world that emerged in the 1890s.

Across Wyoming, but particularly in Johnson County, the elite-rancher-dominated Wyoming Stock Grower's Association (WSGA) was increasingly angry about the intrusion of small-scale ranchers and homesteaders, who they accused of cattle theft. Because of the close connection between ranching and territorial politics, this was also fundamentally a fight over political power in Wyoming. Most of the state's political figures, including the governor at the time and both of Wyoming's senators, were members of the WSGA. The state's livestock commissioners were also members, and had far-reaching powers to police ranges, make arrests, and seize cattle. Yet this was changing. The influx of small-time ranchers and farmers into Wyoming was broadening the state's electorate and its base of political power. The WSGA believed that if it could evict these people from the ranges, wealthy ranchers could return to political as well as economic power.[85]

In late 1891, the WSGA hired private men ostensibly to eliminate cattle rustling (theft), but the process actually amounted to the eviction of small-scale ranchers from the county. Matters came to a head in April 1892. The WSGA men first surrounded the ranch of a local opponent, and eventually killed him and his friend.[86] When word reached the local sheriff, a friend of the murdered man, the sheriff assembled a posse of nearly two hundred people to chase the killers, culminating in a lengthy standoff. The governor, a WSGA supporter, sent a frantic telegram to President William Henry Harrison, asking for federal support against an "insurrection."[87] Troops were dispatched from nearby Fort McKinney.[88] These troops took control, which amounted to overriding the authority of the local sheriff, disbanding the posse, and taking the WSGA agents into military custody. It remains a matter of debate to what extent this was a legitimate move to restore order, or whether it was a miscarriage of justice that saved the cattlemen from the legitimate authority of a local sheriff.[89]

Fundamentally, the conflict was about access to land.[90] Wyoming's ranching elite wanted to use a system of public lands with the WSGA as a gatekeeper. Small ranchers wanted access to these lands and were willing to embrace any system—whether public lands or private ownership—that enabled small-scale farming or ranching. What this conflict in many ways suggests is that corporate ranching was compatible with both open-range ranching and individual access. Public land and a regime of private ownership could both lead to the same industry structure, and therefore struggles over either were part of a process of political and legal jockeying between large and small cattle owners and farmers.

That land politics in the 1880s ended up favoring the large ranchers only magnified the instability in the ranching system. Whereas small-scale ranchers could eke out a modest but stable living, operations that scattered tens of thousands of cattle across as many acres could make huge profits at considerable risk. Size and risk seemed to go hand in hand. Once these risks led to disaster, events like the Johnson County War and the struggles over fence cutting would be remembered. Following the collapse of corporate ranching in the late 1880s, the legacy of these conflicts would inform a broad critique of corporate ranching. But before exploring this story, it is important to understand the place of the cowboy in this history, and the contrast between cowboy myth and cattle-worker reality.

"Cowboy-ism": Cattle Workers and Western Mythology

Though ranch work appears less obviously as a form of wage labor than pushing papers in an office or toiling in a slaughter-house, cowboys and their managers were wage laborers. In art and fiction, cowboys have appeared in many ways noncapitalist and even premodern. Even cowboys themselves often under-stood their work in these terms. Yet at times they behaved like other industrial workers, going on strike or demanding better contracts. Interestingly, these moments often alienated a usually adoring public, revealing that cowboys were only admired up to a point. The disjunct between cowboy perception and reality explains much about how society as a whole understands cattle ranches and cattle labor.

To briefly address middle management, corporate ranches faced the same problem as all large businesses: making individual and firm interests overlap. Scotsman William Sommerville expressed the Texas version of this problem in a critique of a Mr. Farwell, the Matador ranch's American manager. Sommer-ville observed that "Farwell is a very smart man, but he is work-ing for Farwell, not for any share holders or debenture holder in England."[91] For foreign investors, Texans were necessary busi-ness partners, but they were not always to be trusted.

To address this concern, foreign and eastern investors often relied on a friend or compatriot out west who could act as an intermediary between a company's board and local managers.[92]

When Scotsman Murdo Mackenzie applied to be manager of the Matador in 1890, he casually referenced that he had learned the cattle trade "in the Old Country."[93] Yet men like Mackenzie were hard to find; companies often had no choice but to rely on erratic or unreliable agents. William Sommerville was "something of a hypochondriac" and when he temporarily took ill, the Matador's Scottish managers struggled to find a replacement, facing limited options for "individuals of English or Scotch origin" in Forth Worth, Texas.[94]

Good employee relationships could also sour over time. Henry Campbell, the Matador's American superintendent, was a Matador employee for years before an acrimonious split with the company. The company had early concerns about Campbell, but had no other option. Sommerville and Campbell had a tense relationship, with Sommerville accusing Campbell not only of "unfitness for business" but also of jealousy of Sommerville's authority.[95] Following a dispute over a cattle sale, Sommerville sent an angry letter to Scotland, arguing, "I am entitled to give [Campbell] an order and expect to see it obeyed."[96] By 1892, Campbell had left the company and was suing the Matador for unpaid commissions. Matador representatives even believed that, "for the purpose of prejudicing public opinion," Campbell had floated a story to the *Fort Worth Gazette* that small ranchers around the Matador range were upset with the corporation's management practices. This was a dangerous charge given nascent political outrage in Texas about foreign capital and landowners.[97]

Though Scottish managers often overstated the ill effects of incompetent American managers as a way of displacing anxiety about their business, managers could and did cause serious problems. The Prairie Cattle Company had particularly bad luck. For years, their American manager had been secretly "drawing a salary of pounds 4,000—a salary unparalleled in the history of the cattle business, and one which practically made us the laughing-stock of all the cattle interest in America." Worse yet, this situation tapped into Scottish anxieties about their lack of familiarity with American ranching. Apparently, when Americans found out about the manager's inflated salary "they shrugged their shoulders, and said that the people in Scotland must have more money than wit."[98]

The Prairie Cattle Company had even bigger concerns in their partnership with Underwood, Clark & Company, a Chicago-based management and investment company. When the ranch faced bankruptcy in 1889, a report to shareholders explained that "among the causes which have contributed to the misfortunes of the company, the dominating influence of Messrs. Underwood, Clark & Company over its affairs ranks scarcely second in importance to the fall in the price of cattle."[99] Investigators alleged that Underwood, Clark & Company chronically oversold cattle. Because the Chicago firm had only a short-term relationship with the ranch, it took an approach that provided large short-term gains, but arguably hurt the ranch's long-term prospects. Furthermore, "lavish expenditure . . . characterized the management of the company's affairs."[100] Thanks to a foolhardy agreement with Underwood, Clark & Company, the ranch could sever the relationship only at great cost. Though the Prairie Cattle Company was almost assuredly a victim of falling cattle prices and poor management, the company's fate illustrates the difficulty of managing a multinational corporation in the age of the telegraph and steamship.

Managers may have kept investors happy, but the key actors, in the popular imagination and out on the range, were the cowboys. Largely young men, cowboys managed seasonal round-ups during which herds would be (roughly) counted and calves branded; they could also prepare a range for the winter or ride the fences to watch for the encroachment of smaller ranchers and cattle thieves. Cowboys trailed cattle to market and moved herds from range to range. The work was difficult and the pay poor. Most were employed seasonally and scraped through the winter, when there was little to do beyond playing cards.

Born to an upper-middle-class family, Way Hamlin Updegraff learned what he called "the art of cowboy-ism" when he moved from a New York farm to a New Mexico ranch. In a series of letters to his mother and family back in Elmira, New York, he documented 1880s ranch life. Mostly his work was about riding all day, "from six in the A.M. To half-past four P.M."[101]

"Cowboy-ism" required completing a variety of small and large tasks using an even larger variety of tools. Updegraff received a new pair of corduroys of whose fit he was "naturally a trifle proud," but, as he explained, when "[I] went to stick my hands in my pockets to strut around a little" he discovered that his pants had no pockets. He asked, "where will I carry my compass, my matchbook, my pocketbook, my knife, string, keys, and so forth 'ad libitum.' Why, a man can get along a darn sight easier in this country without pants than he can without pockets."[102]

The long hours and coordinated nature of ranch work encouraged the men to form tight-knit groups. Updegraff reflected on these relationships during an account of an argument surrounding the worst of all ranching disasters, a stampede. Scared cattle had gone on a rampage, scattering the herd and nearly trampling the workers, leaving them in sharp disagreement about who was to blame. Updegraff, who "had no hand in it," nevertheless tried to calm things down. Later, he observed that "stampedes are liable to happen in the best regulated families or rather cow-outfits."[103] Updegraff's reference to family strife underscored the importance of emotional bonds to ranch labor.

Though ranch life was difficult, it appealed to Updegraff. Differentiating his views from broader attitudes is difficult, but in reply to a letter asking about his eventual return, Updegraff wrote "[I] don't know when I will come home. The longer I stay the longer I want to stay. I think the chances are better here for making money than they are East—I don't see any prospects for me there, do you?"[104] Cowboys like Updegraff dreamed of eventually owning their own herds.

Despite this enthusiasm, ranch labor was difficult, dangerous, and poorly paid. Updegraff's initial salary was very low, though he soon moved up to the more typical $30 per month.[105] Updegraff was happy with this raise, but for many this sum was pathetic. During an 1883 strike, one sheriff expressed disgust that ranches "expect them to work for $30.00 per month."[106] But Updegraff did not seem to mind, since, like many cowboys, he was young. He turned twenty in 1886, while working at the ranch.

For many like Updegraff, the romantic view of the cowboy pervaded even their self-perception. Workers' self-respect was as much about their vision of the worth and nature of their labor as the work itself. Cowboys who had grown up in rural Texas or New Mexico or Colorado may have understood their jobs radically differently, but the cowboy myth had real power for an Easterner like Updegraff, and it was similarly important to people nationwide.

It is important, however, to note that Updegraff's views likely reflect those of a white cowboy, who had a reasonable hope to rise to the peak of western society. There were many African-American and Indian cowboys, as well as Mexican *vaqueros* (cowboys), who were critical to the ranching system but may not have shared Updegraff's optimism.[107] Nevertheless, they were laborers with their own distinct ranching traditions. These men also participated in the broader cowboy culture, with several African-American cowboys receiving public notoriety. Nat Love, for example, was a former slave who had worked as a cattleman in Texas and published a popular autobiography.[108] Such publications simultaneously put cowboys' labor at the center of Western mythology and downplayed their marginality as laborers and as members of a white-dominated ranching world.

Few cowboys were as colorful or prolific as Way Hamlin Updegraff, but cowboy work songs can provide a window into their world. Told around the campfire, these songs were collective creations. Sung while keeping watch or to soothe nervous cattle, songs kept workers awake during endless nights and grueling days. Many songs are nonsensical, or about day-to-day work or lost love, but a number explore themes of ranch life: the sense that the cowboy life is fading away or that ranch life is tough but honest and pre- or anti-capitalist, and struggles with American Indians.

Many songs spun tales of cowboys giving away their last nickel or squandering their meager wages in a cattle town. At the end of a long journey, a trail crew would go on "a little spree."[109] The ballad of "John Garner's Trial Herd" ends with "the cowboy's life is a dreary life, though his mind it is no load / And he always spends his money like he found it in the road."[110] One cowboy declares, "I ain't got a nickel / And I don't give a dern."[111] Another explains that "when they go to town, boys, you bet their money is spent."[112] While the songs highlight the importance of markets to cowboy life, the mad spending also reflects a kind of anti-capitalist ideology in that the protagonists reject the importance of money and responsible spending.

Songs need villains, and more often than not for cowboys, these were Indians. In the "Cowboy's Meditation," the narrator looks toward the stars and wonders, "Do the cowboys scrap there with Comanches / And other Red Men of the Plains?"[113] One short ditty lists all the things a cowboy would rather do than fight "the bloody in-ji-ans."[114] These songs, again, bind working in the cattle industry with one of the foundational stories of the West and the United States. Yet the songs were largely fictional. Save for the earliest settlers, ranchers, and cowboys, few actively fought Indians. By the 1880s most cattle laborers had little involvement in Indian War.

The disappearing cowboy was a popular theme. "A Cowboy Toast" salutes "the passing cowboy, the plowman's pioneer."[115] In "The Camp Fire Has Gone Out," the narrator laments that "Through the progress of the railroads our occupation's gone."[116] These lyrics belie the reality of ranching; mass cattle drives only existed in the first place because ranchers could take their cattle to eastern markets via already existing northern rail lines. Other songs focused on loss of a way of life more generally, such one ballad lamenting the disappearance of land commonly held "in partnership to god," that now was "only real estate."[117] The introduction to a book of cowboy songs only strengthened this idea, with a lament that "the nester has come, and come to stay. Gone is the buffalo, the Indian warwhoop, the free grass of the open plain."[118]

"The Last Longhorn" takes a similar approach, mourning a dying breed as a way of commenting on the passing of the open range more broadly. The song's narrator is contemptuous of newfangled cattle breeds, explaining that "These Jerseys and these Holsteins / They are no friends of mine / They belong to the nobility / Who live across the brine." In the old days "there was grass and water plenty / but it was too good to last." For the longhorns, then, "their glory must fade and go."[119] The song connects cowboys' way of life with that of the longhorn, using the breed's late nineteenth-century decline to lament what the song's narrator saw as a changing industry.[120]

That said, the songs also reveal self-awareness about cowboy myth making. "To Hear Him Tell It" satirizes the idea that the ranch is fading away. The narrator encounters an old man who recounts the days when beef prices were high, before railroad shipment, and before all sorts of changes. The old man rambles until the narrator's "head it ached." The song's final verse brings it home: "I won't never hail old timers / To have a drink with me / To learn the history of the range / As far back as seventy-three / and the next time that I'm thirsty / and feeling kind of blue / I'll step right and drink alone / Now I'm tellin' you!"[121]

Several songs satirized the power of the cowboy myth back east. In "The Disappointed Tenderfoot," a young Easterner who, like Way Hamlin Updegraff, crosses the country in search of the authentic cowboy lifestyle, discovers that "the west hez gone to the East . . . and it's only in tents such things is done."[122] Other songs, such as "The Dreary, Dreary Life," criticize the widespread assumption on the part of noncowboys that the life of a cattle worker is easy and carefree.[123]

During the late nineteenth and early twentieth centuries, these songs existed at the intersection of cowboy self-understandings and the public consumption of ranch life. Ethnomusicologist John Lomax compiled many of the surviving cattle songs explored here, and self-consciously selected the songs and themes to present to a wider public.[124] It was the interplay between the creation of these songs and their public dissemination that was crucial; Western myth emerged from the commercially driven interaction of western accounts and the tastes of eastern listeners and readers. Perhaps most importantly, the popularity of these songs helps explain why it is difficult to appreciate ranching as a capitalist process and why, as we will see, the public was uneasy with cowboys acting like industrial laborers.

From today's perspective, cowboys are rarely viewed as workers in the way we imagine slaughterhouse worker Jurgis Rudkus, protagonist of *The Jungle*. But cowboys were indeed laborers. Big Bill Haywood, a founder of the Industrial Workers of the World, had worked as a cowboy. Late in life he reflected that "a cowboy's life is not the joyous, adventurous existence shown in the moving pictures, read about in cheap novels or to be seen in World's exhibitions." The life of a cowboy was "dreary and lonesome."[125] Unlike miners and factory workers, however, ranch hands were spread far apart and had great difficulty organizing. But the period of corporate ranching was not without labor unrest. Moments when cowboys behaved like other laborers highlighted the distance between Western myth making and the industry's reality.

In the early spring of 1883, employees of several Texas Panhandle ranches, including the LS, LX, and LIT, went on strike for better wages and conditions.[126] Roughly two to three hundred strikers chose the weeks before the spring roundup to make their demands, in part because the process's time sensitivity meant management was vulnerable. The cowboys camped on the range and threatened to violently oppose any attempt to bring in outside labor.[127] They demanded raises, from about $30 per month to roughly $50.[128] They were not happy about the quality of ranch food and coffee either.

Cowboy grievances were inextricable from the conflict between small and large ranches discussed earlier.[129] Many men kept small herds of their own and, especially during the ranching boom, large operations tried to crowd out these small herds and prevent employees and cowboys from managing their own herds. There were intermittent attempts to organize—such as when Colorado workers tried to organize the Cowboys' Cattle Company to pool wages and buy their own cattle—but cattle workers generally had trouble building their own herds.[130] The rapid spread of barbed wire and private land ownership during the 1880s exacerbated this tension as range land was fenced.

The strikers attacked corporate ranching as changing the business. In explaining the strike, one contemporary observed that early cattlemen like "John Chisum or Charley Goodnight, they were real people. They got right out with the boys on the trail; did just as much work as the boys, ate the same kind of food. Their cowboys would have died in the saddle rather than have complained. See what we have now; a bunch of organized companies."[131] It was a dubious critique, but effective. The public was suspicious of foreign capital, with periodic agitation for measures like a bill against foreign land ownership that was popular in Texas. In the wake of corporate ranching, a similar ideology would be used to valorize small-scale ranching.[132]

The strike quickly became national press. Attitudes on the strikers were mixed, though most coverage reflected a widespread dislike of organized labor. The public was uneasy with cowboys acting like industrial workers. Coverage emphasized the strikers' violence, especially against property and potential strikebreakers. Similarly, many articles stressed the potential for "lawlessness" in the form of fires, fence cutting, or cattle slaughter.[133]

But there was also sympathy for the cowboys. Some newspapers hoped for "compromise," while a few western papers stressed the cowboys' tremendous skill and the unlikeliness of finding replacements. The *Las Vegas Daily Gazette* celebrated that when it came to the "Pride of the Panhandle . . . a stranger cannot take his place simply for the lack of the technical knowledge of the profession."[134] Panhandle workers had intimate knowledge of the local landscape, the "general lore of the ranges," and could make camp in the harshest conditions.

In a familiar story, state power would side with management. The Texas Rangers were deployed to protect strikebreakers and cattlemen's property.[135] As with cowboys and most things associated with Texas, the reality of the Texas Rangers exists in tension with their mythology. Celebrated as forces for order—against Indians or bandits—they also functioned much like the police in New York and Chicago: used to protect property interests during a strike. The Rangers would "do everything possible to preserve order."[136] Ranch owners also requested the state militia or federal troops in case things got too out of hand.

In the end, there was no violent showdown. The strike simply petered out, perhaps in the face of the stock owners' show of force and the ready availability of replacements. Good cattle workers were hard to come by, but passable ones were abundant. Furthermore, experienced men, who might have had the confidence to continue resisting, were scattered. There was no critical mass of men in any one location; a ranch with fifty thousand cattle might only employ fifty men during the peak season.[137] This complicated effective organization and the strike collapsed.

Historian Ruth Allen observed that the strikes were not merely the result of bad conditions, which had not actually worsened during the corporate ranching period, but rather of cowboys' belief that foreign investment and the closing of the ranges were changing the industry.[138] Corporate ranching threatened what the cowboys viewed as the true nature of their work. It ultimately reflected both the complexity and mythology of ranch labor: its simultaneous existence as an exploitative form of wage labor as well as its central place in Western mythology and as an expression of independent manhood.[139]

The writings of Way Hamlin Updegraff, the failure of the 1883 strike, and the reproduction of cattle songs reveal the enormous symbolic power as well as marginality of ranch labor. Even as cattle songs helped ranch workers find meaning in their work, they made it harder for cowboys and the public to see them as laborers. On a ranch, the desire to celebrate one's work also made it harder to recognize one's marginal and exploitative situation.

There is another reason to focus on the art of cowboy-ism, to borrow Updegraff's phrase. Cattle work is fundamentally about the ecological relationships between people and the landscape and its fauna. In aggregate, these relationships produce the ranching system, and therefore this system's emergence and operation can be found, in microcosm, in the daily work of each ranch. Studying cowboy labor, from guarding the herd overnight to the yearly branding of calves, is key to understanding the place of humans in this for-profit ecosystem.[140]

"Doomed of Its Own Excesses [?]": Hard Winters and the Collapse of the Industry

Each spring, the Matador ranch's investors and managers back in Scotland awaited word from William Sommerville on how their herds had fared over the previous winter. Without Sommerville's letters, the investors had only disconnected anecdotes and alarmist newspaper reports. In 1886, a winter that Matador herds endured without difficulty, Henry Campbell, the American assistant manager of the Matador ranch, worried that "newspaper reports of the effects among stock of the late cold weather may cause uneasiness among the Matador stockholders," and promised to keep Sommerville briefed so he could relay things back to Scotland.[141]

In 1888, Sommerville had only bad news. He explained that "the loss of this last winter is the heaviest we have yet experienced; for I have never at any time, seen as many dead cattle in the course of ordinary journeying over the range as on this occasion."[142] Bad winters killed the most valuable animals: suckling cows. Adult males can fend for themselves, and, as Sommerville would explain, calves have "nothing to do but eat" and "pull through very well." But new mothers weaken as they suckle their young and are so exhausted by early spring that they become trapped in mud holes created by melting snow, and starve.[143] Since these animals are also prime breeding stock, the losses diminish the herd long term as well.

This winter came on the heels of two of the worst winters in the history of the industry: the 1885–86 winter on the southern Plains, and the hard winter of 1886–87 that devastated ranches in Wyoming, Montana, and the northern Plains.[144] According to the traditional story, these winters were so severe that they decimated Plains cattle herds, sending the entire industry into a tailspin. Ultimately, they would spark the decline of corporate ranching.

Bad winters began with dry summers. Dry weather meant grasses were not as nourishing and fires became a serious risk. For instance, in July 1886, Way Hamlin Updegraff complained they had only received "three sprinkles," and that if it stayed as dry as the previous year "the results would be serious as the cattle have eaten off the grass closely for miles around."[145] Similar effects had been seen the previous year on the southern Plains and preceding the 1886–87 winter on the northern Plains.[146] These droughts could cause immediate death and long-term damage as well; starving animals destroyed ranges as they ate the land beyond bare.[147]

Both winters brought mass starvation and death. Cattle froze against fences as they sought cover. Entire herds drowned and froze in rivers after crashing through the ice in their desperation to reach shelter from brutal winds.[148] Cowboys trying to protect their herds rode until their horses' feet were bloody from walking on icy ground.[149] In Kansas, railroad employees worked around the clock to clear dead cattle from rail cuts where they had sought cover.[150] Even surviving cattle were often too thin to be salable in any reasonable amount of time.[151] Reflecting on the disaster, the *Economist* gloomily explained, "while the cattle may get through a few winters without great loss to their numbers, there will then come a winter which will sweep them off by thousands, and the profits of former seasons are swept away."[152]

Montana rancher Granville Stuart connected the disaster to a larger message, which echoes in histories of ranching. Stuart explained, "this was the death knell to the range cattle business on anything like the scale it had been run before."[153] The purpose of Stuart's framing was to simultaneously condemn corporate ranches and tell a story of an industry learning from its mistakes and following a sounder model. By echoing this view, historians have inadvertently endorsed an oversimplified account that elides ongoing similarities—for good and ill—between the corporate period and what followed, whether in terms of environmental degradation, labor exploitation, or business practices.[154] David Wheeler, for instance, has gone so far as to argue that the blizzard of 1886 "lay prostrate an industry doomed of its own excesses."[155] For ranchers and historians, these winters were a turning point in the industry.

But these winters are a strange turning point, primarily because it is likely that they were not as bad as has been suggested. Since the winters first occurred, scholars have been skeptical of the extent of the overstocking of the ranges. Recent work has even challenged the idea quite aggressively. The most vocal recent critics of this argument are Randy McFerrin and Douglas Wills, whose article "Who Said the Ranges Were Overstocked?" accused earlier scholars of reading contradictory eyewitness testimony selectively in order to fit a narrative of environmental degradation or "excesses," to use Wheeler's phrase.[156] The evidence that the ranges were overstocked is spotty on two counts: (1) at the time there had been little systematic study of the carrying capacity of a range, and (2) there is little accurate evidence of the hard winters' effects. Though the evidence is clear that some areas saw extensive overstocking and land deterioration, particularly in the Southwest, there is limited evidence for overcrowding as a tendency across the Plains.[157]

Regarding the first point, intensive cattle ranching had only existed on the Plains for at most a few decades by the 1880s. Range management texts generally attribute the range of publications produced in the wake of the hard winters of the 1880s as the beginnings of the field.[158] Even using buffalo populations as a baseline is problematic, since there is evidence of buffalo eating pastures bare during bad seasons and dying in huge numbers during the winter. This raises questions about the very idea of overstocking (is there any "natural" capacity of land independent of human influence and, if so, where and when has this existed?), but, more conservatively, it is clear that ranchers had limited evidence or experience to support their claims.[159] Cattle populations on the range had surely increased dramatically, but the evidence that this exceeded capacity is limited.

Regarding the second point, as discussed in the section "As Large as All Yorkshire," on counting cattle, it was unclear if anybody had any idea how many cattle were actually on the ranges.

In 1886, the *Breeder's Gazette* complained about people asking it to estimate the previous winter's losses without realizing "this is simply impossible. When the ranchmen themselves cannot do this . . . it is all guesswork, as in no instance does he get an actual count on his cattle."[160] The difficulty individual ranchers had counting cattle was only compounded when it came to estimating broader cattle populations. When D. E. Salmon, first head of the Bureau of Animal Industry, tried to provide accurate statistics on the "beef supply of the United States," he opened with the observation that "it is probable that no accurate census of the range cattle has ever been secured, and nearly all the estimates . . . have varied widely from each other, and probably from the true figures."[161] In 1885, Texas rancher George Loving estimated that the number of cattle in Texas was as much as two million more than the official tally, because "few, if any, of our largest ranchmen render the full number of cattle owned by them for taxation."[162] This meant there was the opportunity for exaggeration as well as the motive: unscrupulous managers could use cattle losses to cover up their own greed or incompetence. Most likely, there was a series of unusually bad winters for which crowded ranges were unprepared, but that they did not cause the kind of mortality rates claimed. For every tragic account, there are published reports to the contrary: "not only in this country but in Texas the reported loss of cattle has been exaggerated."[163]

Though it seems likely the winters were not as bad as many have argued, this does not mean that scholars like Osgood, Dale, and Wheeler are entirely wrong. Hard winters did decimate the industry, but this was because they exposed the fiction on which many ranching corporations were founded, and, against a backdrop of long-term price declines, triggered a panic that would lead to the industry's collapse. In this reading, hard winters could, in the words of Wheeler, "lay prostrate an industry doomed of its own excesses," but it said as much about financial instability as the harsh western environment.

As discussed earlier, in nineteenth-century ranching, instability and profit were necessary bedfellows. Profit came from leaving cattle on their own, and the more risks taken in this regard, the higher the potential profit. It was not merely an inability to rationalize nature, then, it was the way a ranch necessarily worked, even if a ranch prospectus or investor report needed to suggest otherwise to secure capital.[164]

While well-managed operations could insulate themselves from the immediate effects of these disastrous winters, once a substantial number of ranches encountered difficulty, a cascading effect began. It started with struggling ranches, whose investors and creditors pressured managers to liquidate their herds in order to recoup losses. Thousands of cattle would be taken to market and sold for fire-sale prices. For instance, nearly seventy thousand cattle left Wyoming for market in 1887.[165] Better-run ranches would then have to compete with businesses desperate to sell at any price.

As rancher George Tyng angrily explained, outsiders "rushed into the business three or four years ago when cattle were selling as far too high as they now are too low; and are now helping to lower the market by urging their agents to raise money by making sales." This was hurting Tyng's operation, for "this year of 1887 is one of enforced liquidation for the range-cattle business. It would be unfortunate for us to be now compelled to compete in glutting the market for range cattle."[166] Tyng could afford to wait, but those ranchers who did try to operate in these glutted markets found conditions enormously difficult.[167] When a Matador ranch associate tried to sell cattle in Denver, he sent a telegram back with the words "it is hell" underlined.

He wanted to know the lowest price managers would accept.[168] The market would hold well-run ranches accountable for the mistakes of the soon-to-be bankrupt.

The struggles of western ranchers as a whole after the disastrous winter of 1886–87 on the northern Plains revealed that the new national ranching system was predicated on large-scale risk. Texas ranchers had become dependent on a thriving market for year-old Texas cattle coming from northern ranches in Wyoming, Montana, and elsewhere. These northern operations fattened cattle on good northern grasses for a year or two before selling in Chicago. As these ranches went out of business, Texas ranchers lost their buyers. George Tyng complained to a business partner that Montana blizzards in 1886–87 had "disabled and discouraged" purchases of Texas cattle at "prices anything like those heretofore paid."[169] Bad winters on the northern ranges could cause panic a thousand miles away. The complexity of this continent-spanning ranching system is the focus of chapter 3.

The fate of the Francklyn Land & Cattle Company illustrates what happened to big ranches as cattle markets began to deteriorate. Founded in 1881 by a group of English investors, the company initially held more than six hundred thousand acres and had raised over a million dollars in capital. With these funds, ranch managers bought a number of smaller herds and ranges from small-scale ranchers in the Texas Panhandle. At its peak, the ranch owned somewhere between seventy and one hundred thousand cattle.[170]

Times were initially good, but the ranch's fortunes soon turned. When the Francklyn Land & Cattle Company became insolvent in late 1886, George Tyng faced difficult financial decisions on behalf of investors. Past mismanagement had left the ranch nearly broke, putting Tyng in the unenviable position of tallying necessary expenses and determining just how much more investors would sink into the failing enterprise. He wrote, "the coat can be cut according to the cloth. I will be grateful to you for indication of the quantity of cloth available." If investors could not afford the $2,000 needed to make improvements to help the ranch's stock survive the winter, "some trust must be placed in providence and more in the chance of a mild winter." After all, "poor folks must follow poor ways."[171] As ranches across the West started cutting corners and taking these kinds of risks, they became further exposed to the risk of harsh winters.

There were, however, opportunities for experienced ranchers. In June 1887, Tyng wrote to headquarters about an exchange with Charles Goodnight of the JA ranch. Apparently Goodnight had been touring cattle markets and had provided "a discouraging statement of his views as to prices." But Tyng had his suspicions, for "[Goodnight] knows we have pretty good cattle; of course acclimated, convenient for driving to his own range. He knows we want to sell badly, which we admit, and that we still stand some sacrifice in order to get out of the cattle business entirely and at once." Though he was a respectable rancher, "Mr. Goodnight is in the cow-business where God favors no one who does not look out for himself."[172] The Francklyn Land & Cattle Company did not end up selling to Goodnight, preferring to hold out for higher prices.

The winters caused panic but the fatal problem was a long-term decline in the price of cattle. When the boom had started during the late 1870s, cattle prices were relatively high. By 1885 or so, when western stockyards were crowded with cattle, prices were slumping. In November 1885, William Sommerville described the Chicago cattle markets as "weak from the start" of the season.[173] In an 1885 review of the industry, the *Economist* was already explaining that "low prices obtained for cattle" were hurting British investments.[174] By early 1886, Kansas City and Chicago prices were "unprecedentedly low," and by 1887, the Chicago Board of Trade was reporting prices of nearly $2 per head less than the already flagging 1885 prices.[175] The Swan Land & Cattle Company saw average prices drop from just over $40 per head in 1884 to $26 in 1886 and 1887.[176] In 1888, Sommerville described the Chicago markets as "demoralized."[177] It became apparent that the high prices justifying the ranching boom had been a self-fulfilling prophecy. Investors worldwide had been lured into a business on the promise of high cattle prices, which were high because ranchers could sell year-old animals to new ranches eager to stock their own ranges and hopefully sell to even newer ranches.

Worse yet, once panic hit, the deck was stacked in favor of the buyer. By the time cattlemen had sent their cattle all the way to Kansas City or Chicago—perhaps on old price information— they were desperate to sell. Buyers had more flexibility, and the glut of cattle from ranches going bankrupt made for a buyer's market. Even when prices recovered in the early 1890s, the situation remained difficult. Other price fluctuations could cause similar problems; after a precipitous increase in corn prices temporarily made the cattle-fattening business prohibitively expensive, fatteners rushed their cattle to market and all cattle "of necessity sold at prices favoring the purchaser."[178] The sellers were many and even the largest corporate ranches were relatively small compared with the Chicago packinghouses, making the situation nearly hopeless.

Nevertheless, ranch managers were eternally optimistic. Sure, prices had been low, but steep rises were on the horizon. This line could be used to calm anxious investors in the worst of market conditions. Poor industry performance eventually became evidence that prices would recover. If so many ranches were liquidating their herds as they went out of business, then a shortage of cattle was imminent. Following a lengthy and perceptive analysis of the interlocking forces causing cattle prices to collapse, XIT manager John Farwell observed that these forces would bankrupt so many ranches that "the supply of cattle next year will be very much decreased from all sources, and it is the opinion of responsible cattle men throughout the business that the prices next year will be undoubtedly very much higher." As a result, he erroneously believed that "it was unquestionably the best policy for the company to hold their cattle until another season, particularly as the outlook for both grass and water during the winter months for all cattle now on the ranche was so very good."[179] In an otherwise pessimistic report for investors of the Prairie Cattle Company, John Stuart Smith shared his belief that the difficult markets meant that "the candle is burning at both ends," and that a shortage of cattle would soon mean high prices for surviving operations.[180] He was mistaken. Though prices would eventually recover slightly, the days of corporate ranching were largely over.

Conclusion

The boom was over by 1890. Having taken the greatest risks, the largest ranches were the biggest losers. The Francklyn Land & Cattle Company faced foreclosure suits in 1886. The Swan Land & Cattle Company went into receivership in 1887.[181] Collectively, the British-American operations had lost roughly $25 million by the early twentieth century.[182] Eastern investors lost on a large scale as well. Though several multinational ranches survived into the twentieth century (the Matador was not sold until World War II), they were no longer a popular investment.[183] Smaller family-owned ranches or small-scale partnerships would predominate.[184] Winter feeding with hay replaced year-round grazing. The farmer/rancher distinction broke down as small-scale ranching became the norm; many people engaged in both.[185] Less profitable, these businesses took fewer risks, making the industry marginal but more stable.[186] Though cattle prices would recover in the 1890s, ranching would never again be conducted on the scale of the 1880s.

For corporate ranching's critics, the industry's collapse confirmed long-held beliefs about the dangers of mixing big business and ranching. As far back as 1886, the *Breeder's Gazette* had predicted—hoped—that "the mass of men seeking a field for personal effort will wear out the unequal conditions which prevail," and defeat those "large cattle companies, represented merely by a manager or superintendent."[187] After the collapse, succeeding ranchers created a story of the excesses that had led to the disaster. These men would use the myths of the cowboy and the open range to create a new ranching ideology—one that traced the decline of the old ranching system to the corrupting influence of eastern (or, even worse, foreign) capital. This new ideology foregrounded family, localism, and tradition.[188]

Though the collapse of ranching was a macro-level event, it grew from the micro-level processes of ranching. A ranch was an ecosystem created in the interest of profit. Rancher and cattle had replaced nomad and bison in the quest to metabolize grass into salable human food. But it could never be a wholly artificial system, a factory for producing animal flesh. All ranchers knew the very possibility of profit depended on ensuring "natural increase." As a result, a ranch was an ecosystem in tension: it relied on active creation and maintenance (as endless complaints about wolves and prairie dogs suggest), as well as leaving nature to its own devices. This tension was even reflected in breeding, where the imperative to "grade-up" collided with the desire to maintain cattle's "rustling qualities."[189]

To be profitable, this system required indeterminacy. Cattle had to be allowed to wander and live far out of sight. Yet investors demanded precise numbers. This was the core contradiction of nineteenth-century ranching. To function, the system relied on masking this contradiction. Despite their endemic problems, methods like range delivery and documents like the herd book had to be used as if they were accurate. The mismatch between ranching's micro-level practices and investment's macro-level needs would be corporate ranching's undoing. Winters (and droughts) introduced further unpredictability. If every season were the same, honest managers could build those effects into their profit calculations. But investors and managers had short memories and used mild winters as a baseline for their expectations. The unpredictable Plains climate collided with not just investor psychology, but also the heart of investment and business: reliable and quantifiable inputs.

This story highlights important aspects of how landscapes are incorporated into commodity markets. Attention to the practice of "range delivery" reveals that an ability to crudely, but persuasively, represent an ecosystem for investment capital may be more important for initially integrating a landscape into an economy than actually transforming that landscape. The crude estimation methods that made range delivery a workable if problematic practice enabled capital to flow, even when its reliability was more investor delusion than ecological reality. Understanding why range delivery was acceptable and other practices were not helps explain how and when ecological transformations happened.

The rise and fall of corporate ranching decisively shaped the cattle-beef complex. The long-term reduction in cattle prices that resulted from the boom and the dramatic increase of cattle production across the Plains was key to beef's move to

the center of the American diet. With the collapse of corporate ranching, later ranchers could promote a vision of their
business as authentically American; hardworking men out on
the Plains, free of the dirtiness of wage labor or big business.[190]
Further, the Chicago meatpackers, perhaps the best example of
nineteenth-century big business and exploitative wage labor,
would ultimately use this mythology to market their products,
featuring idyllic western scenes on beef cans and trade cards.

Corporate ranching's failure during the 1880s, a time when
the Chicago meatpackers, armed with new refrigeration technology, were beginning to distribute nationwide, also helps
explain the cattle-beef complex's ultimate structure.[191] Ranches
would be small and dispersed, unable to coordinate opposition
to the meatpackers. This structure would resolve the friction
between the hands-off nature of nineteenth-century ranching
and the capitalist demand for precision. Thousands of small
ranchers would shoulder the risk of cattle raising, insulating the
highly capitalized portion of the supply chain, meatpacking,
from the unpredictability of natural increase. The Cattle Kingdom was indeed a reality, but it would ultimately be dwarfed by
a much larger and more profitable "Beef Trust."

3

Market

BY 1900, CHICAGO'S dominance of the nation's commodity markets seemed as though natural law. According to the Chicago Board of Trade, "every portion of the West as naturally as rivers find their way to the Ocean, sends to this entrepôt its farm animals."[1] From remote tributaries in Texas, Montana, Ohio, and elsewhere, cattle flowed into ever-larger markets such as Fort Worth or Kansas City, before reaching the chief commodity market in the country, and possibly the world, Chicago.[2]

Yet the river metaphor elides the work that made this system operate. Cattle traveled trails and rails whose location was not simply a feature of the landscape. Town boosters eager for business, farmers angry about invading herds, and railroad managers hungry for fares all shaped the flow of cattle. Even as yearly migrations strengthened routes as a river carves a canyon, the cattle system was ever shifting. A railroad-spurred transportation revolution made the national cattle market possible, but the politics of city boosterism, railroad building, and state regulation determined its contours.

Despite the limitations of the Chicago Board of Trade's metaphor, it does capture a core truth about this system: like a river, it was principally about movement. What made cattle markets national was the mobility of information, people, and animals. Cattle did not merely move longer distances than ever before, but did so at unprecedented speed; ranchers in Texas and Montana could compete in Chicago and Denver. This chapter examines the processes and forces that enabled this mobility, from railroad technology to the labor organization that allowed ten humans to drive a herd of cattle a thousand miles.

Mobility promoted two overarching tendencies: (1) government regulation commensurate with the mobility's breadth, and (2) standardization of the spaces through which cattle and people moved. Though these were continent-spanning developments, they grew from local struggles. As people negotiated with strangers, traveled unfamiliar terrain, or dealt with passing herds, they sought government regulation of practices like cattle pricing or transportation. Because mobile goods crossed jurisdictions, people sought expanded federal authority to match the new scale of national markets. Meanwhile, specific places and immobile actors appealed to mobile actors like ranchers with familiar amenities—hotels, well-regulated stockyards, and clearly marked trailing routes—that amounted to standardization, requiring correspondingly less local knowledge from market participants. In the end, these tendencies would be self-reinforcing. Standardization, for instance, only accelerated the movement of cattle and capital, which in turn promoted further standardization.

These tendencies resulted in two ironies. The irony of regulation was that local and regional actors, in seeking to solve problems such as sick cattle illegally crossing borders and jurisdictions, promoted the development of a muscular federal state, which ultimately favored elite national actors. Regulations favor large businesses, since they have the capital to meet high compliance costs, and the federal state prefers large actors, since business concentration lowers enforcement costs. Meanwhile, the irony of standardization was that the cattle-beef complex was born in particular places, but would eventually exist independent of any of them. The national market that so many local people and communities helped create would abandon them. Once dominant, Ohio Valley cattle raising declined as western ranching expanded. Born in Texas, Plains ranching became independent of the Lone-Star State as ranchers in states like Colorado, Wyoming, and Montana built self-sustaining herds. Even Chicago's importance as a packing center and cattle market declined in the twentieth century as trucking decentralized meatpacking. Residents of the neighborhoods surrounding the city's once-powerful Union Stockyards were left with dilapidated infrastructure and few jobs.

Those who witnessed the rise of the national cattle market struggled to adjust to its scale and possibility. When information was scarce and trails poorly developed, profitable opportunities were few. Soon, however, there was an abundance of places for ranchers and meatpackers to buy and sell cattle. Could ranchers play markets off each other by waiting for telegraph information about prices? Could railroads force towns into a bidding war to ensure lines passed nearby? Would Chicago meatpackers be able to crush (or control) rival operations in Kansas City or Omaha?

Competitors often sought advantage through superior mobility. Success was about being able to operate in multiple markets at once as well as preventing competitors from doing the same.[3] Once a herd was unloaded in Omaha, a rancher had to sell or risk dramatic losses. Meatpackers exploited this reality. Armour & Company could decide between buying cattle in Omaha or a comparable herd in Chicago or Sioux City. Facing high transport and feed costs, ranchers often settled for lower prices rather than test their luck elsewhere.

Understanding the resilience, breadth, and power of the nation's cattle markets requires appreciating the sheer diversity of places and spaces in which cattle were raised, sold, and butchered. Particular geographic areas may have been important in the history of the cattle industry, but the system as a whole was not dependent on any single part. The cattle system was not merely greater than the sum of its parts, it in some sense existed independently of them. Exploring what that means, and the implications of that reality, is the focus of this chapter.

The chapter proceeds in two parts. The first outlines the cattle-ranching, trailing, and marketing system with an emphasis on the changing locations of cattle marketing and raising. As this system evolved, it provided the framework that ranchers, meatpackers, and others navigated in their search for profit. Yet these actors' efforts to transcend the local and operate as regional or national actors also shaped this infrastructure. The second section follows a hypothetical group of cattle from pasture to slaughterhouse. An examination of the ecology of cattle trailing and transportation will highlight the centrality of mobility to this system. This section also studies how mobility promoted regulation and standardization.

The Cattle Marketing System

There are four ways to make money from cattle: raising them, fattening them, moving them, or butchering them.[4] The largest cattle raisers were generally west of the Mississippi, where a dearth of people and an abundance of grasses meant that cattle were cheap to raise and breed.[5] Sometimes sold directly to meatpackers, these animals were often sold first at one, two, or three years of age to cattle fatteners. These were either northern ranchers—in Wyoming, Colorado, and elsewhere—who would fatten an animal on nutritious northern Plains grasses,

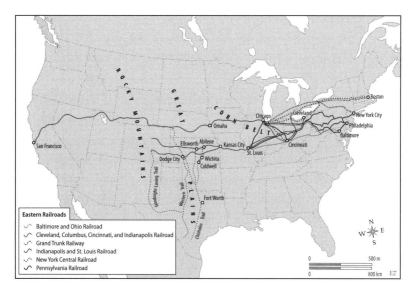

MAP 2. This map represents the key components of the cattle-beef complex.
During the early period, western cattle were largely trailed out of Texas to
cattle towns. From there, cattle traveled to meatpacking centers or to western
ranges on the central and northern Plains. By the 1880s, cattle were heading to
market from ranches across the Great Plains. Cattle feeding was concentrated
in the corn belt. Finally, the sheer mass of railroads eastbound from Chicago
shaped the rise of the Big Four meatpackers, a story explored in chapter 4.
Squares indicate major stockyards; circles, cattle towns. Map by Ezra Zeitler.

or they were corn-belt farmers operating nineteenth-century
versions of feedlots.[6] These farmers, based in midwestern
states like Kansas or Illinois, fed cattle on cheap corn as a way
of "finishing" the animal before sale in Chicago.[7] Cattle trailers, commission merchants, and shippers greased the wheels
of this ever-moving system. Finally, slaughterers and butchers
purchased all kinds of animals, purchasing finished cattle from
fatteners as well as bidding against these same fatteners when
they wanted unfinished, lower-grade animals for canning.

All of these aspects of the cattle business happened relatively far apart. This is because cattle thrive in rural areas. Pigs were a fact of life in nineteenth-century American cities, but cattle were and still are country animals.[8] To grow profitably, cattle had to be spread over wide swaths of (relatively) empty land. As populations moved westward, centers of cattle raising did as well. This was why mobility was crucial to the cattle-beef complex: beef was perishable and its production was necessarily far from its consumption.

The fact that cattle were rural animals spread across the United States meant that providing a bovine census was nearly impossible during the nineteenth century. When D. E. Salmon was tasked with producing such a census, his report required two years and, despite having a number of assistants, he had to admit his numbers were a little fuzzy. Nineteenth-century cattle statistics were imprecise, both because they were likely exaggerated and because of the dynamics of nineteenth-century ranching. Therefore, the numbers below are rough estimates. Similarly, cattle numbers do not tell us everything about available beef. Due to breeding and refinements in cattle fattening, animal weights increased dramatically over the period, meaning that although the number of beef cattle per thousand people in the United States increased only very slightly from 1860 to 1890, there was much more available beef.[9]

Despite these challenges, it is possible to give a sense of the system's broad contours. In 1880, roughly half of American cattle were west of the Mississippi, and by 1900 that number had increased to over sixty percent. When one takes out dairy cattle, the numbers are even more stark: in 1900, nearly eighty percent of American beef cattle were west of the Mississippi.[10] That eighty percent translated into nearly twenty million animals. These were largely split between the Plains (with the majority in Texas) and the corn belt. Though there were likely more cattle scattered across the Plains, their density in the corn belt was much higher; the region was a funnel through which many western cattle passed on their way to market. Nineteenth-century cattle, like nineteenth-century Americans, were constantly on the move. Nevertheless, state-level statistics provide a rough idea of the industry's shape. In 1870, there were three million beef cattle in Texas, and a negligible additional amount scattered across the Plains. In the corn belt, there were a million in Illinois and another 750 thousand or so in Ohio and Missouri each.[11] In the following three decades, cattle production would spread across the Plains and intensify in the corn belt. By 1900, there were roughly 6.5 million cattle in Texas and another 4 or 5 million in the range/ranch country. In the corn belt, there were 2.8 million in Kansas, 2.6 million in Iowa, and another 1 to 2 million in Nebraska, Illinois, and Missouri each.[12] Growth in the West and the corn belt was comparable, and these regions became increasingly linked.[13] Whereas in 1870 many corn-belt animals were raised and finished there, many more fatteners purchased western cattle at the turn of the century. In both 1870 and 1900 there was a relatively smaller, but still significant, number of animals scattered elsewhere across the United States as well.

Over time, different regions specialized in different parts of the bovine life cycle. Regarding western ranching, one cattleman explained that "Texas generally only makes the skeleton, which is driven North and fattened for the various markets."[14] Places like Colorado and Montana had more nutritious grasses and the cold weather encouraged weight gain.[15] A four-year-old animal raised entirely in Texas could weigh eight hundred pounds, but if driven north at one or two years of age, might weigh closer to a thousand pounds by age four. Though a few brave entrepreneurs attempted to fatten cattle in Texas, almost all of them failed.[16] Rather, Texas was the West's cattle nursery.

But Texas and the Great Plains were not the only cattle-raising regions west of the Mississippi; the Pacific Northwest as well as the Southwest were important as well, supplying midwestern markets but also supplying one of the country's other great cattle markets, California.[17] Stock growing in California was big business. Atypically, a large corporate ranch, Miller & Lux, dominated the state's ranching as well as meatpacking, operating several of its own facilities.[18] Mining in Nevada and gold in California drove massive population growth and spurred the expansion of beef production to supply it.[19]

Despite the importance of the West, one should not underestimate eastern cattle raising. In fact, midwestern cattle raising had its roots in Ohio River Valley ranching during the first half of the nineteenth century.[20] Ranchers and farmers would drive cattle and hogs across the Allegheny Mountains toward east-coast markets.[21] Before the spread of railroads corn was expensive to transport, but could be used to fatten an animal that walked itself to market.[22] Following the Civil War, Ohio Valley corn fatteners and cattle raisers would take their expertise west, to the corn belt and Plains. Though eastern beef production became less and less important following the Civil War, it remained a sizable part of the overall industry.

Although cattle are rural animals, much of the business of ranching happened in towns and cities. Cattle towns, particularly in Kansas, were a vital part of beef production. Situated at rail junctions where trailing cattle could board trains headed north or east, towns like Abilene, Caldwell, or Ellsworth were the first connection western ranchers made with the national market. At times, these bustling towns contained far more cattle than people.

During the 1870s and 1880s, these towns were engaged in cut-throat competition for a share of the cattle trade. The focus was generally on securing a town's railroad access, which often determined that town's success or failure. Thanks to the Kansas Pacific Railway running through Abilene, Kansas, the town was nearer to Chicago in terms of travel time than a comparable town that might be fifty miles closer geographically but without rail access. Similarly, quarantine laws to curtail the spread of cattle disease shaped the location of cattle towns. These issues were all political: what kinds of coalitions could be built at the Kansas statehouse or what kind of subsidy (or bribe) a community's leadership could provide to railroad executives.[23]

From these cattle towns, animals often headed either to market or to the cattle fatteners of the corn belt (in states like Kansas, Missouri, and Iowa). When corn prices were moderate or low, fattening cattle was profitable business.[24] Fatteners who grew their own corn would essentially graze the cattle in their fields until the animals had nearly picked it clean. Pigs then followed, eating the trampled husks, stalks, and even undigested grain in cow manure. In this manner every part of the cornfield could be turned into salable animal flesh. In terms of cattle, this not only resulted in profit on the increased weight, but, because meatpackers preferred fattened cattle, also brought a premium of a few cents per pound on the entire animal. Some fatteners did not even bother growing corn, but would simply wait for prices to drop and then buy it in large quantities for feeding to lean western cattle. Fatteners in Ohio or Kansas were also close to major cattle markets, meaning little weight would be lost in transport, a serious problem when an animal was shipped from Texas or Montana all the way to Chicago.

Fatteners had other advantages as well. They could time the market, selling corn or fattening cattle depending on prices.

They also had the flexibility to produce whiskey with corn or fatten hogs, which was less profitable, but entailed less risk.[25] The stockyards in Peoria had their start when a distiller decided he would try to attract animals he could fatten on his distillery's swill.[26] Overall, fatteners had the flexibility to wait until markets were glutted with cattle and ranchers were desperate to sell.

For western ranchers, the corn belt was a profitable if risky outlet for their cattle. In 1890, for example, much of the corn crop failed and prices skyrocketed, spurring fatteners to sell grain directly rather than fatten cattle. Though the Matador Land & Cattle Company's William Sommerville remained optimistic about selling to Kansas feeders, he knew prices would be bad since demand was weak.[27] While a poor corn crop surely hurt cattle fatteners, corn growers could at least sell their corn directly, receiving high prices for their limited harvest. Ranchers, on the other hand, were left without a critical set of cattle buyers.

Whether or not animals made a stop in the corn belt, the ultimate destination was always the slaughterhouse. During the first half of the nineteenth century, cattle buying and selling were largely local or regional, clustered around consumer markets.[28] There were a few well-developed cattle markets, most notably in New York and Boston, where the Brighton cattle market had been a major commercial center since the eighteenth century. Large formal markets were unusual; most places relied on weekly or monthly cattle fairs and auctions since seasonality and lower production meant there was not a supply to justify permanent markets. Beyond hog slaughter, large meatpacking operations could only produce salted beef, which was less perishable than fresh beef.[29]

This changed during the Civil War.[30] Northern rail networks integrated, and surging demand for cattle formalized markets.

Whereas markets were relatively casual when the cattle trade was small and seasonal, the tens of thousands of animals passing through places like wartime Chicago led to the creation of permanent market facilities, most famously the Chicago Union Stockyards in 1864–65. In the South, Union control of the Mississippi River severed the link between Texas and New Orleans, causing the number of cattle in Texas to skyrocket as Southerners lost their key market. The war also sent Mississippi River metropolises like St. Louis into decline, contributing to Chicago's emergence as the undisputed gateway to western commerce. With the establishment of Chicago's Union Stock Yard & Transit Company in 1865, the city became the center of US cattle marketing and meatpacking.

Though Chicago was indisputably the center of American meatpacking by 1890, its strength came not from the fact that it was the only major meatpacking center, but rather from its relationship to smaller markets like Omaha and Kansas City.[31] Rather than one urban center and a vast rural hinterland, nineteenth-century meatpacking centers were akin to a series of nodes in a network centered in Chicago. The big Chicago houses often directly and indirectly controlled other cities' markets and facilities. One of Armour's senior managers started the Cudahy packing plant in Milwaukee, while Armour's brother controlled a Kansas City facility.[32] Omaha's market never really took off until town leaders convinced the major Chicago houses to expand there. By 1907, Armour owned a considerable stake in Omaha's stockyards. Nelson Morris (of Morris & Company) and Gustavus Swift would come to control the St. Louis market.[33] Throughout the 1880s stockyards were built in Sioux City (1884), Denver (1886), Fort Worth (1887), Wichita (1887), and elsewhere. Cattle passing through all of these markets were likely to end up at the facilities of the major Chicago packinghouses.

One might wonder why meatpacking facilities were not moved closer to ranching areas, in the same process of decentralization that would happen in the twentieth century. In the nineteenth century this was much more difficult. Railroads meant city production was ideal, as opposed to truck transport, which favored suburban and rural production.[34] Further, the existence of large and diverse cattle markets in Chicago and the other packing centers gave them a huge advantage over upstart markets. Ranchers tried and failed to build their own facilities in places like Texas. Though one observer lamented ranchers' "absolute dependence on a fluctuating, contracted, and distant market," he was skeptical that a beef processing facility could succeed in Texas since "a continuous supply of fat beef the year round is a necessary condition."[35] That supply could only be found in centralized cattle markets that could draw from the entire Plains.

The cattle export trade was the only major alternative to Chicago. Most animals went to England, but many went to the European continent and locations like Cuba.[36] Chilled beef shipment grew throughout the 1870s, but live shipping was also common. These animals were high quality, in order to minimize European reluctance to purchase and eat animals that had crossed an ocean.[37] Legitimate European fears of American livestock diseases also contributed to this unease. Though the trade was modest in the early 1870s, by late in the decade, more than fifty million pounds of beef were going to England each year.[38] Despite periodic threats of protectionist measures in Europe, this quantity would only grow. Much of this meat was slaughtered in New York to minimize the risk of spoilage as it crossed the Atlantic, making New York one of the last remaining destinations for live animals shipped east from Chicago.

Nevertheless, the Chicago houses had a great deal of influence over the export trade. As one ranch manager explained to shareholders, the Chicago market "is a great monopoly which we want to see broken," but shipment to English ports was "out of the frying pan into the fire." Apparently the manager argued that these ports were either indirectly or directly "in the hands of the same large monopolists as they now are at Chicago viz: Armour, Swift, and others."[39]

Linking these ranches, fatteners, cattle towns, and meat-packing centers were the people who made money moving cattle. Commission merchants assembled the deals that sold cattle from one party to another, and often decided where cattle would be shipped. Working for clients hundreds of miles away, these men operated largely on trust. Though some commission companies volunteered their books for inspection, there was little defense against misreporting the sale price and pocketing the difference. As one rancher explained, "The only thing that can be done is to send the cattle to a good house and take all reasonable [care] to see that they are honestly accounted for."[40] Beyond commission merchants, cattle drovers often bought and trailed cattle or did so for a fee, connecting sellers and purchasers.

A relatively stable national cattle marketing and raising system emerged following the Civil War. Over the final three decades of the nineteenth century, large ranches opened farther and farther west, and the dominance of Texas waned as ranching intensified on the central and northern plains. The corn belt continued to grow in importance. Cattle trailing faded with the growth of rail networks and as new stockyards were created across the country. Yet the overall structure remained the same: some people raised cattle, some people fattened cattle, some people moved cattle, and they all thought they were getting fleeced by the people slaughtering cattle.

From Ranch to Slaughter

Whoopee ti yi yo, git along little dogies,
It's your misfortune, and none of my own.
Whoopee ti yi yo, git along little dogies,
For you know Wyoming will be your new home.

(TRADITIONAL TRAIL BALLAD)[41]

The cattle marketing system was fundamentally about movement. In a ledger this might amount to an entry indicating that a thousand animals were sent to Kansas City, but on the trail this involved physically moving a massive herd of stubborn, thirsty, and, at times, angry animals. Trail bosses had to manage their herd and their employees, as well as navigate cattle quarantines and survive frenetic cattle towns. From there it only got trickier. At the end of the journey were the great cattle markets of the West, where the deck always seemed to be stacked in favor of buyers.

The war that had devastated southern cattle markets had created a hunger for beef in northern ones. In 1865, an animal "worth five or six dollars in Texas . . . was worth in the northern markets more than ten times that amount."[42] Men who had driven to southern markets for years turned north, taking their cattle to Kansas and other markets already connected to the northern rail network.

When cattle trailing began in earnest, the Civil War was still fresh in people's minds. Fear of disease and trampled crops meant farmers and ranchers always resented cattle passing through their area, and it was even worse when former Confederates owned the animals. Armed men would surround southern drovers, whipping them, stealing cattle, and allegedly even killing some of them. Apparently, "in that day and country a man's, especially Southern drover's, legal rights, without physical force . . . were as useless as a piece of refuse paper."[43] Cattleman Jack Bailey's journal echoes this point in a particularly ominous entry: "passed a parcel of men around a little bunch of Texas beef in the act of shooting them on the prairie . . . they swear people shant drive through the country. If the law don't stop it, they will."[44] J. M. Daugherty reported a similarly terrifying encounter with some Kansas "jayhawkers" in 1866, when he was apprehended and "tried" for bringing diseased cattle into the area.[45] Daugherty's captors debated hanging or whipping him to death. Daugherty eventually managed to persuade them to release him. Though the men were rumored to be disgruntled former Union soldiers, by Daugherty's reckoning they were "nothing more than a bunch of cattle rustlers," who claimed to be worried about cattle disease but actually "used this just as a pretense to kill the men with the herds and steal the cattle or stampede herds."[46]

Over time, however, cattle trade profits healed all wounds. As cattleman and booster Joseph McCoy claimed, by 1873 "the western cattle trade has been no feeble means of bringing about an era of better feeling between northern and Texas men by bringing them in contact with each other in commercial transactions."[47] While McCoy's assertion might be overblown, it was true that following early turmoil in the 1860s, the business grew rapidly in the 1870s as Texas ranchers developed personal connections with Kansas businessmen and northern ranchers.

What emerged was a relatively stable system of cattle trailing that lasted from roughly 1870 to the mid-1880s. Rather than taking valuable hands away from the ranch, owners would often contract out cattle transportation to professional drivers who could trail cattle at rates of $1.00 or $1.50 a head, quite affordable at the time.[48] These firms in turn became so efficient that they could move cattle for under $0.75 a head per fifteen hundred miles, earning significant profits.[49] Furthermore, when ranchers could not pay fees up front, trailers worked on credit or for a fraction of the cattle sold. Assuming the cattle drover was reasonably reputable and established, the original owner generally assumed the risk of transport, freeing the drover from liability for disasters along the trail.[50] On the trail, drovers carried little more than a trailing contract and a note authorizing the firm to move a herd.[51]

Over time, cattle trailing became big business. Ike Pryor moved forty-five thousand head of cattle in 1884, and the firm Blocker, Briscoll & Davis moved fifty-seven thousand animals in 1886.[52] Charles Goodnight had built his herd on trailing profits.[53] Moving tens of thousands of cattle was no mean feat; the animals are stubborn and aimless. The real trick was convincing them to walk themselves to slaughter.

Horses, Water, and Stampedes: The Ecology of Cattle Trailing

A cattle-trailing outfit was an unstable entity, brought into existence by a particular configuration of horses, cattle, and people. Thunderstorms, stampedes, swollen rivers, and quarantine lines threatened to tear that relationship apart, while potable water and abundant Plains grasses gave the outfit the strength to make the journey. Attention to how the trailing outfit traveled from ranch to market and the forces that threatened or sustained this entity will reveal the material process through which rural animals and businesses participated in the development of a national cattle market.

A trailing outfit was not a stable or self-contained set of actors. As long as relatively similar numbers of cattle arrived at market as departed the ranch, the journey was a success. Men would join or leave along the trail. At the end of a five-month trip, Sam Neill was the only man left in his outfit who had made the thousand-mile trek from Frio County, Texas, to Ogallala Nebraska.[54] Cowboys were often lured by better offers; animals, on the other hand, left in considerably worse circumstances. Cattle that could not keep up "gave out" and were left to die along the trail.[55] Calves met similar fates since they were too young to survive long drives. According to one trailer, when calves were born on the trail, "it was custom to kill them before starting the herd each morning."[56] The mothers would become especially unruly early in the subsequent drive as they tried to return to their dead calf.[57] While some sources suggest a cart was used to transport calves, others indicate this measure was not cost-effective.[58] Killing the calves was considered merciful, since it was not merely that they slowed the herd, but calves were "unable to stand the tortures of thirst" that life on the trail required.[59]

To make up for these losses, trail outfits collected stray cattle. When these animals clearly belonged to someone, they were exchanged on the trail, but otherwise they were simply incorporated into the herd. One trail driver explained that he reached market with the same number of cattle as when he left because his expedition had "picked up as many crippled trail cattle as we lost."[60] This practice did not endear them to ranchers and farmers along trailing routes, who "made bitter complaints of moving herders 'incorporating' their stock." Yet this practice was understandable; "a trail boss who did not reach his destination with an equal or greater number than he started was considered incompetent."[61]

When possible, sore-footed cattle and horses were traded for fresh ones along the trail. A local rancher or merchant received a more valuable animal in exchange for a fresh steer or horse. If "incorporating" animals into a herd caused tension, this practice was win-win: local farmers profited and trail outfits avoided leaving an animal to die along the trail. In Jack Bailey's trail diary, one of the few journals produced while actually on a cattle drive, he describes "a negroe [who] came to camp last night to trade dry cows for cows + calves fixing to start."[62]

Yet the shifting agglomeration of cattle amounting to a herd was not an undifferentiated mass, for, as cattleman John Jacobs explains, "cattle of different temperament take their different places in the herd while traveling—they, like men, have their individuality."[63] The strongest members of the herd were known as "lead cattle." They were particularly useful for getting the herd moving and for leading the herd on river crossings.[64] At the opposite end of the herd were the drags, which had trouble keeping up. Tom Welder complained about younger cattle that could not endure the trials of the trail and "gave out," becoming drags for the entirety of the drive.[65] John Jacobs believed some cattle were drags by nature, and "they are drags from the day they leave the ranch to the end of the drive."[66] These animals were also known as "tenderfeet," and the term was also soon used to describe inexperienced cowboys or ranchers.

More than individual personalities, the overall composition of a herd had a major effect on the course of the journey. Herds were generally either steer only or mixed. Steers were preferred for trailing, as they generally had more energy and were never slowed by pregnancy. Furthermore, they were usually of a relatively standard age, whereas mixed herds had cattle of all ages. A herd could only move as fast as its slowest drag, and when a very young calf had to be left on the trail, getting the mother to move on was difficult.[67] At its core, cattle trailing was about convincing a herd of cattle to walk themselves where you wanted them to go. When that distance was measured in miles and not feet, this process depended on the relationship between rider and horse. This relationship was so fundamental to trailing and to a cowboy's identity that, according to Joseph McCoy, "[the cowboy] has a fixed, constitutional prejudice against doing anything on foot that can possibly be done on horseback, not to speak of the almost universal fear they entertain of being among their stock on foot."[68]

Whereas a herd of cattle could easily overwhelm a small number of people on foot, a relatively small number of mounted cowboys could manage massive herds. Professional cattle trailer Ike Pryor estimated that he used only 165 cowboys to "[drive] fifteen herds in 1884 from south Texas to the Northwestern States." He divided the cowboys into teams of eleven, with each group taking roughly three thousand head of cattle.[69] Bill Jackman also used eleven-man teams, but since one was the cook and another managed the horses, his scheme used only nine men to manage three thousand animals.[70]

Controlling this many animals depended above all on the maneuverability horses afforded. Even one thousand cattle could stretch into a line a mile long, and managing this large a group with only eleven people required speed and organization. Two lead riders would manage the herd's front and control the outfit's direction, while the remaining riders rode along the column, keeping the cattle in line. The supply wagon brought up the rear and watched for stragglers. By the 1880s, experienced drivers had mastered this process, a factor in the dramatic expansion of trail herd size in the 1860s and 1870s from a few hundred cattle to many thousands of beasts.[71]

Though horses have incredible stamina, maintaining the mobility and speed required to manage a herd required constantly substituting fresh horses for tired ones. Baylis Fletcher estimated that there were eight horses to each man and many horses were exchanged for fresher mounts along the trail.[72] Ike Pryor's outfit supplied six horses per man.[73] The herd of riderless horses was kept at the rear, with the supply wagon, in what was known as the "cavvie-yard."[74]

The best illustration of the power of a group of riders was the "cutting-out" process, in which a herd of cattle was separated into smaller groups, often by brand. This was necessary when stray cattle mingled with a herd or during sales of small numbers of cattle. Cattle from a wide area would slowly be driven into one large mass and then individual riders "were sent into the common herd to cut, or run out, such cattle as they severally claimed, putting the cuts of each brand into separate herds held by men detailed for that purpose."[75] This process was easier described than done. The harder part began once a single animal was separated from the herd and it began aggressively trying to return. According to Joseph McCoy, it was at this moment "where the skill of the cow-boy is put in requisition." A team of two riders would surround the beast and slowly work it farther and farther away from the herd. Though "often the race is close and the contest exciting," the result was always the same: the animal accepted its lot.[76]

If the human-horse relationship enabled cattle trailing, water dictated the herd's route. Cattle towns and Indian raids dominate popular accounts of trail life, but actual narratives were almost universally organized around rivers and lakes, whether overflowing or completely dry.[77] As Granville Stuart explains, "a day's drive on the trail is from ten to fifteen miles, but it is always governed by water."[78]

Access to potable water was a perpetual concern. Even conservative estimates placed the daily water needs of a herd of a thousand cattle at roughly twenty thousand gallons per day. Worse yet for the herd, humans and horses took first priority as strong horses were needed to control dehydrated and cranky cattle. Animals were often underhydrated for as much as a week at a time, and hundred-mile drives without water were not unknown.[79] At times, cattle became so thirsty that when they did reach water they were at risk of overdrinking and dying from water intoxication.[80]

James Shaw's trail narrative, *North from Texas*, provides a particularly vivid example of dehydration's toll. After two hot days without water, Shaw's herd smelled water on the breeze. A thousand cattle began "bawling, switching their tails and clashing their horns together." Shaw and his compatriots tried to calm the cattle but soon "every animal had started to bawl, with that sad and lonely bawl the cowboys know so well."[81] The animals became more and more disruptive until they finally reached the river. The inability to control thirsty cattle was a common issue, for, as one driver explained, it was like "[handling] a bunch of mixed turkeys."[82]

When Andy Adams wrote a self-consciously realistic novelization of trail life, he made a long waterless drive the climax of his narrative. He emphasizes its effect on the animals, describing how "the cattle lolled their tongues in despair," making "piteous yet ominous appeal[s]."[83] By the third day, the herd was "feverish and ungovernable," refusing even to lie down at night.[84] It was only on the fifth day, after some of the cattle had gone blind from extreme dehydration, that the herd finally reached a lake.[85]

Even when water was abundant, looks could be deceiving. Sam Garner discovered a spring "flowing out of the side of a mountain, and inviting us to partake freely," but it turned out the water was too salty to drink.[86] Garner was so thirsty that when he met a traveling merchant later that day, he paid him the outrageous sum of three dollars for five gallons of water. But Garner had no complaints: "while I have drank some good liquor in times gone by and thought it was the best stuff that ever went down a cowboy's neck, that five gallons of water . . . beat any liquor."[87]

Salty water proved more dangerous for cattle, since they were often dehydrated enough to drink fatal quantities. Near one river crossing, Baylis Fletcher's outfit found nearly a hundred cattle that had died from ingesting salty water.[88] Worse yet, Fletcher's own herd was drawn to the lethal water. Fletcher and his compatriots stampeded their animals across the nearly-dry river to keep them from stopping to drink. Once across, however, the animals tried to turn back. It took the rest of the afternoon to get the herd just a mile away, and even then severely dehydrated cattle spent the entire night trying to "escape to the river to drink," forcing the cowboys to keep watch all night.[89]

As much as potable water shortages, river crossings were a central feature of trail life. Cattle are strong swimmers and with a little bit of coaxing could swim a river. The cowboys would swim alongside, often on horseback. A reliable trail partner was "a man to ride the river with."[90] River swims generally went smoothly, but at times cattle would get trapped in quicksand or mud and become "bogged." These animals had to be bound with ropes and pulled out by oxen. It was an unpleasant process for man and beast.[91]

And river crossings were not without other risks, especially if an outfit did not ensure an easy exit from the river. G. H. Mohle's team met catastrophe when they failed to account for a narrow river bank. When crossing the North Fork of the Canadian River, the outfit "had no trouble getting the cattle into the water," but on the other side, the cattle "crowded in so that they could not get out . . . and began milling"; 116 animals drowned.[92]

Usually, however, getting the cattle across was the easy part. Moving the wagon proved more complicated as it had to be floated across the river without losing the supplies it carried. James Shaw's outfit would "hitch four yoke of oxen, with a man to swim on each side and swim [the wagons] across."[93] Joseph McCoy described a slightly different technique: ropes pulled the wagon across the river and then the oxen would swim the river and be re-yoked on the other side to pull the wagon onto shore.[94]

More than water shortages or treacherous river crossings, the ever-present threat of a stampede highlighted the fragility of the human-horse control of a herd. Seemingly at once, hundreds or thousands of cattle would scatter. Usually attributed to the unanticipated, whether storms, wayward buffalo, or cattle thieves, stampedes lurk in the background of narratives, journals, and cowboy fiction alike.[95]

Many a wet and sleepless night was the result of sudden lightning storms that would frighten the herd and cause a stampede.[96] The severity of these disruptions could range from minor to catastrophic and it was never entirely clear which was happening. Jack Bailey nonchalantly recorded in his August 9, 1868, diary entry that his team "had a stampede last night though nothing serious."[97] Just three days later, Bailey recounted "the hardest time last night imaginable." A few hours before dawn "came a loud clap of thunder," and Bailey was caught in the middle of a stampeding herd in total darkness.[98] The darkness created total confusion, with men "holering at the cattle when the cattle were not near them," because "[the men] swore [the cattle] wer comeing right towards them." The outfit eventually gained control, but spent the next morning rounding up more than two hundred lost animals.[99] Some were never recovered. Beyond stock losses, these stampedes could lead to serious human injury. After James Shaw and a partner regained control of a herd their boss ordered them to seek shelter in an adobe, "for fear the cattle get to running [again] and trample you to death."[100] In the aftermath of a particularly bad stampede, George Brock recounted that his friends "all looked like they had been to an Irish wake, all bloody and bruised."[101]

Indians or cattle thieves, sometimes real, often imagined, were also blamed for stampedes. A frequently described scam was secretly stampeding cattle and then offering to recover wayward cattle for a fee. Trailers frequently saw through the ruse, but it was often easier to go along with the scheme than to oppose the thieves. Indian-caused stampedes loomed large in cowboys' minds, but accounts of actual incidents are usually hazy. These alleged "depredations" often focused on horses: "[the Indians'] plan was to stampede droves of horses working the trail, with the intent of stealing such animals as were lost in the stampede."[102] Whether or not true, stampede fears crystallized cowboys' uncertainty and unease with trail life.

Homesteaders and town folk, angry with herds on or near their property, could also provoke stampedes. Baylis Fletcher explained that while passing through the town of Victoria, "a lady, fearful that the cattle would break down her fence and ruin her roses, ran out to the pickets and, waving her bonnet frantically at the cattle, stampeded those in front."[103] Fletcher credits his trail boss with stopping the stampede and avoiding serious damage to "city property."[104] The story seems a little farfetched, but it's not surprising that people would resent trail outfits. Later on Fletcher's trip, cattle destroyed a woman's dugout home by wandering over its roof and caving it in. Though "extremely sorry," Fletcher and his partners could not gain the woman's forgiveness.[105]

Most outfits followed the same few trails: chiefly the Chisholm trail, the Western trail, the Goodnight-Loving trail, and, in an earlier period, the Shawnee trail.[106] Major trails were like ocean shipping lanes: they had a relatively stable course, say from the Red River to Caldwell, Kansas, but were remade on each journey, with trailing outfits following one another in an ongoing stream. Trail driver M. J. Ripps described trails like rivers: "a river changes its course in the course of time; likewise, the channels of trade are changed with the passing of the days."[107] Along these channels, individual routes varied slightly depending on weather, availability of water, or news from the trailing outfit just over the horizon.

To get from Texas to northern markets, most of these routes passed through Indian Territory (today Oklahoma). This made interactions between trail drivers and American Indians inevitable. The drivers' accounts are generally unflattering, emphasizing the extent to which Indian Territory was a wilderness and its inhabitants routinely demanded unearned tribute or undeserved charity. Outfits generally describe encountering a man claiming to be an Indian leader or one of his emissaries. Drivers' lack of understanding of Indian politics complicated these interactions, and cowboys often complained of the number of men claiming to be leaders. Emissaries asked for what cowboy V. J. Carvajal described as a customs duty: cattle given in exchange for trail access.[108] Facing this situation, trail bosses often tried to pass off sore-footed or crippled cattle, and their counterparts either accepted the offer or held out for better payment. A. M. Gildea reported with outrage an account of Mescalero Indians who not only refused to take drags, but insisted that they choose the cattle they would receive.[109] Though outrageous to trail drivers, this tribute was something approximating a toll. Cattle did not merely pass through harmlessly; they tore up soil, drank any available water, and grazed freely.

The use of cattle stampedes as retribution against outfits that would not hand over cattle suggests that Indian leaders viewed payment of animals as obligatory. A. Huffmeyer described an incident when his outfit was in the Osage Nation in which "an Indian chief and four bucks came to our camp . . . and wanted us to give them a steer or two for allowing us to graze our cattle through their reservation." When the trail boss refused to do so, "the Indians went away in an ugly humor, threatened to come back and stampede our herd that night and get one anyhow."[110] Huffmeyer must have been well aware of the risk, as cowboys discussed such exchanges frequently. Reflecting on his time trailing cattle, Thomas Welder explained that he "always complied with the [cattle] request and had no trouble, but others who failed to do so had their cattle stampeded at night and probably lost more in the end than I did."[111]

In most cases, cattle were not trailed all the way to their final destination. Cattle trailing was a means to connect the animals through north–south arteries to the nation's largely east–west rail network. Therefore, the drives often ended in cattle towns, which were access points for the major western railroads. But before we talk about the frenetic life in these towns—for human and animal—it is important to understand the forces off the trail that shaped where cattle could travel. This was in part a story of town boosters and railroad policy, but it was also a story of cattle quarantine and the expanding federal state.

Cattle Disease and the Regulation of Mobility

Within and beyond Indian Territory, trailing cattle trampled crops, grazed private land, and generally annoyed local farmers and ranchers. But these were minor concerns compared with an unwelcome companion Texas outfits sometimes brought: disease. During the 1880s, local cattle that grazed fields traveled by Texas longhorns would sicken and die. According to the *Western Recorder*, "when an animal gets sick with the disease, it mopes around with hair turned forward, head down, eyes sleepy, until finally it falls over and expires."[112] The response to an outbreak was usually quick and severe, with ill cattle shot and exposed cattle quarantined.[113] The cause, effect, and extent of the disease were sharply debated at the time, but subsequent estimates indicate that it caused as much as $63 million in damage between 1866 and 1889.[114]

The disease was mysterious; at times harmless, it was often lethal. Theories abounded: contaminated grass and dirt traveling in animals' hooves, disease-carrying ticks, miasmas traveling with herds, and many more. In light of the threat, ranchers and farmers in Kansas wanted quarantines to keep Texas cattle out of their state. Texans dismissed the risks and claimed the complaints were the cynical attempt of rival ranchers to cripple their trade. Though Texans first tried evading or ignoring quarantines, they eventually accepted them and embraced their own regulatory solution to the Texas fever problem: a federally sanctioned cattle trail that would keep their herds away from local animals.

In emphasizing on-the-ground conflicts, this discussion highlights how federal-level regulation can emerge from local political dynamics. Furthermore, problems enforcing state-level quarantines—ranchers evaded authorities by moving rapidly between jurisdictions—reveal that the scale of markets and the scale of regulation are interlinked; a mismatch between the two sparks conflict and a diminishment or growth of either market or state. If the ecology of cattle trailing was a set of relationships that allowed cattle to move, the spatial politics of cattle quarantines shaped where and how the animals traveled.

Even the name of the disease, known here for consistency as "Texas fever," was contentious. It was known variously as Texas fever, Spanish fever, tick fever, southern cattle fever, and splenetic fever. During the quarantine fight, those who supported aggressive measures against the disease called it Texas fever, emphasizing the threat of the Texas cattle trade. Unsurprisingly, the name faced Texans' contempt. A. E. Carothers, chief veterinarian of the Southern Texas Live Stock Association, referred to the name as a "misnomer," and observed that the disease itself "is far from proven to have any connection with Texas cattle."[115]

Despite Carothers' claim, evidence was strong that Texas cattle spread the disease. D. E. Salmon, first chief of the Bureau of Animal Industry and recipient of the first degree of veterinary medicine in the United States, built his career fighting the disease.[116] In "Texas Fever: A Matter of National Importance," first published in the Breeder's Gazette, he argued that not only was the disease endemic to the South, but that greedy ranchers and cattle investors "utterly refused" to be convinced about the disease's threat.[117]

Texans remained skeptical. Carothers mocked Salmon's claim that the still-controversial germ theory explained the spread of Texas fever, joking that these germs have "no existence except in the vivid imaginations or one-sided spectacles of these learned scientists."[118] Senator Richard Coke of Texas referred to Salmon's explanation as a "monstrous theory."[119] To Joseph McCoy, a convention dedicated to the disease was "a collection of quondam quacks, impractical theorists, and imbecile ignoramuses."[120] These critics were always quick to observe that veterinarians had no hard evidence about the causes of Texas fever.[121]

Despite this skepticism, there was little doubt in the minds of northern ranchers and farmers who had seen cattle drop dead in their pastures after mingling with Texas cattle. These people pushed aggressively for quarantines. In 1867, the Kansas legislature prohibited Texas cattle from passing through the populous areas of the state, requiring instead that they travel through Kansas's far western end. The law was updated and revised throughout the 1870s. During the early 1880s, northwestern states like Wyoming and Colorado passed quarantines as well.[122] A patchwork of overlapping and confusingly worded state and local quarantines eventually covered the West.

Ultimately, however, these quarantines were enforced selectively or incompetently. Perhaps the most glaring example is that the massive stockyards at Abilene, Kansas, actually violated Kansas's 1867 quarantine. This meant that the state's largest cattle market was formally illegal. Joseph McCoy, the stockyards' mastermind, had won the support of the Kansas governor, who ignored local farmers' complaints.[123] Even an updated quarantine requiring cattle to spend the winter in Kansas before sale had little effect on the town's markets. Joseph McCoy joked that he was "[astonished] the following summer how many 'wintered cattle' arrived at Abilene. In fact it was [hard] to get a steer or cow, four or five years old, without it having been 'wintered' somewhere."[124]

At least at first, the quarantines had only limited success. They met determined opposition—cattle trailing was hugely profitable—and the fact that the exact cause, extent, and effects of Texas fever were unclear also contributed to the quarantines' failure. Though Texans' skepticism was at times cynical, the mystery surrounding the disease underpinned genuine skepticism and a corresponding anger with seemingly protectionist quarantines.[125] On the other side, ranchers and marketers were willing to make exceptions to quarantines or allow borderline cases, but the problem was that few knew for sure how to make an appropriate (or safe) exception.[126] This was particularly true of requirements that drovers receive permission for trailing near locals' property. The buffer between Texas herds and local cattle was often either too large or too small. Similarly, the region in which Texas fever was endemic was unclear, so that harmless herds were sometimes quarantined and dangerous ones permitted.

Lack of effective enforcement and brazen violation on the part of Texas ranchers spurred vigilante quarantine enforcement. The "Winchester quarantines," in which rifle-wielding farmers or ranchers prevented passage through their land, are a central (and real) part of ranching lore.[127] When Charles Goodnight heard that an acquaintance was planning to trail potentially infected cattle over his land, he wrote a letter explaining that "even friendship will not protect you in the drive through here . . . I simply say to you that you will not pass through here in good health."[128] In places like Kansas, this type of approach was viewed as legitimate enforcement of restrictions that were already on the books.

Despite the quarantine failures of the 1870s, by the early 1880s it looked as though the restrictions would finally have teeth. After an outbreak of pleuropneumonia, a similarly devastating cattle disease, threatened American cattle exports to Britain, lawmakers and bureaucrats began to treat cattle diseases as a serious economic and political issue.[129] Furthermore, farmers and small ranchers in Kansas built a coalition with northern ranchers—who had self-interested reasons for opposing the Texas industry—to push for enforcement.

Texas ranchers and their allies recognized that they could not evade the quarantines forever and sought their own regulatory solution. They wanted the federal government to establish a national cattle trail running from the Red River in Texas to the Canadian border that would be wide enough to satisfy quarantine requirements and protected from the encroachments of settlers. Similar proposals had been debated for years, but this time the trail's supporters chose a dramatic venue for unveiling their plan: a national ranching convention, convened in St. Louis in November 1884.

On the third day of the convention, Texas rancher Judge Carroll introduced a proposal to ask Congress for a national cattle trail.[130] Stephen Dorsey of New Mexico quickly lent his support, announcing that "the people from Texas have a right to a trail."[131] But the proposal had many critics. At least one Kansan was skeptical that the trail could check the spread of Texas fever.[132] Some criticisms had little to do with cattle disease. A. T. Babbitt of Wyoming explained that "we did not object to it on the ground of the liability of infection, or of cattle disease . . . we have objected to the trail simply on the ground of safety of our investments."[133] Babbitt and his allies in Colorado, Montana, and elsewhere opposed the trail because they viewed it as a measure to protect Texas ranching interests at a time when northern ranchers were already subject to sagging prices. Despite this vocal opposition, Texans comprised a majority of the convention attendees and voted to send a national cattle trail request to Washington.

With the national trail proposal, both sides of the Texas fever fight were now pushing for a regulatory solution. This was an important step: the outlines of the intervention remained a matter of debate, but the value of regulation was presupposed. Moreover, both sides were turning toward federal solutions; according to both sides, local interests had captured state regulation and were using it to "vexatious" ends.[134] Texas ranchers and their allies wanted federal intervention to protect interstate commerce, which they believed state-level interests threatened. This was a vital step in the regulation of cattle markets; it became apparent that the scale of regulation needed to match the scale of markets. Once goods started to move across state boundaries, federal solutions appeared necessary.

On April 28, 1886, Texas representative John Henniger Reagan presented Congress with a bill for the establishment of a national livestock highway. Though a former Confederate who had briefly served time in Boston's Fort Warren for treason, by the 1880s Reagan was known as a supporter of federal power, especially if it helped Texas. When he introduced the trail measure, he announced that the secretary of the interior endorsed the proposal and that it had passed the Senate "without objection." Despite this groundswell of support, there was strong but silent opposition, likely owing to the belief that the proposal would chiefly benefit Texas' big corporate ranches. When put to a vote, the bill received sixty-nine ayes and twenty-nine noes, but this fell short of the quorum needed for any motion to pass.[135] The bill died and was not raised again.

Within a couple of years, however, the federal government did intervene. This was the result of increased activity on the part of the Bureau of Animal Industry, the growing strength of animal quarantine as a practice more generally, and the fact that government veterinarians had already successfully campaigned for quarantines to control pleuropneumonia. In July 1889, the Department of Agriculture quarantined fifteen southern states.[136]

Cattle trailing was already declining rapidly with effective enforcement of local quarantines and the failure of the drovers' last hope: the national cattle trail. By the late 1880s, the number of cattle driven on the hoof had declined more than eighty percent and yearly totals were at their lowest since 1867.[137] The flow of yearlings from Texas to stock the northwestern ranges dried up, and rail routes carrying cattle directly to Chicago expanded. Yet the national market for cattle, as well as government regulation of that market, was a product of the cattle-trailing period, and it became central to the business.

The story of Texas fever did not end in the mid-1880s. The disease continued to kill western cattle and the solution embraced during the quarantine fight—using rail transportation to keep cattle quarantined—actually contributed to Texas fever's spread since it allowed contagious cattle to travel farther and farther. It would not be until 1893 that scientists largely agreed that ticks transmitted the disease—an explanation first offered more than ten years previously.[138] Over the next twenty years, Bureau of Animal Industry scientists would work to eradicate the disease, a process that included mandatory cattle disinfecting devices, which were prohibitively expensive for smaller ranchers and farmers. This campaign dispossessed smaller farmers of their cattle, an interesting contrast with the quarantine struggle when the epidemic threatened small farmers' livelihoods.[139]

Texas fever as an epidemic was ultimately an economic-biological creation. Initially susceptible to the disease, Texas cattle had developed a resistance during the two centuries following their arrival in North America. As part of local markets, these animals had moved little during their lives and therefore the disease's extent remained limited. It was only when Texas cattle were transported north for sale that the disease reached fresh populations. Commodity flows and consumption patterns drove the disease's expansion. In this sense, Texas fever was not a disease that emerged naturally (or as a product of simple biological forces) to wreak havoc on the cattle-trailing industry. The disease as an epidemic was a product of that system.

The story of Texas fever highlights the broader inextricability of government regulation from the emergence of national markets. Cattle mobility created economic and social tensions that could not be resolved without government intervention. Though Texas ranchers initially rejected quarantines, they eventually concluded that they had no alternative to embracing regulation. Even if competitors disagreed on the nature of regulation, both sides accepted state authority. Further, the political maneuvering around Texas fever reveals that the scale of regulation tends to match the scale of markets: when goods and people move across jurisdictions, local solutions start to fray. Nevertheless, these local conflicts were what ultimately sparked calls for large-scale solutions. Market development and government expansion were interlinked processes rooted as much in local contestation as in regional or national institutional developments.

Between Trail and Market

From the trail, herds arrived in cattle towns, the first connection ranchers made with the nation's rail network and, therefore, the emerging national market. These towns were frenetic places, perpetually in a process of becoming; boosters were ever-eager to promote their town as the next Chicago or St. Louis. Towns depended on the business of highly mobile actors: either ranchers passing through or railroads looking for a town in which to build. To appeal to outsiders, towns built and advertised familiar, reliable, and convenient facilities like hotels and stockyards. Because a multiplicity of towns were doing the same thing, this promoted a process of town standardization that would become a core aspect of the emerging national cattle market.

This idea hinges on a particular understanding of the concept of standardization. Here, the term means any tendency toward similarity between places that reduces the local knowledge required to navigate them. Ranchers wanted assurances that they could find clean and reliable stockyards, even in a place they had never been before. Similarly, standardized trails guiding ranchers to town stockyards meant that ranchers no longer needed to know the specificities of the route. For boosters, this was a double-edged sword: when a town had something no one else could offer, there was reason to go there, but once everybody offered reliable and good service, ranchers could take their business anywhere.

Abilene, Kansas, was the first major cattle town. Though there was a supply of cattle in Texas and demand in Chicago following the Civil War, railroads only extended as far south as Kansas. Furthermore, cattle loading facilities were poorly developed, making rail transport even more complicated. In 1867, Joseph McCoy and some partners decided that there was an opportunity to make Abilene the key nexus between Texas ranching and national markets.[140] McCoy lobbied railroads, contacted ranchers, and began an aggressive promotional campaign to lure business.

Much of Abilene's economy became organized around cattle shipping. Just as town boosters hoped to make their town the next western metropolis, small-business owners hoped to cash in on the thriving cattle trade and become the next western magnate.[141] Most towns included hotels and boardinghouses, as well as local banks to finance trailing operations and grease the wheels of the cattle trade. Provision stores helped trailing outfits restock. Cowboys were often paid upon arrival and, according to a cattle-town cliché, spent all their earnings in town. Dance halls and bars provided entertainment, and businesses appealed to Texans with names like "Alamo," "Lone Star," or "Long Horns."[142] Cattle towns were sites of tolerated though technically illegal prostitution; town growth brought police crackdowns.[143] These places were highly seasonal: busy from spring to late fall, but mostly vacant in winter.

The story of Ellsworth, Kansas, the next great cattle town after Abilene, reveals the life cycle of a cow town as well as the processes that standardized the nation's cattle markets.[144] Built on traffic headed east, Ellsworth had initially looked west. The town was organized in 1867, when boosters envisioned Ellsworth as the eastern end of the Kansas Pacific Railway and a supply point for western Kansas, Colorado, and New Mexico.[145] This early scheme failed miserably. A flood forced the town to relocate to higher ground, and a Cheyenne raid caused further chaos. After the ensuing failure to persuade railroad executives to make the town a supply point for lines headed west, it appeared that the story of Ellsworth was at an end.[146]

Yet Ellsworth's boosters remained determined. In 1869, they made a bold move for the cattle trade. Town leaders lobbied the Kansas legislature for a state-sanctioned trail to Ellsworth that would be exempt from the Texas fever quarantine laws. Finding limited success, the town's boosters, with the help of the Kansas Pacific Railway, wrote a bulletin "to cattle owners and dealers," advertising the "large and commodious" stockyards at Ellsworth, complete with quality pasturage and other amenities. Boosters also played up the threat of Texas fever quarantines, noting that their stockyards were in "strict conformity to law," before implying their loyalties were with Texas ranchers since trailing to Ellsworth would protect drovers from "unjust prosecutions."[147]

The sympathy with Texas ranchers was disingenuous, since Ellsworth's boosters actually worked behind the scenes to ensure prosecutions elsewhere in the state. Further, they began warning ranchers that the quarantine law threatened herds headed for Abilene.[148] Joseph McCoy railed against Ellsworth's boosters as "utterly unscrupulous as to means employed, destitute of honorable manhood and incapable of doing a legitimate business in an honest manner; full of low cunning and despicable motives, these ghouls resorted to every device their fertile brain could conceive."[149] This "low cunning" soon put Ellsworth on the map.

In 1871, the Kansas Pacific purchased and expanded the Ellsworth stockyards, making them the biggest in the state.[150] Meanwhile, rail employees and Ellsworth boosters continued to promote the town in Texas. As in 1869, recruiters distributed maps promoting "the best and shortest cattle routes from Texas,"[151] as well as elaborate pamphlets such as a guide complete with cost estimates, a mile-by-mile guide, and engravings of the pasturage, rail, and cattle-buying facilities in Ellsworth. Because these guides were so clear, ranchers could decide where to send cattle based on price expectations, rather than preexisting familiarity with travel routes.

For Ellsworth's boosters and the Kansas Pacific's promoters, these efforts paid off quickly; they were rewarded with almost thirty thousand cattle in 1871, and during the off-season before 1872 businesses began relocating to Ellsworth.[152] Sometime in 1871 or 1872, the proprietor of Abilene's Drover's Cottage hotel arrived in Ellsworth with boards taken from his failing business.[153] Ellsworth saw nearly one hundred thousand cattle in 1872, making it the largest market in Kansas that year. It had become the new end of the famed Chisholm trail and, as one reporter explained, it became "the Abilene of last year."[154] Almost overnight, Ellsworth had become a bustling town with hotels, saloons, supply stores, and the only sidewalk west of Kansas City.[155]

The town was thriving, but there was already trouble on the horizon. Boosters in Wichita, Kansas, began angling for a share of the Texas trade. Newspaper editors in Wichita and Ellsworth began publishing articles promoting their town and denigrating their rival. When Ellsworth's leaders established a fund to attract business to the town, Wichita followed suit.[156]

Over time, Wichita gained the edge. The town was slightly closer to Texas, and Wichita's boosters were running a better ground game there. Wichita also developed amenities—hotels, groceries, stockyards—functionally identical to those in Ellsworth. In 1873, the Santa Fe became a major cattle shipper as its line extended to Wichita. Four hundred thousand cattle passed through the city that year. Meanwhile, other railroads began building into Texas, taking even more of Ellsworth's business. Ellsworth ultimately fell prey to the same practices that had brought its brief dominance. As cattle historian Donald Worcester observed, "when the Wichita market opened, some of the merchants had who deserted Abilene for Ellsworth loaded their wagons once more and headed for the new cattle center."[157]

Ellsworth's rapid downfall was not unique. Caldwell, Kansas, had a similar fate. During the late 1870s, both the Atchison, Topeka, & Santa Fe Railroad (AT&SF) and the Kansas City, Burlington, & Southwestern (KCB&SW) were considering passing through or near Caldwell. Managers from both lines met with town leaders to secure a local subsidy. After some political maneuvering, including a showdown between rival factions of town residents, the AT&SF won the support of the town. But the rail line was slow to arrive. Residents watched as rival towns captured the Texas trade. By 1880, town boosters wooed yet another railroad in hope of motivating the AT&SF to build more quickly. But in trying to play one line against the other, boosters brought disaster. Due to Caldwell's efforts, the Kansas City, Lawrence, & Southern Railway (KCL&S) had become interested in the area, but thanks to an even larger subsidy from a neighboring town, moved there. This town, Hunnewell, Kansas, soaked up a significant amount of the cattle trade and, with the AT&SF finally in Caldwell, the towns entered vicious competition. The AT&SF eventually won out, but at high cost to Caldwell. In a few years the cattle trade moved elsewhere, and though the railroad remained, Caldwell went into decline.

Caldwell's story reveals the added layer of railroad competition, which was central to this process. Railroads were massive national businesses, but they were enmeshed in local politics. Competition between rail lines meant that railroad managers had to forge alliances with town boosters. Railroads were important drivers of standardization, but it was only possible with the cooperation of aspiring cattle towns.

The process (and risks) of standardization is evident in two pairs of images from 1874. Two images depict "Abilene in Its Glory" and two depict "Ellsworth, Kansas." Train cars stretch to the horizon. Cattle, horses, and cowboys populate the foreground. These are not merely depictions of similar places, the two pairs of images are the same. Kansas artist Henry Worrall produced the images during a collaboration with Joseph McCoy; it turns out that Ellsworth's boosters were as "utterly unscrupulous" as McCoy had claimed.[158] Either Ellsworth residents or Kansas Pacific Railway promoters had taken Worrall's

ABILENE IN ITS GLORY.

FIGURE 4. A promotional image of Abilene, Kansas, taken from Joseph McCoy's *Historic Sketches*. Reproduced by permission from Kansas State Historical Society.

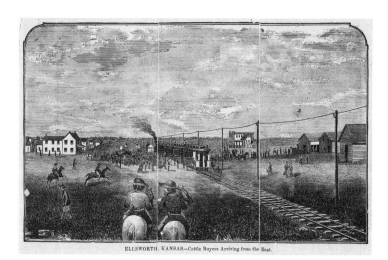

ELLSWORTH, KANSAS—Cattle Buyers Arriving from the East.

FIGURE 5. A promotional image captioned "Ellsworth, Kansas," taken from the Kansas Pacific Railway's *Guide Map of the Great Texas Cattle Trail*. The pamphlet makers appear to have simply reused the Abilene image. Reproduced by permission from Kansas State Historical Society.

images of Abilene and put them in their own promotional pamphlet.[159]

What matters more than the theft of Worrall's images is the fact that they could plausibly have represented either town, and that Ellsworth promoters would employ direct imitation. They wanted Texas ranchers to see Ellsworth as a town like any other, interchangeable with the previous year's most popular market, Abilene. It was a strategy that would bring Ellsworth a lot of business for a few years, but it was also part of a process of standardization that pieced together the national cattle distribution system and made an abstracted national market, bigger than any individual place.

From the perspective of ranchers, these cattle towns all served the same purpose: access to distant markets. Once a trail herd reached a town like Ellsworth or Abilene, managers fed their cattle generously to provide them with the strength to survive the upcoming rail journey. Cowboys left for home—usually not before spending generously in town—while ranchers or trail managers tried to figure out where they should send their animals: Chicago, Kansas City, or elsewhere. As quickly as possible, the cattle were loaded onto trains.

Rail transportation required a careful balancing of risks. If the train was too slow, or the final destination too far, cattle would lose valuable flesh on the journey. But if the train went too fast, the animals had a higher chance of injury. Sudden stops or sharp curves could lead to goring.[160] Further, if cattle were packed too tightly, larger animals or those with well-developed horns could injure smaller specimens. Deprivation of food and water was another concern. When trailed, animals could take periodic breaks for grazing or drinking, but this was impossible on a train. As animals became dehydrated, hungry, or simply tired, they tried to lie down, putting them at even greater risk for injury. Shippers used long poles equipped with a sharp prod to jab downed animals until they returned to their feet. Some cattle simply died. The American Humane Association condemned shipping practices and even tried—without success—to encourage the development of a more humane car.[161]

In the early days of the cattle trade animals were moved in standard boxcars. Cattle filled the car and shippers scattered hay and feed among the animals. The owner or the owner's fiduciary occupied the end of the car, at times sleeping alongside the cattle.[162] This situation was not ideal for the shipper, car owner, or rancher; animal waste would fill the car.

By the late nineteenth century, small numbers of specialized cattle cars had entered use. These cars often belonged to a particular company—there were seven well-known companies by 1889—and were operated as a private shipping line on contract with particular railroads.[163] The most well-known and high-end of these specialized cars was the Palace Stock Car. Developed by A. C. Mather in the early 1880s, the car could hold twenty-five animals. Animals faced the sides of the car in alternating directions, with slats keeping them separate and space for hay just above them and water pans below.[164] While expensive, it was estimated that this specialized car significantly reduced cattle shrinkage.[165]

Cars of this type never became popular.[166] The problem was that live cattle only went in one direction: toward Chicago. Specialized cars could not be loaded with other kinds of freight, so these cars often remained empty on the way out of Chicago, frustrating railroad managers who wanted their cars perpetually full. As one alarmist railroad manager explained, "these two species of equipment, namely, the refrigerator car and the palace stock car, are two of the greatest vampires that are now sucking the life blood of the railroads."[167] While this was certainly an exaggeration, it highlights the core tension in the cattle transportation system between the need to provide cattle with comfortable and safe transportation—largely for economic reasons—and the needs of the broader freight system. For this reason, shippers generally preferred the flexibility of standard freight cars.

When a load of cattle reached market, they were unloaded and entered the care of the local stockyard company, which charged a flat daily rate per animal—around twenty-five cents per head—for taking care of the animals.[168] Unloading the car was an involved process. Tired and dehydrated animals were driven out with prods, and yard workers dragged out dead and dying cattle with ropes.[169] Surviving animals were generally fed and watered before being weighed—a point of contention, since buyers claimed they were purchasing useless weight. The animals were then taken to a pen where they awaited sale under the care of the stockyard company, which also refereed any sales, weighing and certifying the transactions.[170]

Stockyards were chaotic places and ranchers often relied on agents known as commission merchants. For a flat fee—fifty cents per head in 1880s Chicago, or a percentage cut of the sale ranging from five to ten percent—a commission merchant monitored prices in the local market as well as elsewhere, acting as a rancher's "general intelligence office."[171] For example, when a representative of the American Live Stock Commission Company had trouble finding buyers in one market, he notified his client that he "thought best to forward [the cattle] on to Chicago."[172] In this sense, commission merchants managed the complicated calculus of where and how to sell, helping ranchers transcend their immediate market. Since stockyards charged daily fees for feeding, watering, and storing cattle, ranchers wanted a rapid sale. Ranchers at times stated a preference—such as when William Sommerville directed his merchants to consider sending to Chicago but explained they should "keep in mind we prefer sale in Kansas City"[173]—but generally sales came down to commission merchants' decisions as they used their expertise to balance speed and price.

These merchants were often former cattle trailers or small-time ranchers who had concluded there was more reliable money in facilitating sales. R. D. Hunter of Hunter, Evans & Company, one of the largest commission firms, fit this profile well, having made money trailing and selling cattle before entering the commission business with Albert Evans.[174] These men combined their knowledge of cattle markets with their credibility as cattlemen to expand rapidly. Hunter and Evans' firm grew large enough for multiple markets, making their operation one of the larger ones. There were scores of one- or two-person local operations working in the West. In Kansas City alone, there were roughly fifty commission firms by the 1880s. Most of these firms were local, and there was a great deal of tension between local firms and the large companies that worked in multiple markets and even sent recruiting agents to ranching country.

Ranchers had to give commission merchants broad discretion; markets moved quickly and there was rarely time to communicate. Trust, then, was a necessary but shaky foundation. To attract customers, one firm bragged about its detailed records and offered "to hold their books open for inspection."[175] Even this, however, was not entirely persuasive. Commission merchants generally only recorded the total weight and number of cattle, and when a rancher was dealing with hundreds or thousands of animals, this provided ample room for grift. One disgusted rancher lumped commission merchants in with the railroads and other parties who were "making more out of [an animal], than us who raise him."[176]

As markets expanded, formalized livestock exchanges sought to regulate and standardize the commission business. Codified rules eased rancher fears, simultaneously facilitating trade as well as reducing the personal connections a rancher needed to ensure fair treatment in an unfamiliar market. Yet it was also an attempt by small merchants to oppose large companies, as the history of the Kansas City Live Stock Exchange highlights.[177] In the 1870s, a few multicity commission firms controlled most of the trade, chiefly because they had developed the extensive personal connections needed to assemble regular cattle deals. Using a system of rebates and kickbacks to reward large-volume clients, these firms effectively undercut smaller companies, which generally lacked the capital to offer similar deals.[178] In 1886, upstart commission merchants established the Kansas City Live Stock Exchange, which charged a standard commission of fifty cents per head, independent of volume. Though small companies eagerly joined the livestock exchange, the large commission houses were reluctant to surrender their autonomy.[179]

The resistance of these larger firms was short-lived. The exchange's organizers used their knowledge of local conditions in Kansas City to force compliance and the participation of these larger businesses. When the exchange threatened to publicize the big firms' shady rebating practices, the larger firms joined. Once the first few large companies agreed to participate, the pressure on the holdouts became enormous. Soon, the Kansas City Live Stock Exchange managed almost the entirety of the city's cattle trade.

Although the victory of the upstart commission merchants in Kansas City was a victory of small local merchants over the

large multimarket ones, the end product—standardization in
the form of a livestock exchange—promoted the growth of a
national commodity market by making it easier for ranches of
all sizes to act in Kansas City's markets. It also made it easier
for a rancher who had never been to Kansas City to do business
there. Therefore it helped small, and generally local, commission merchants, but ultimately enabled the expanded movement of cattle around the West.

The fate of the American Live Stock Commission Company, which had tried to operate in many markets before falling prey to local actors, presents a more complicated picture
of standardization. Organized in 1889, the company managed
multiple markets, used large-client rebates, and offered faster
price information than rivals. The company is the subject of
some historiographic debate, with certain historians of populism identifying the company, which was in part organized by
ranchers, with progressive ideas.[180] Scholars more friendly to
self-regulation and business, however, believe this is mistaken
and that the company was actually a large-rancher attempt to
crush small commission merchants and circumvent organi-
zations like the Kansas City Live Stock Exchange. Eventually
the Kansas City exchange, as well as exchanges in Chicago and
Omaha, organized a boycott and legal action against the company.[181] When ranchers caught wind of this, they began to look
for other partners. Murdo Mackenzie asked his colleague Alexander Mackay about changing commission merchants since
"for the past two years the American Live Stock Company sold
the bulk of your cattle but this year it has got into trouble ... and
it was expelled from the stock yards exchanges and boycotted
by the buyers ... if we ship to this company we are liable at any
moment to be left with our cattle in the yards and nobody to
make an offer for them."[182] The company survived the boycott,

but it was dealt a serious blow, illustrating how standardization could hurt some multimarket companies even as it empowered others, such as the Chicago meatpackers.

Whether involving ranchers, commission merchants, railroads, or meatpackers, competition in the cattle business was about scale. Mobile actors tried to operate in multiple markets and those fixed in one place, such as local commission merchants, were torn between trying to keep the scale local and promoting standardization in order to secure distant customers. The overarching tendencies were nevertheless present: parties involved sought some form of regulation to solve coordination problems and mobile actors sought standardization.

Making a Deal

Though commission merchants helped ranchers navigate cattle markets, there was no escaping the fact that selling cattle was a messy and unpleasant process. In theory, it was a good system for sellers: they received competing bids from potential buyers and payments were always in cash. In practice, however, buyers had the upper hand. Buyers did not have to worry about a herd of cattle grazing on the stockyard's dime. Whereas sellers unhappy with prevailing prices had to weigh the risks of shipping a herd of cattle to a different market, unhappy buyers could simply telegraph an associate elsewhere and buy their animals there. As a result of this dynamic, prices were rarely what ranchers hoped.

Another complication of the cattle market was that there was no one price; different kinds of cattle brought different prices. As one rancher explained, "what an immense difference 100 lbs make in the sale of an animal of this kind," for "we have two classes of buyers to deal with in Chicago, and the difference in the prices they pay is enormous."[183] He was referring to cattle purchased for dressed beef (higher quality) and cattle produced for canning (lower quality). There were markets for Texas cattle, native cattle, and high-end animals. This multiplicity of prices and markets was confusing for ranchers and good for meatpackers. If prices were low for high-quality animals the packers could stock up, or they could rely on a past surplus to ride out relatively high prices for canning steers.

This practice was particularly effective—and brutal for ranchers—when markets were poor. As a consequence of oversupply—discussed in chapter 2, especially the section "Doomed of Its Own Excesses [?]"—prices were on a long-term decline through the 1880s and, with a few exceptions, during the 1890s as well. When prices were bad, ranchers noted desperately that "the market must be met," and accepted prices scarcely higher—and sometimes lower—than what they had paid in feed and transportation. At these moments commission merchants would request a telegraph with the lowest prices ranchers could accept.[184] At one point prices were so poor that "cows have been marketed to net prices very little in excess of the value of their hides."[185]

That said, only a rube believed oversupply was the entire story. There was a good deal of evidence that collusion marred the bidding process. When the US Senate studied the cattle-selling process, the investigation concluded that "the overwhelming weight of testimony . . . is to the effect that cattle owners going with their cattle to the Chicago and Kansas City markets find no competition among buyers, and if they refused to take the first bid are generally forced to accept a lower one."[186] G. Buarmann, a former employee of meatpacker Morris &

Company, claimed that the big meatpackers "set the price of beef" each morning.[187] One cattle feeder testified to how the packers "skin poor men," and that when he went to sell cattle he received one bid and "no other man made us a bid. Nobody came around our cattle who was buying."[188] There were even claims—though this evidence is more limited—that the packers would collectively bid on enormous lots of cattle or hogs and divide them privately.[189] To be clear, there was some evidence against collusion; Samuel P. Cady reported receiving varying bids for many of his sales, though investigators later noted the reluctance of many active commission merchants and ranchers to openly claim collusion.[190] Perhaps as important as whether there was actual collusion was the Senate investigators' observation that "there was no hesitation on the part of witnesses even when obviously prejudiced in favor of the packers, in stating that the control of the market was absolutely within the grasp of these four houses if they saw proper to exercise it."[191]

When prices were bad, ranchers rarely succeeded when trying their luck in a better market. L. C. Baldwin, a stock raiser from Council Bluffs, Iowa, explained, "as a rule, in my experience, in the case of no sale being made in Omaha, and in moving from Omaha to Chicago we expect to realize a better profit . . . but in almost all instances in my experience we receive less." Baldwin went on to explain his belief that raisers were "punished" for taking this approach and that packers were well aware of movements because "communication is frequent and rapid between Omaha and Chicago and the market is seldom opened in Omaha until the telegraphic communications come from Chicago as to the state and condition of the market in Chicago."[192] Baldwin went on to claim that the Chicago packers were so strong that he could not sell directly in Council Bluffs,

FIGURE 6. 1909 photograph of Chicago's Union Stock Yards.
Workers would walk along the top rail of fences between
pens to move around the yards. Library of Congress.

having to send his animals to Omaha or elsewhere, despite the
fact that the big packers then shipped the meat back to Council
Bluffs for sale. In limiting Baldwin's and others' options, the
large meatpacking companies were operating at a national scale
while forcing their suppliers to act in a single market.

Rancher resentment extended to other meatpacker practices. Texas ranchers were particularly angry about the "broken
rib steal," in which the packers docked an animal's sale price
by $5 if it was badly bruised or injured. The packers allegedly
overstated the extent of injury to save money and because this
deduction was made after the lot had been weighed and priced,
ranchers anxious to sell had little recourse. Ranchers tried to
demand purchasers separate bruised animals prior to sale, but
had little power to ensure the practice.[193]

The fact that the ranchers were largely powerless—
meatpackers could operate in several markets at once and had
an endless number of suppliers—sparked a great deal of resentment. Transactions were grounded on trust and cattle owners
were often far from the point of sale, allowing ample room for
deception and suspicion. Evidence of the packers' collusion is
overwhelming, but what is important from the perspective of
this chapter is that they colluded in a way that allowed them to
exploit the scale of their business—operating regionally and
nationally—while keeping their suppliers inescapably bound
to a particular place, be it range, train car, or stock pen. Ranchers tried to compare prices in different markets, but buyers
always had the upper hand; once a lot of cattle had arrived
in Kansas City or Chicago, there were considerable costs to
moving them. It is no surprise, then, that ranchers sought state
solutions—regulation—to address these problems of scale and
mobility.

Eventually, however, cattle in Chicago or Kansas City or any
other packing center ended up with a buyer, whether or not
the amount paid to the rancher was "remunerative." The animals would then be weighed, the cash would change hands, and
either the owner went home or the commission merchant went

to telegraph news of the transaction. Whether to drown their sorrows or to celebrate, a trip to the saloon was likely along the way. For the animal, the future was always bleak.

Conclusion

Between 1870 and 1900, western cattle markets evolved from a series of regional centers into an integrated national system. The emergence of this national market and its supporting infrastructure occurred in tandem with contestation over who would dominate this new regime. Cattle raising on the Plains, fattening in the corn belt, and slaughter in Chicago were not the inevitable outcomes of technological changes or market forces, but the aggregated effect of thousands of decisions of cattle raisers, farmers, meatpackers, town boosters, and railroad executives as they fought over who would benefit from the growth in commerce.

Fundamentally, the story was about mobility. The cattle marketing system was a set of continent-spanning spatial relationships keeping cattle moving. The rise of the cattle-beef complex was predicated on the ability to put more and more distance between where food was produced and where it was consumed. This put a premium on those forces—whether railroads, cattle drovers, or commission merchants—keeping cattle in motion materially as well as abstractly (through finance).

This mobility, and the social and political conflict it sparked, resulted in two tendencies: (1) regulation at the scale of its breadth, and (2) standardization of the spaces through which commodities and people moved. In the case of Texas fever, political contestations over cattle mobility led to a regulatory arms race in which participants escalated from local solutions to state-level measures and finally toward federal intervention. This tendency contributed to a broader expansion of federal authority as government bureaucrats found new roles regulating growing markets and studying economic problems like cattle disease. Meanwhile, as people working in one place (town boosters and business owners) competed for highly mobile business (cattle trailing), they promoted a process of standardization that ultimately made one place look much like any other. Standardization explains how the cattle-beef complex was born in particular places but became bigger than any of them. Western ranching began in Texas but spread across the Plains, as the Texas fever discussion illustrates. For a time specific cattle towns had particular advantages, but once one looked like any other, ranchers could quickly move from town to town. Similarly, once every stockyard worked in roughly the same way, meatpackers could operate nearly simultaneously in all of them.

Regulatory changes brought their own challenges. Governments see the world in particular ways and people and businesses that can exploit this tendency thrive.[194] Regulatory compliance is often expensive, and this favors large operators who can afford the substantial cost. Similarly, the political process of creating regulations can be, and often is, unduly influenced. Oddly, these issues are a consequence of a muscular federal state, and the same small actors clamoring for federal quarantine enforcement or a national cattle trail would eventually become dependent on national actors, whether the Chicago meatpackers or government veterinarians.

This is not to suggest that either standardization or regulation is inherently problematic, but rather that they have specific consequences. Standardization not only enabled the consolidation of national markets, but also made it possible for people to move around the West or find new economic opportunities. However, it also meant businesses could easily move, disrupting entire communities. Not every resident of Abilene could follow the lead of the proprietor of the Drover's Cottage and move to the next cattle town. Similarly, regulation and increased federal authority protected consumers and often ensured fair competition, but also enabled regulatory capture and a tendency toward centralization and size that could marginalize people on the peripheries, in this case, ranchers.

Ultimately, however, regulation and standardization were more tendencies than laws of nature. No two cattle towns or stockyards were ever actually the same, and even a federal bureaucrat could be bribed or a federal quarantine circumvented. More broadly, capitalism has proved enormously successful at accommodating and even profiting from difference.[195] Yet a tendency toward powerful centralized states and a general reduction of the local knowledge needed to operate in a specific context is an ever-present aspect of the mobility of goods and people.

These tendencies resonate today. Small-scale producers of products such as meat, milk, and cheese all face high compliance costs with federal regulations that favor large processors.[196] Similarly, the fact that standardization means meat processors can pit ranchers and slaughterhouse workers in Texas, Colorado, Wyoming, and even Argentina against one another entrenches the inequality of the modern food regime. More broadly, standardization has had high costs for communities that increasingly all look the same from the vantage of a highway exit sign. This is as true of cities like Detroit or Pittsburgh as it is of towns like Abilene or Ellsworth.

A place is inescapably local: a rancher is in the Texas Panhandle or a lawyer is in Chicago. Spaces, however, are constituted by social and economic relationships and can be functionally identical. From one vantage, Chicago's Union Stock Yards were no different from stockyards in Kansas City or Wichita. The ability to operate as though one were in one of many interchangeable spaces, and not specific places, was crucial to success in the cattle-beef complex. Meatpackers developed information and transport networks so sophisticated that cattle in Kansas City and Chicago were functionally interchangeable. Meatpackers could play those tied to a given place—ranchers lacking the means to choose where to ship their cattle—against one another. The outcome of these struggles determined western space and economic power.

4

Slaughterhouse

TO HEAR HIM TELL IT, cooperation was not Philip Danforth Armour's strong suit. When the head of the enormous meat-packing firm Armour & Company appeared before the US Senate's Select Committee on the Transportation and Sale of Meat Products in 1889, his company and the others comprising what was popularly known as the "Big Four"—Swift & Company, Morris & Company, and Hammond & Company—stood accused of manipulating the prices they paid ranchers on one end of their supply chain and using predatory pricing to bankrupt butchers on the other.[1] In just over a decade, the Chicago packinghouses had grown from regional players to global behemoths. The select committee, popularly known as the "Vest Committee" after Chairman George Vest, was tasked with investigating a variety of charges against the Big Four. Armour and his colleagues were allegedly conspiring to "destroy the rule of supply and demand," and Texas Senator Richard Coke argued that the Big Four "have both ends of the string."[2]

Armour responded to the Vest Committee's questions with a mixture of evasion and indignation. On the charge that he and his competitors refused to bid against one another, Armour claimed not only was the accusation false, but that he and his

FIGURE 7. A portrait of meatpacker Philip Danforth
Armour. New York Public Library.

rivals were "like two flints rubbing together all the while."[3]
Armour did concede that he occasionally set prices with competitors, but that this was only in the consumer's interest. He
then refused to say with whom he was colluding, offering instead to tell examiners with whom he was not colluding. When
the examiners responded that he could perfectly well name
most of Chicago on that count, Armour asked for time to con-
sult his attorney.

In response to other charges, Armour gave accurate, but
incomplete answers. To the claim that he colluded with railroads to choke small competitors, he replied that the railroads
had spent much of the past decade colluding against him. That
was true, but it did not change the fact that after winning a
lengthy struggle, the Chicago meatpackers used their market
share to force desperate railroads to do their bidding. To the

charge that Armour and his compatriots were depressing cattle markets, Armour replied that the decline in prices was a consequence of the overproduction of cattle during the 1880s ranching boom. This was also true, but it did not address the abundant evidence that meatpacker collusion was exacerbating the problem.

Armour then offered a prepared statement explaining what was happening to struggling ranchers and butchers. His position was that structural changes in food production—refrigeration and railroads—meant that the industry had new rules. According to Armour, "to market the vast herds of cattle raised on what used to be called the plains of the West and Southwest, to slaughter the same and prepare every part of the animal for the market in which the consumer buys in the thickly populated parts of this country and in Europe" required aggressive tactics.[4] Traditional occupations would disappear. Armour's account worked much like his answers to the charges of predatory pricing and collusion: accurate, but only half the story.

In this sense, Armour's account is a lot like popular and academic narratives of the rise of big meatpacking. These accounts have a standard story that stresses technological and organizational change. The expansion of livestock markets provided the means, and railroads provided the infrastructure. The refrigerator car made fresh distribution possible, and, once slaughterhouses could process thousands of cattle daily at lower cost than traditional butchers, centralized production was secured. This story casts the shape of the food production system as an inevitable consequence of technological change. For Armour in the nineteenth century, and his successors today, this account protects against criticisms of the food system's inequities.

One of the earliest proponents of this narrative was Rudolf Clemen, whose career spanned both academia (Northwestern

University) and meatpacking (editor of the trade journal the *National Provisioner*). His comprehensive 1923 work, *The American Livestock and Meat Industry*, uses technological change to explain the evolution of meatpacking and business acumen to explain who benefited from it most. Clemen first lists the factors that created the modern meat industry: cattle supply, railroads, refrigeration, and "men to organize."[5] About the heads of the Big Four, he goes on to explain, "it was the work of these men with the refrigerator car which revolutionized the meat industry, created the dressed beef traffic on a commercial basis, and organized the distribution system of the modern meat industry. In this task they showed courage seldom equaled in commercial history."[6] Clemen does cover railroad and butcher resistance to dressed beef, but treats it as an irrational reaction to "enterprise and progress."[7]

The great-man narrative disappeared from subsequent histories but the emphasis on technology and the organizational changes it accompanied has remained center stage. These accounts neglect the social conflict at the heart of the story of the rise of centralized meatpacking, with the dual effect of taking away some of the glory from men once hailed as business geniuses, but also absolving them from responsibility for their actions; structural forces, not men like Armour, were to blame for bankruptcy and labor unrest.[8] These accounts present the modern food production system as an inevitable result of technological change and business optimization rather than one aggregate outcome of many social and political struggles.

A complete picture of the rise of centralized meatpacking must portray human conflict alongside technological changes and business developments. Armour and his managers, like his competitors and their managers, were organizational adepts and, at times, business geniuses, but this did not preclude strong-arming suppliers, colluding on prices, or breaking strikes. Cattle slaughter was as much about exploitation as innovation; beef distribution as much about collusion as invention.

The refrigerator car and the managerial revolution explains how a small group of firms could dominate a world in which cattle were slaughtered in one place and eaten a continent or an ocean away, but the meatpackers' victories over labor, the railroads, and local butchers explain how this state of affairs went from one that horrified people—pale gray meat in stuffy railcars—to one that was accepted as not only natural and inevitable, but also laudable. The key to the meatpackers' success was that they would align their cause, centralized mass production of meat, with the interests of consumers. Rancher, worker, and butcher would take a back seat. Government policy hindered unionization, and displaced butchers—finding little support for their protectionist measures in the courts—gave up or left the business. Ranchers, meanwhile, failed to effectively mobilize against the Chicago packers and accepted their subordinate role. By 1900, these once-loud voices of criticism had become a whimper. Reconstructing these social conflicts, then, helps explain how and why the federal government ultimately embraced the Big Four's vision of food production.

In the 1880s, however, the Chicago meatpackers faced determined opposition from slaughter to sale. Cattle slaughter was as much about new technologies as forms of labor discipline, which were often the source of conflict with slaughterhouse workers. Meanwhile, attempts to ship dressed beef faced opposition from a collusive group of railroads seeking to protect their obsolete equipment for shipping live cattle. Once dressed beef reached the nation's many cities and towns, the packers fought to displace traditional butchers and woo skeptical consumers. Armour & Company will often take center stage in this story, but only because the firm's policies are indicative of those of the Big Four more generally.

The consequences of each of these struggles persist today. A small number of firms still control most of the country's—and by now the world's—beef. They draw from many comparatively small ranchers and cattle feeders and depend on a low-paid, mostly invisible workforce. The fact that this set of relationships remains so stable, despite the public's abstract sense that something is not quite right, is not the inevitable consequence of technological change, but the direct result of the political struggles of the late nineteenth century.

Labor

In the slaughterhouse, someone was always willing to take your place. This could not have been far from the mind of fourteen-year-old Vincentz Rutkowski as he stooped, knife in hand, in a Swift & Company facility.[9] For up to ten hours each day, Vincentz trimmed tallow from cattle paunches. The job required strong workers who were low to the ground, making it ideal for boys like Rutkowski, who had the beginnings of the strength but not the size of grown men.[10] For the first two weeks of his employment, Vincentz shared his job with two other boys. As they became more skilled, one of the boys was fired. Another few weeks later, Rutkowski's last remaining colleague was removed and Vincentz was expected to do the work of three people.

The morning his final compatriot left, on June 30, 1892, Rutkowski fell behind the disassembly line's frenetic pace. After just three hours of working alone, the boy failed to dodge a carcass swinging toward him. It struck his knife hand, driving the tool into his left arm near the elbow. The knife cut muscle and tendon, leaving Rutkowski gravely injured.

In early 1893, Rutkowski filed suit against Swift & Company. His lawyer argued it was "the duty of the defendant ... to employ a sufficient number of servants in and about the slaughtering and dressing of said cattle, so that by reason thereof the said work of the plaintiff [Rutkowski] would be free from danger to himself while in the performance thereof, using all due care and diligence on his own behalf." Swift & Company, however, responded that Rutkowski was to blame since he was aware of the risk but had continued working.[11]

Though lower-level courts sided with Rutkowski, the Supreme Court of Illinois sided with the company on June 8, 1897. The court ruled that the lack of sufficient help was not enough to prove that Swift & Company was negligent. Though the firm was obligated to provide "suitable and safe machinery and appliances," this requirement covered situations where employees were oblivious to risks they faced. As the ruling explained, "when the employee discovers that the machinery or appliances are unfit for use, or dangerous or insufficient, it is his duty to quit the service of the employer, but, if he remains, he does so at his own risk." Swift & Company was not liable because Rutkowski had continued working.[12]

The labor regime that led to Rutkowski's injury was integral to large-scale meatpacking. A packinghouse was a masterpiece of technological and organizational achievement, but that was not enough to slaughter millions of cattle annually. Packing plants needed cheap, reliable, and desperate labor. Fortunately, they found it in the combination of mass immigration and a legal regime that empowered management, checked the nascent power of unions, and limited liability for worker injury. The Big Four's output depended on worker quantity over worker quality, as long as the public accepted the fate of people like Vincentz Rutkowski.[13]

Meatpacking lines, pioneered in the 1860s in Cincinnati's pork packinghouses, represented the first modern production lines. The innovation was that they kept products moving continuously, eliminating downtime and requiring workers to synchronize their movements to keep pace.[14] This idea would prove enormously influential. In his memoirs, Henry Ford explained that his idea for continuous motion assembly "came in a general way from the overhead trolley that the Chicago packers use in dressing beef."[15]

The aspect people today would most associate with assembly-line work, the employment of machines, was not a significant part of the Cincinnati or Chicago packing plants. Differences in animal size, musculature, and fat deposits required human flexibility more than machine precision. The same packing line had to process a nine-hundred-pound steer as well as an eleven-hundred-pound beast.

Rather, these plants relied on a brilliant intensification of the division of labor. The disassembly line was no different from the pin factory that Adam Smith uses to exemplify the division of labor in the opening pages of the *Wealth of Nations*, but represented Smith's logics intensified to a previously unimaginable degree, enabled by an abundance of raw materials (cattle) and a reserve of cheap labor. Instead of allowing mechanization, the division of labor in meatpacking increased productivity because it simplified labor tasks in a process of de-skilling that made workers replaceable as well as allowing for a more total exploitation of labor through worker synchronization and pace setting. Workers like Vincentz Rutkowski could be worked nearly to death.

If the nation's motto is *e pluribus unum*—out of many, one—the slaughterhouse's motto is *ex uno plures*—out of one, many. When cattle first entered a slaughterhouse, they encountered an armed man walking toward them on an overhead plank. Whether a

FIGURE 8. 1906 photograph of a Swift & Company slaughterhouse in Chicago. The animals are hung from hooks to allow ease of movement and then split (right side of image). Library of Congress.

hammer swing to the skull or a spear thrust to the animal's spinal column, the (usually achieved) goal was to kill with a single blow.[16] Assistants chained the animal's legs and dragged the carcass from the room. The carcass was hoisted into the air and brought from station to station along an overhead rail.

Next, a worker cut the animal's throat and drained and collected its blood while another group began skinning the carcass. Even this relatively simple process was subdivided throughout the period. Initially the work of a pair, nine different workers handled skinning by 1904.[17] Once the carcass was stripped, gutted, and drained of blood, it went into another room where highly trained butchers cut the carcass into quarters. These quarters were stored in giant refrigerated rooms to await distribution.

Though this description may make readers today squeamish, the nineteenth-century public's fascination with the process was linked to a dark humor in which the animal's suffering was never out of mind. One early twentieth-century Armour & Company postcard depicted hogs hanging from a wheel, with the caption "Round goes the wheel to the music of the squeal."[18] Similarly, the pamphlets of Milwaukee firm Cudahy & Company bragged that modern food processing had allowed the industry to "save the world from starvation and confound the disciples of Malthus" before joking that, from the steer's perspective, "the purgatory of the stockyards is but the entrance to the inferno of the packing-house," with its "clouds of steam, ever evilly rising, suggest[ing] never-ending torments."[19] An Armour pamphlet joked about "Billy the Bunco Steer" as a kind of employee.[20] His job was:

> to lead the unsuspecting train load of cattle from the cattle pens to the slaughterhouse ... when the time to move arrives "Billy" takes his victims in hand, and having probably communicated to them in bovine language that there is something good to eat over the way he marches deliberately at the head of his regiment and delivers them safely within the slaughter-house pens. Having thus betrayed his friends, he turns cooly and marches off to perform the same service for another load.[21]

This fascination with the animal's perspective accompanied a total lack of interest in the disassembly line's other participant, the worker. The pages of *Scientific American* were filled with descriptions of disassembly lines for pork, cattle, and even sheep, but laborers were largely ignored in popular accounts of meatpacking.[22] Yet, as much as the division of labor, the disassembly line owed its existence to a labor regime and labor pool that enabled it.

The profitability of what happened inside Chicago's slaughterhouses depended on the throngs of men and women outside them, hoping to find a day's or a week's employment.[23] An abundant labor supply meant the packers could easily replace anyone who balked at paltry salaries, or, worse yet, tried to unionize. Similarly, productivity increases risked worker injury, and therefore were only effective if people like Vincentz Rutkowski could be easily replaced. Fortunately for the packers, late nineteenth-century Chicago was full of people desperate for work.

Seasonal fluctuations and the vagaries of the nation's cattle markets conspired to marginalize slaughterhouse labor. Though refrigeration helped the meatpackers "defeat the seasons" and secure year-round shipping, packing nevertheless remained seasonal.[24] Packers had to reckon with cattle's reproductive cycles and the climate's effect on the cost—if not the possibility—of summer distribution. The number of animals processed varied day to day and month to month. For packinghouse workers, the effect was a world in which an individual day's labor might pay relatively well, but busy days were punctuated with long stretches of little or no work. The least skilled workers might only find a few weeks or months of employment at a time.

This seasonality and oversupply kept workers fighting for their jobs. Packers could choose the healthiest candidates and overwork them, a practice captured in *The Jungle*. Early in the novel, the protagonist, Jurgis, is hired out of a surging crowd. The powerfully built hero scornfully studies the broken faces around him. Later in the book, when his time in the slaughterhouse and a fertilizer plant has left Jurgis sickly and weak, he stands in a crowd watching foremen ignore him in favor of young, stronger men.[25]

Desperate workers also made it easy for the packers to blacklist people with even a whiff of union affiliation. In the wake of an 1886 work stoppage, the local sheriff issued a statement that men who wanted their jobs back would assemble into lines and packinghouse managers would "select from the lines such men as they desire to have come to work on that or any other day, giving each man a pass, with the name of the firm stamped upon it, and said pass to be good on presentation at any entrance to the stock yards." Known organizers were denied passes. Once this process was done, the workers were sent home and told to report back with their passes if they wanted to be rehired.[26]

The work was so competitive and the workers so desperate that, even when they had jobs, they often had to wait, without pay, if there were no animals to slaughter. Workers would be fired if they did not show up at a specified time before nine o'clock in the morning, but then might wait, unpaid, until ten or eleven for a shipment.[27] If the delivery was very late, work might then continue until late into the night.

Though the division of labor and throngs of unemployed people were crucial to operating the Big Four's disassembly lines, these factors were not sufficient to maintain a relentless production pace. This required intervention directly on the line. Fortunately for the packers, they could exploit a core aspect of continuous-motion processing: if one person went faster, everyone had to go faster. The meatpackers used pace setters to force other workers to increase their speed. The packers would pay this select group—roughly one in ten workers—higher wages and offer secure positions that they only kept if they maintained a rapid pace, forcing the rest of the line to keep up. Resented by their coworkers, these pace setters were a vital management tool.[28]

Close supervision of foremen was equally important. Management kept statistics on production-line output and overseers who slipped in production could lose their jobs. This allowed management to indirectly encourage foremen to use tactics that management did not want to explicitly support. According to one retired foreman, he was "always trying to cut down wages in every possible way . . . some of [the foremen] got a commission on all expenses they could save below a certain point."[29] Though union officials vilified foremen and novels like *The Jungle* peppered corrupt foremen throughout, their jobs were only marginally less tenuous than those of their underlings.

The effectiveness of de-skilling on the disassembly line rested on an increase in the wages of a few highly skilled positions. Though these workers individually made more money, the packers secured a precipitous decrease in average wages. Previously, a gang composed entirely of general-purpose butchers might all be paid thirty-five cents an hour. In the new regime, a few highly specialized butchers would receive fifty cents or more an hour, but the majority of other workers would be paid much less than thirty-five cents. Highly paid workers were given the only jobs in which costly mistakes could be made—damage to hides or expensive cuts of meat—protecting against mistakes or sabotage from the irregularly employed workers.[30] The packers also believed (sometimes erroneously) that the highly paid workers—popularly known as the "butcher aristocracy"—would be more loyal to management and less willing to cooperate with unionization attempts.

Despite sporadic worker attempts to control pace and set wages, the overall trend was an incredible intensification of output. Splitters, one of the most skilled positions, provide a good example.[31] Economist John Commons explains that in 1884, "five splitters in a certain gang would get out 800 cattle in 10 hours, or 16 per hour for each man, the wages being 45 cents. In 1894 the speed had been increased so that 4 splitters got out 1,200 in 10 hours, or 30 per hour for each man—an increase of nearly 100 per cent. in 10 years."[32] Even as the pace increased, the process of de-skilling ensured that wages were constantly moving downward, forcing employees to work harder for less money.

Meatpackers argued that ever-lower wages were necessary because of the low prices they received for the products they sold. This may have in a sense been true, though it was disingenuous, since razor-thin margins were key to their business strategy. The packers' efforts to constantly undercut local butchers' prices created a climate in which prices were unsustainably low without extremely low wages. Once the entire industry became organized around this principle, packers could reasonably reply to union demands with the claim that increased wages would ruin competitiveness.

The fact that meatpacking's profitability depended on a brutal labor regime meant that conflicts between labor and management were ongoing, and at times violent. Yet the broader social and political climate ultimately favored the meatpackers, as the story of an 1886 strike, part of a larger worker struggle for an eight-hour workday, reveals. Workers sought not simply a shorter workday, they wanted their standard daily wage to remain the same, effectively providing an hourly raise. Initially, the packers appeared amenable to the proposal. In very early May 1886, facing a tide of organizing and worker involvement in the Knights of Labor, the major meatpackers, as well as the smaller Chicago houses, accepted an eight-hour day.[33]

On May 4, however, this all changed. A bombing at a labor demonstration in Chicago's Haymarket Square led to fighting between workers and the Chicago police, turning public sentiment against the Knights of Labor. Business sensed weakness, and in many industries the eight-hour-day agreements collapsed.[34] Though the agreements in meatpacking survived for a few months, each week brought renewed tension. In October, the packers reverted to the ten-hour day. In a letter to Knights of Labor leader Terence Powderly, Chicago organizer P. M. Flanagan explained that the packers had said that "under no circumstances can they afford here in Chicago to do business on the eight hours a day basis when in all the rest of the country men work ten hours."[35] Workers found this claim particularly galling because the Chicago packers directly and indirectly controlled most of the major plants outside Chicago. Armour's own brother ran a major facility in Kansas City. In response to the abandonment of the eight-hour day, pork workers struck first, and beef-packing workers—who had yet to revert to ten-hour days—joined in solidarity.

The packinghouses responded by hiring private detectives— the infamous "Pinkertons"—to fight strikers and protect strikebreakers, who they began recruiting from all over the country. In newspaper advertisements in the South, Midwest, and East, the packers promised good wages and agreed to provide room and lodging for the new workers, though this was primarily a safety measure. With the support of local law enforcement, the packers prepared for a lengthy fight.[36]

The packers refused to compromise. Armour's foremen announced permanent replacements. Strikers would not be rehired. A reporter explained that "[Armour's firm] is not disposed to trifle any longer, and announce[s] that it will employ whom it pleases, and run its own business to suit itself."[37] This angry declaration came just days after an agreement to resume work had collapsed when Armour tried to require his employees to sign a document condemning the Knights of Labor and the labor movement more broadly.[38] Though the packers presented a united front, Armour was the driving force. Knights of Labor representative T. R. Barry told the press that "from my interviews with various packers I have come to the conclusion that Armour alone stands in the way of an amicable settlement of the Stock Yards troubles."[39]

Armour's hatred of organized labor was extreme even for a nineteenth-century capitalist, and conspiracy theories about Armour's machinations abounded. In the months before the 1886 showdown, an unidentified unionist claimed Armour was buying rivals' debt to compel their cooperation:

[Armour] is preparing for a protracted struggle. And what Armour does, the others will do, not sympathetically, but as a matter of compulsion. People do not generally know, but it is nevertheless a fact, that for the past few months, Armour has been industriously buying up all the sixty and ninety day paper that his smaller competitors have issued. Ordinarily, this paper could be staved off, and an extension obtained. With Armour as the holder of their notes the packers can do so, too—provided they dance as he fiddles.[40]

Though the specifics of the theory seem implausible, there is something to the general sentiment. As head of the most powerful of the Big Four, Armour exerted a large degree of influence over his rivals.

But the packers' strength consisted of more than the resolve not to cooperate with organized labor. They had state support.

As tensions in the stockyards intensified, authorities "garrisoned over 1,000 men . . . to preserve order and protect property." When National Guard soldiers marched past the Chicago Board of Trade, brokers supposedly cheered from the building's balconies.[41]

The strike collapsed within a week. Following early setbacks, the Knights of Labor's national leadership decided to call the strike off, reasoning that it was a losing proposition. Local chapters initially resisted, but grudgingly accepted the return to ten-hour days. Many workers had lost their jobs, but the packers, short workers despite the influx of strikebreakers, hired most of the men back. The workers, however, were finally forced to sign antiunion statements.[42]

Despite sporadic efforts following the 1886 disaster, packinghouse workers could not organize effectively during the nineteenth century. This was in part an effect of the assembly line's de-skilling of labor—striking workers were easily replaceable—but it was also a consequence of meatpacker strikebreaking and the broader turn of the government, and the public, against organized labor in the wake of the violence in Chicago's Haymarket Square.[43] Much of the public believed unions threatened social stability. Labor did win scattered victories, and by 1897 workers organized the Amalgamated Meat Cutters and Butcher Workmen of North America, but their successes were limited. Over a generation, gradually shifting baselines had forced workers to accept production-speed increases and stagnant wages, meaning that union victories were needed merely to keep labor conditions from becoming worse, rather than achieving genuine improvement.

The genius of the disassembly line was not merely productivity gains through the division of labor, it was also that it simplified labor enough that the Big Four could benefit from a growing surplus of workers and a business-friendly legal regime. If the meatpackers needed purely skilled labor, they could not exploit desperate throngs outside their gates. If a new worker could be trained in hours and government was willing to break strikes and limit liability for worker injury, workers became disposable. This enabled the dangerous—and profitable—increases in production speed that maimed Vincentz Rutkowski. Adam Smith's praise of the division of labor is appropriate, for it is brilliant, but its power was as much in how it enabled management to coerce productivity gains as in the ways it increased worker efficiency.[44]

Management innovations and technological changes in animal slaughter made the industry more profitable to the extent that meatpackers could coerce productivity gains from workers. Ultimately, this depended on public acceptance of, or blindness to, workers' marginality. The public accepted this marginality as a consequence of the broad turn against organized labor in the 1880s as well as a fascination with the technological marvels of mass slaughter, and this fascination subtly devalued human labor. These processes all unfolded in the late nineteenth century, but persist today.[45]

Refrigerators on Wheels

From Chicago's slaughterhouses, beef was sent nationwide. This was no trivial task—fresh meat spoils quickly. From the first domestication of cattle to the late nineteenth century, if you wanted fresh beef, you needed to live near cattle. That changed with refrigeration. An animal could now be butchered in Chicago and eaten in Boston, New York, or London. Yet simply because a technology created a possibility did not make its adoption inevitable.

Refrigeration sparked nearly a decade of conflict between the meatpackers and railroads that would have far-reaching implications for the beef industry, the power of Chicago's Big Four, and the history of federal regulation. Railroads had invested heavily in equipment to ship live cattle and fought dressed-beef shipment ton by ton. Their ultimate failure to stop its distribution illustrates that even if, as so many scholars have argued, the railroads stitched together a national market to serve their own ends, the meatpackers would wield that market as a cudgel against them.[46]

J. B. Sutherland of Detroit received the first patent for a refrigerator car in 1867 and many rival designs would appear over the next few years.[47] Essentially standard cars loaded with ice on either end, these designs were relatively crude. They kept products cold, but did not promote effective air circulation, leading to uneven cooling and meat spoilage. Freezer burn was also a problem and early designs that required hanging meat—in order to keep the precious cargo from touching the ice directly—could cause the car to sway dangerously around sharp curves.[48] Despite these difficulties, Swift & Company began experimenting with dressed-beef shipments in the mid-1870s.

Dressed-beef shipment promised high profits. When an animal is shipped live, almost forty percent of the traveling weight is blood, bones, hide, and other inedible parts of the animal. The small slaughterhouses and butchers that bought live animals in New York or Boston could sell some of these by-products to tanners or fertilizer manufacturers, but their ability to do so was limited. If the animals could be slaughtered in Chicago, the large packinghouses could realize massive economies of scale on the by-products. In fact, these firms could undersell local slaughterhouses on the actual meat and make their profits on by-products. In an interview, Armour left little doubt where he thought his profits came from: "after a while we shall see other fortunes made, like mine has been, out of the things we now waste."[49] Yet the success of the entire approach required centralized slaughter in Chicago, which was more complicated than simply adopting refrigeration technology. For one thing, the railroads had invested heavily in live-animal shipment and were reluctant to change.

Traditionally, railroads owned the cars and shippers paid a fee for the conveyance of their product. But in the case of refrigerator cars, the railroads were suspicious of an experimental technology that also threatened their existing investments. Consequently, they forced the meatpackers to build their own refrigerator cars, which would ultimately prove hugely profitable for the packers, who came to control refrigerated shipping technology.[50] This became even more lucrative in the early twentieth century as the meatpackers moved into national fruit and vegetable distribution.

When Swift's early efforts were successful, the other Chicago firms followed his lead, and by the early 1880s what had once been a tiny market threatened the profitability of traditional livestock shippers and the railroads themselves. If dressed-beef shipping became universal, the railroads would have a fleet of obsolete livestock cars, would be substituting a less profitable commodity to ship (beef) for a more valuable one (cattle), and would lose revenue from their facilities that fed and cared for animals en route.

The railroads decided to fight back. They used a strategy they had developed to ease competition among themselves: pooling agreements. During the 1880s the railroads had formed agreements to prevent "ruinous competition" over rates. Consequently, the major railroads from Chicago to the eastern seaboard formed the Joint Executive Committee to coordinate their business. Revenue and traffic would be "pooled" and allocated based on a predetermined agreement. The Joint Executive Committee, which the Chicago Board of Trade attacked for leaving its city "bound in iron bands," made the chilled-beef traffic one of its primary targets.[51]

In order not to "unjustly discriminate," the committee members decided that they would set different rates for shipping a pound of dressed beef as opposed to a pound of live cattle.[52] The underlying logic (or so it was claimed) was that a fair rate would be one that would "place the dressed beef and live stock shippers upon an equal footing, so that a man who buys in the eastern market dressed beef shipped from Chicago as such, and dressed beef that is derived from live stock which is shipped from the west and slaughtered here, will have to pay the same money per pound."[53] Whether fairness was the actual intent, determining differential shipping rates proved enormously complicated. The committee's first attempt enraged both the packers and livestock shippers, spurring the Joint Executive Committee to hold a conference in 1883 that would try to reach a fair determination of the respective costs involved in the preparation, distribution, and marketing of beef from these two sources and then set rates correspondingly.

This, however, proved impossible. The only sources on these costs were the meatpackers and livestock shippers, and both had good reason to lie. Even the committee acknowledged that their estimates had little value. In the course of assessing costs, the committee's final report conceded that with "these estimates being made by parties specially interested in each kind of traffic, it is reasonable to assume that the truth lies somewhere between the highest and lowest estimates for each kind of traffic."[54] In the end, the relative rates were set at roughly seventy cents per hundred pounds of dressed beef and forty cents per hundred pounds of cattle.[55] The rates, however, would only hold if the railroads all agreed to honor them, and with the amount of money that could be made shipping dressed beef, it was only a matter of time before the agreement collapsed.

Canada's Grand Trunk Railway (GTR) had always been merely an also-ran of the major commodity shippers, given the circuitous route the GTR took east from Chicago—north into Canada and then back south into the United States. In a competitive market, the increased shipping cost made the GTR a poor option. But the GTR's management recognized an opportunity with dressed beef. They offered generous rates to the meatpackers in order to secure business they would never have had otherwise. The GTR's first dressed-beef contract was with Swift & Company in 1878, but the trade really took off with the Joint Executive Committee's relative pricing decision. Soon, business was booming.

Through the mid-1880s, the GTR's dressed-beef traffic increased rapidly. At a time when dressed-beef shipments were increasing dramatically relative to live-cattle shipments—from 1882 to 1885 live-cattle traffic was down roughly twenty percent, or 100,000 tons, across all railroads, while dressed-beef shipments had increased from a mere 5,500 tons to 232,000 tons—the GTR was capturing most of the traffic. In 1885, the GTR carried under one percent of the eastbound live cattle, but controlled nearly sixty percent of the dressed-beef trade.[56]

Although the GTR's business was almost entirely due to the collusion of American railroads, the Grand Trunk's managers told shareholders a different story. Managers argued that the traffic was due to the railway's merits as a cold-weather line. It was not that the American roads left the packers without better options, but rather that "the Grand Trunk route . . . from its more northerly position, is specially adapted for this kind of traffic."[57] This phrase "specially adapted" was also used in the company's annual report that year.[58] According to this logic, the already cold Canadian weather lowered refrigeration costs, giving the line a competitive advantage. These claims were likely made to keep investors distracted from the fact that the GTR soon became dependent on business that could disappear completely if even a single American line broke the Joint Executive Committee's agreement.

Once the American lines caught wind of what the GTR was doing, the Joint Executive Committee tried to stop the Canadian trade. William Vanderbilt tried to cut off the GTR's access to Chicago by purchasing the Michigan Central Railroad, which connected Chicago and Port Huron, an important town on the US-Canadian border. The GTR outmaneuvered him, buying the line and creating the "Chicago and Grand Trunk," which, according to the GTR's president, put the company "in a perfectly independent position in Chicago, and enable[s] us to make our own rates and control our own traffic from that important centre."[59] The Joint Executive Committee then tried to incorporate the Chicago and Grand Trunk into their existing agreements, but the understandably suspicious Canadian line stuck with the meatpackers.

The GTR's unwillingness to cooperate with the American lines was rooted in its belief in itself as an outsider. This self-perception allowed the GTR to simultaneously subvert American railroads' attempts to collude and blame the American lines for the collapse of pooling agreements. Throughout the 1880s, the GTR's president repeatedly announced that, despite his line's efforts to participate in the agreements on fair terms, the agreements had broken down. In 1883, the board of directors notified shareholders that "unfortunate strife between the Trunk Lines" was hurting business, and in 1885 they announced that the collapse of the pooling system was a consequence of "an indisposition on the part of the Railway Companies interested to cordially cooperate with each other."[60] While it appears that the major lines were indeed trying to marginalize the GTR, the general tone of the GTR's complaints suggests it would never have been satisfied and merely used the collapse of negotiations to justify its deals with the meatpackers. When the Joint Executive Committee met to decide relative rates—described above—the GTR's participation was noteworthy only for the line's vocal objections to live-cattle shippers' cost estimates.[61] The GTR's representative was also the only railroad manager who loudly sided with the meatpackers on their cost estimates.

Though largely about protecting their business, the GTR's stance on pooling agreements was framed as a legitimate objection to the American lines' collusion. As the GTR's president told shareholders in 1883:

> There are a great many interested in the livestock traffic who complain about [dressed beef] being taken at too low a rate. They want to kill this traffic, and promote the livestock traffic; but our reply is, "you have no right to complain of our carrying this traffic at too low a rate; it pays us four times as much as to carry the same amount of grain, and as long as we get it at those remunerative rates we mean to carry it."[62]

According to the GTR, the dressed-beef trade's sheer profitability proved the illegitimacy of the Joint Executive Committee's rates.

Now that the meatpackers had a route to market, their investment in refrigeration technology was paying off, as were their investments in meat distribution. Meatpackers not only owned the railcars, but they also owned the icing stations needed to reload refrigerator cars every couple of hundred miles. What the American railroads and livestock shippers had once hoped was prohibitively expensive—meatpacker ownership of railroad infrastructure—was becoming a source of strength.

For the meatpackers, the beauty of this system was that they controlled everything but the rails, meaning they could easily switch from one railroad to another. Thanks to the GTR, the major American railroads were ready to give in by 1885, and the meatpackers could begin playing the railroads against one another. First, the packers began putting pressure on the GTR. In 1887, the railroad's director began alluding to meatpacker demands that the line could not meet, but hoped "it [was] only a lovers' quarrel."[63] Six months later, the prognosis was much more bleak. The GTR president told investors that "we have helped to build up that traffic; we have assisted to make [the packers] powerful; and they have become so powerful that they have become exacting and arbitrary."[64] He went on to complain about shipping rebates, free ice, and other incentives the American lines were using to woo the Big Four.[65] The GTR had created a monster.

Soon, all of the railroads were feeling the packers' pressure. At a special meeting of the GTR, the line's president noted that "the shippers are trying to use the railway companies one against another, so as to put down the rates for that traffic, and the shippers are very powerful."[66] Swift and Armour were specifically cited as the most powerful of the shippers.

The major American lines were forced to offer rates so low that the GTR, with its circuitous route, could no longer carry dressed beef profitably. The Chicago and Grand Trunk's collapse would be as rapid as its rise. Its dressed-beef market share decreased to 44.8 percent in 1887 and then to 28.42 percent in 1888.[67] Worse yet, the GTR's now diminished share was carried at breakeven or a slight loss. By 1893 the GTR's market share was down to 2 percent and by 1900 the Chicago and Grand Trunk Railway was in receivership.[68] Meanwhile, members of the once-mighty Joint Executive Committee were busy cutting their own throats as they vied for the packers' affections.

The packers would now use their power over the railroads to crush nascent opposition. When Texas rancher and entrepreneur J. C. Beatty and a few associates tried to start an independent dressed-beef facility, they faced immediate opposition. Shortly before commencing operations, their shipper, the South Pacific, announced that it could not provide the men with any railcars. The railroad eventually explained that Armour & Company had ordered it not to help the fledgling business. This was despite the fact that the ranchers were planning to work the Texas to Southern California route, which was a relative backwater for the Chicago packinghouses. When Beatty and his partners tried shipping live cattle to Los Angeles instead, Armour & Company allegedly expanded their Los Angeles operation and undercut Beatty's prices, driving him out.[69]

The railroads, whom the meatpackers had once complained subjected them to unfair pricing, were now lamenting the packers' power. John King, president of the New York, Lake Erie & Western Railroad, complained that Swift, Hammond, and Armour "go together in solid column wherever they go. They manage to get on all the roads at the same price, and if anything is to be done they fight together."[70] As with their opposition to labor, the ability of the meatpackers to cooperate as they gained control of supply and distribution was a key source of their strength.

The extent of the packers' power was so great and the railroads' dependency so unexpected, that antitrust investigators initially misunderstood their relationship. The Senate investigators who had grilled Armour understood that the Big Four's power was in some sense dependent on railroad collusion. Rebates had been made illegal, but the packers were receiving essentially the same thing in the form of mileage rates—an amount railroads returned to shippers for using their own railcars. The investigators mistakenly assumed these favorable rates grew out of a relationship between equals. In reality, the railroads had essentially been coerced into these agreements.

Horace J. Hayden, president of the New York Central & Hudson River Railroad Company, made this argument when he testified before the US Senate.[71] Hayden explained that the overbuilding of the rail network east from Chicago meant that "these [refrigerated cars] carry the business, and you have this immense business, and when you may tender it to one of eight roads you are very apt to find one weak enough to make a concession, and we have no way of preventing it."[72] Because the packers could play different lines against each other, railroad executives claimed they had to collude just to keep themselves in business.

The railroads were victims of their own machinations, although it might be more appropriate to say these companies were victims of individual stakeholders' machinations. As Richard White has argued, the railroads were built inefficiently because they were simply money-making schemes for managers and investors. When it came to east–west routes across the country, railroads built more lines to and from a given city than necessary. This overbuilding left the packers with a wealth of shipping options and made brutal competition between eastern rail lines almost inevitable. This meant the efficiency of centralized meatpacking depended on the inefficiency of the country's rail network.

The struggle to ship dressed beef would have far-reaching implications for the livestock-processing industry as a whole. If the Big Four could control beef distribution, they could control livestock slaughtering, which would give them the lucrative canning and by-product industries that benefited tremendously from the packers' economies of scale. But first the Chicago meatpackers had to convince suspicious consumers to actually eat their beef, and displace traditional butchers in the process.

The Decline of Wholesale Butchering and the Rise of Dressed Beef

In 1889, Henry Barber entered Ramsey County, Minnesota, with one hundred pounds of contraband: fresh beef from an animal slaughtered in Chicago. Barber, however, was no fly-by-night butcher and was well aware of an 1889 law requiring all meat sold in Minnesota to be inspected locally prior to slaughter. Shortly after arriving, Barber was arrested, convicted, and sentenced to thirty days in jail. But with the support of his employer, Armour & Company, Barber aggressively challenged the local inspection measure.

Barber's arrest was part of a plan to provoke a fight over the 1889 law. Even when the Minnesota law was being framed, Armour & Company had lobbied against the measure.[73] In federal court, Barber's lawyers alleged that the statute under which he was convicted violated federal authority over interstate commerce, as well as the Constitution's Privileges and Immunities Clause. The case would eventually reach the US Supreme Court.

At trial, the state argued that without local on-the-hoof inspection it was impossible to know if meat had come from a diseased animal. Local inspection was therefore a reasonable part of the state's police power. If this argument was upheld, the Chicago houses would no longer be able to ship their goods to any unfriendly state. In response, Barber's counsel argued that the Minnesota law was actually a protectionist

measure that discriminated against out-of-state butchers. There
was no reason meat could not be adequately inspected in Chicago before sale elsewhere. In *Minnesota v. Barber* (1890), the
Supreme Court ruled the statute unconstitutional and ordered
Barber's release. Armour & Company would go on to dominate
the local market.[74]

The Barber ruling was a pivotal moment in a longer fight on
the part of the Big Four to secure national distribution. The
Minnesota statute and measures like it across the country were
fronts in a war waged by local butchers to protect their trade
against the encroachment of the "dressed-beef men." The story
of this struggle highlights the local conflicts behind seemingly
inevitable structural changes: the adoption of centralized meat
slaughter and a national food economy. The rise of the Chicago meatpackers was not a gradual process of newer practices
displacing old, but a wrenching process of meatpackers strong-
arming and bankrupting smaller competitors. For the packers,
the Barber decision made these fights possible, but it did not
make victory inevitable. It was on the back of hundreds of small
victories—in rural and urban communities across the United
States—that the meatpackers built their enormous profits.

Central to the dressed-beef fight was the distinction between
wholesale and retail butchers. A wholesaler bought cattle at
local markets or from a nearby farm, slaughtered the animal,
and processed a dressed carcass (keeping the other parts to sell
to by-product businesses). This dressed carcass would be sold
in quarters or individual cuts, whether fine or coarse, to retail
butchers, who sold the meat by the pound to consumers. While
some butchers functioned as both wholesalers and retailers,
this division clarifies the business model of Armour and his
colleagues. They did not want to deal directly with customers. That required knowledge of local markets and entailed a

considerable amount of risk. Instead, they hoped to replace wholesalers.[75] Their message to these butchers was to stop slaughtering cattle and instead focus on selling meat, the packers would handle the rest. Of course, once the packers controlled a city's wholesale market, they could set terms for retail butchers. Repeated thousands of times, this process turned the packers' slim margins into big profits.

When the packers first entered an area, they wooed a respected butcher. If the local butcher refused their advances, the packers would move on to more aggressive means. For example, when the Chicago houses entered Pittsburgh, they approached veteran butcher William Peters. Peters told the Senate Committee that when he refused to work with Armour & Company, the Chicago firm's agent told him, "Mr. Peters, if you butchers don't take hold of it [dressed beef], we are going to open shops throughout the city."[76] Still, Peters resisted and Armour went on to open its own shops, underselling Pittsburgh's butchers. Peters told investigators that he and his colleagues "are working for glory now. We do not work for any profit . . . we have been working for glory for the past three or four years, ever since those fellows came into our town."[77] Meanwhile, Armour's share of the Pittsburgh market continued to grow.

The packers' message to butchers was "give up." Mathias Schwabe of Luzerne County, Pennsylvania, told Senate investigators that an agent of Armour had delivered a menacing telegram, saying: "you may just as well give up and go along with us, or else we will break you up anyhow."[78] Philip Armour, speaking on behalf of his firm, initially denied the telegram, but investigators produced an internal memo that read: "can not allow Schwabe to continue killing live cattle. If he will not stop . . . make prices so as can get his trade."[79] Armour eventually acknowledged the note was authentic, but blamed an overzealous employee.[80]

When pressed on claims of predatory pricing, the Big Four had a clever defense: they sold a perishable product. If customers would not buy it at a particular price, the packers could not be expected to let the meat spoil. They had to cut prices. In his prepared statement to investigators, Armour stressed that the rapid sale of meat was critical, because of a "fact which seems to be very generally overlooked . . . that fresh meat is a perishable commodity."[81] When Armour was forced to concede that there were a few situations in which the Chicago packers set prices collectively, he explained it was not to "destroy the rule of supply and demand" as his examiner insisted, but rather "because [dressed beef] is a perishable article."[82] The perishability argument also justified the Big Four's aggressive practices with labor and their suppliers. Any hiccup in business could be catastrophic because, as Armour explained, the packer "must dispose of his meat as soon as it is ripe enough, and to retain his market and keep his customers he must be ready, day after day and every day, to supply the trade he caters to."[83] Perishability, then, made meatpacking a tough business.

Meanwhile, local butchers' criticisms of the Chicago packers had an air of elitism, which did little to help their cause in front of lawmakers and the public. While one butcher claimed that the Big Four were selling inferior products, his descriptions of the packers' customers were tinged with contempt. The packers sell their beef "to a grocery man, and that grocery man sells it to a poor woman who comes in there, and he sells it too low."[84] Regarding lard, another product over which wholesalers and the Big Four competed, the same butcher explained that "of course, poor people who do not know any better buy the eight and a half cents lard and leave my twelve and a half cents lard stand. That is an outrage, I think, on the butchers, and the worst kind of an outrage."[85] He goes on to claim the woman is being scammed, but blames his plight on her ignorance. F. H. Brice believed that the collapsing prices on coarser cuts of meat were the result of common people's changing expectations about what meat they deserve. He lamented that "even a laborer on the street or a negro will come in and ask for a porter-house steak, and he has got to have it, because he can get it almost everywhere. That has created a demand in that respect for fine cuts of meat, and nobody wants anything else."[86] This elitism would backfire badly, as the packers took up the mantle of public good.

The Chicago packers rightly argued that they had democratized meat consumption, and for that, even butchers should thank them. As Armour observed, the dressed-beef men should be thanked "for the successful efforts of [dressed beef's] promoters in opening up new markets in communities which were not formerly beef consuming. They have firmly established themselves among the artisans and laborers of the East and North, and are to-day actively engaged in opening new markets throughout the South of the introduction and sale of western beef."[87] According to this logic, increased meat consumption would improve business across the board.

Butchers were contemptuous of consumers because they felt betrayed. A failed boycott in Akron, Ohio, stung particularly badly. Retailer Warren Buckmaster explained that during a Chicago meatpacking strike, the Trades and Labor Assembly of Akron, Ohio, passed a resolution refusing to support sellers of Armour & Company meat. After local butchers supported the boycott, Armour's agent in the area opened a store to underprice local competition. Buckmaster explained that the butchers persisted with the boycott to see "if the people would stand by us as we were willing to stand by them." But it was a tough proposition: at a time when meat in Akron was selling for roughly six and a half cents per pound, the Armour house was asking for half. Armour was so aggressive in its quest to bankrupt Akron's butchers that "any person asking for meats were furnished whether they had money to pay for the same or not."[88] Armour's shop quickly took over the market and Akron's butchers were crushed. Buckmaster's sense of betrayal was palpable; he complained that "the very parties who asked us to not get the meat and forbade us to buy it were the very ones who went there and bought it, simply because they could get it for a cent or two a pound less."[89] Consumers overwhelmingly embraced cheap beef.

Failing with fickle consumers, traditional butchers organized a legislative agenda. Around the country, protective associations sought to check the dressed-beef industry's rapid expansion. Organized in 1887, the Butchers' National Protective Association of the United States of America aspired to "unite in one brotherhood all butchers and persons engaged in dealing in butchers' stock."[90] They described the Chicago packers as "soulless corporations" and argued that they had to organize themselves to oppose the fact of "capital having organized monster monopolies."[91] Self-conscious about the elitism the butchers' position risked, they organized to "protect their common interests and those of the general public" through a focus on sanitary conditions. Health concerns were an issue on which traditional butchers could oppose the Chicago houses while appealing to consumers' collective good. They argued the Big Four "disregard the public good and endanger the health of the people by selling, for human food, diseased, tainted, and other unwholesome meat." The association further pledged to oppose price manipulation of a "staple and indispensable article of human food."[92]

Smaller related associations began to appear nationwide at roughly the same time.[93] The Eastern Butchers' Protective Association in New York City was particularly aggressive. The organization began organizing to oppose Chicago beef in March 1884. It was especially worried about apathy among retail butchers, who were happy to buy beef from any distributor, as long as it was cheap.[94] When retailer Aaron Buchsbaum of Ninth Avenue could not be persuaded to join the association, two Protective Association members marched outside his door with leaflets warning, "Beware! Beware! Beware! Don't buy Chicago-dressed beef!" The men were arrested.[95]

These associations pushed what amounted to a protectionist agenda using food contamination as a justification. On the state and local levels, associations demanded local inspection before slaughter, as was the case with the Minnesota law mentioned at the start of this section. Decentralizing slaughter would make wholesale butchering again dependent on local knowledge that the packers could not acquire from Chicago. Measures like the one that spurred the arrest of Henry Barber began to appear nationwide.[96]

Though these measures ultimately faced insurmountable legal difficulties, the packers hoped to stop them before they became law. Butcher George Beck organized a "little association in Detroit for self-protection," encouraging members to put cards in their windows condemning Chicago dressed meat and circulating a state-level petition for local cattle inspection. According to Beck, the Big Four were so concerned about his measures that they were willing to forgo entering Detroit's market; a Hammond & Company representative approached him and said, "if you men will take down those cards, and if you will withdraw the petition you are now circulating... I will agree to keep out of Detroit myself with my dressed beef and to keep Mr. Armour and Mr. Swift out."[97] The packers denied that a Hammond & Company representative claimed he could influence the other houses—though Beck was insistent the agent had said it—but an offer to stay out of a market was a major concession.

Local and state inspection laws were passed despite the packers' efforts, and so began a series of legal challenges that went to the Supreme Court as part of a broader defense of interstate commerce during the period.[98] Though the specifics varied by case, the courts affirmed the argument that local, on-the-hoof inspection violated the Constitution's Interstate Commerce Clause. The local inspection measures also failed because judges accepted that inspection did not need to be local to ensure safe food.[99] Animals could be inspected in Chicago before slaughter and then the meat itself could be inspected locally. Though butchers claimed centralized inspection would likely be corrupt—and, in some cases, it was—the fact that it was theoretically adequate was enough to placate jurists and lawmakers. Further, a centralized inspection regime worked well with an emerging federal bureaucracy that found working with large actors easier than disparate small ones. Ultimately, the real winners of butchers' protective efforts were these federal inspectors. Federal sanitary measures would provide the public benefit that protective associations advocated, but without the corresponding benefit to butchers.

In ruling that states could not restrict or regulate traffic from elsewhere in the United States, these rulings helped create a nationally bounded free-trade unit that was vital to the growth of centralized mass production.[100] Yet, rather than inevitable developments in the rise of a national market, these court rulings were an outgrowth of specific debates over the nature of mass distribution as well as judges' acceptance or rejection of arguments about food inspection. The refrigerator car might have made it possible for fresh Chicago beef to reach Minnesota, but a Supreme Court decision was necessary to sell it there.

With legal barriers eliminated, the Big Four's wholesale market share grew unchecked, which they used to bully retail butchers. The story of a federal contract to supply the Washington, DC, Freedman's Hospital provides an example. When the federal government opened bidding on an 1889 contract to supply meat there, William Hoover, a retail butcher who bought his beef wholesale from the Big Four, wanted to bid. Unfortunately for him, the big packers had planned to bid directly on the Freedman's Hospital contract, and a few other large contracts, as an early foray into retail sales. According to Hoover, a Chicago agent, C. C. Carroll, told him that if he or his colleagues "got any part of said government contracts the Chicago houses would not sell us any meat, and that they would compel [them] to leave the market."[101] Hoover was apparently a stubborn man and despite the urgings of his brother, also a butcher, Hoover placed a bid.

Though Hoover lost the contract, the Chicago houses followed through on their threat. Hoover's key suppliers, Morris & Company and Armour & Company, would only offer him wholesale beef at double price. His brother also faced boycott. When William Hoover telegrammed Chicago hoping to work things out, the packers denied everything. A June 1889 telegram from Armour & Company described the high prices as a "misunderstanding" and said that the firm would never deliberately overcharge.[102]

Yet the high prices persisted. George Omohundro, a Morris & Company salesman, testified that he was ordered to overcharge Hoover, though he did not know why.[103] A former Armour & Company employee said much the same thing, explaining that he "understood" it was punishment for Hoover's bid.[104] A few months later the boycott was mysteriously lifted—around the same time that the US Senate announced its investigation of the meatpacking industry.

Local butchers could not stop the Chicago packinghouses' encroachment. Yet butchers' struggle to oppose the Chicago houses reveals how social conflict drove the spread and extent of structural changes, such as the emergence of a national market and the centralized mass production of dressed beef. Furthermore, the meatpackers' cutthroat business tactics reveal how seemingly value-neutral business developments—the rise of dressed-beef distribution as a consequence of refrigeration technology, organizational innovation, and infrastructural development—both accompanied and built upon predatory pricing and collusion. Finally, in butchers' failure to appeal to consumers and their frustration with the expectations of the "common laborer," we see an elitist undercurrent that reveals tensions over beef's democratization in the 1880s, a focus of the final chapter.

Early Regulatory Approaches

Despite the failure of the butchers' protective associations, cries from ranchers and butchers did spark federal inquiry into beef and cattle prices. To return to the US Senate's 1889 Vest Committee investigation that opened this chapter, it was the charge that the Big Four were engaged in anticompetitive practices that resonated with elected officials. Their central concern was whether the meatpackers had a "combination"—that is, a system for collectively setting prices. Generally, investigators believed that collusion and anticompetitive tactics were a direct consequence of market centralization. This was why, in their final report, they argued the "principal cause" of the decline in prices ranchers received at market in the face of stable consumer prices was the "artificial and abnormal centralization of markets, and the absolute control by a few operators thereby made possible."[105] This was an attitude that butchers, ranchers, and commission merchants shared. As cattleman Samuel P. Cady explained, "competition is the life of the trade," and the problem is that "the big fish are eating up the little ones."[106]

For at least some interviewees, however, centralization—the increasing scale of industry and the expanding geographic area controlled by individual urban markets—was not inherently a problem. Several cattlemen, though concerned about the packers' anticompetitive tactics, argued that centralization had an upside. W. H. Maurer of Kansas City argued that competition could be paired with centralization. When the examiners asked whether combination was "an inevitable result of the concentration of all the cattle of the country," Maurer disagreed, explaining that "I would rather take my chances in shipping to a market with a great many buyers than to a number of markets with a few buyers, from the fact that they handle all kinds of stuff in the market with a great many buyers." He argued that with many disparate markets—as in the industry's early days—different markets would be good at different times, and shippers faced considerable risks when choosing a market. One massive market would be ideal, if it had "the proper healthy competition." Maurer was, however, unsure whether a small number of buyers could be forced to compete fairly. In regard to centralization in meatpacking (as opposed to markets), Maurer admitted, "whether it can be divided or got into more hands is a question to me."[107] The fact that there was a potential upside to centralization, if concerns about collusion and prices could be solved, meant that remedying the problem of meatpacking concentration could go in two directions: either taming the Big Four, or dismantling them.

Though Senate investigators broadly agreed with meatpacking's critics that centralization was a threat, they were uneasy with proposed solutions. Legislators accepted and even celebrated the Big Four's claims that they had democratized beef consumption.[108] This meant that butchers had to persuade the senators that not only would reform increase the prices ranchers received for their cattle and make wholesale local butchering again viable, but also that it would not increase consumer prices. Because this was almost impossible—centralization was at its core about reducing prices—industry critics were set up for failure.

Detroit wholesaler George Beck faced this bind when he presented his critique of centralized meatpacking. Beck's testimony began uneventfully, with his account of how the Chicago packers systematically moved throughout the eastern United States cutting prices, bankrupting wholesalers, and forcing retail butchers to sell their product. Beyond a few obvious dressed-beef partisans, the butchers who appeared before Senate investigators presented the same story. When asked for names of struggling butchers driven out of business, Beck was vague—perhaps because he did not want to drag people into the debate who might not want to testify—but he argued that most butchers were in a precarious position. He explained, "we [butchers] are doing this business ourselves for nothing, and a goodly number of our dealers are doing it for less than nothing. We simply do not like to be driven out of the business in which we have spent the better portion of our life."[109] Beck went on to discuss how he and several other local butchers pursued state-level legislation to restrict the Chicago packers. Once investigators started questioning Beck, the issue quickly moved to prices. Investigators were particularly concerned that measures such as local inspection would make meat more expensive.[110] According to Beck, the rise of Chicago dressed beef had not increased prices for high-end cuts of meat, but cheaper cuts were significantly cheaper. Beck was on uneasy ground, and when one questioner observed that the "poorer class are really getting the benefit of the reduced price," Beck was forced to agree.[111]

Senate investigators quickly clarified that Beck's proposed measures were only acceptable if they did not hurt consumers. An examiner summarized the conflict as one of "two interests . . . one of them is the producer of the cattle, who says, and justly, that his prices are not adequate to bring him a fair profit, and he is seeking a remedy. Of course whatever he wants to have at the hands of the law must be consistent with the general interests of the public." By implication, the same was true of measures for butchers. Beck's only rejoinder was that restoring competitive markets and breaking the Big Four would not increase prices. This was difficult ground, as Beck had to acknowledge that new consumer expectations put independent butchers at a disadvantage: "circumstances have placed us in a position where very often a man earning a dollar or a dollar and a quarter a day will demand porterhouse steak."[112] From here, Beck's testimony became more and more tense as he struggled to defend his views, producing a sad parallel between his own words and Armour's evasive testimony.

At the same time the Vest Committee was studying the Beef Trust, the Sherman Antitrust Act was working its way through government.[113] The Act is noteworthy in relation to the history of meatpacking. Current academic debates about Progressive Era regulation have focused on a tension between consumer welfare and producer interest. Were measures protectionist or of genuine benefit to the public good? In meatpacking, regulation actually achieved both goals, but at the cost of specific interests (small ranchers and wholesale butchers). Protecting interstate commerce—as the Sherman Antitrust Act, coupled with rulings like *Minnesota v. Barber,* did—promoted a kind of regulated bigness, which tolerated the Big Four and ensured cheap beef. But it also meant that ranchers, wholesale butchers, and slaughterhouse workers were out of luck.

It was not until 1905, in the Supreme Court case *Swift & Co. v. United States,* that decisive state action was taken against the meatpacking industry. The court concluded that the packers colluded to provide low bids in stockyards; manipulated market prices to induce ranchers to ship cattle, and then lowered prices when the cattle reached Chicago; fixed dressed-beef prices to gain market control; and colluded with railroads on shipping rates.[114] By 1905, these practices had been ongoing for almost twenty years. In affirming a lower-court ruling, the Supreme Court embraced the idea that "the defendants cannot be ordered to compete, but they properly can be forbidden to give directions or to make agreements not to compete."[115]

The ruling, however, did accept that regulated centralization was the only viable course of action. As a result, it did little to break up the Chicago firms' oligopoly, beyond stopping its coordination. For the packers' critics, the ruling closed the barn door after the animals were already out; by 1905 the packers' local competition was already bankrupt and ranchers were subordinate. A ruling intended to stop collusion did nothing to erase the benefit they had gained from doing so in the past.

Because judges, politicians, and bureaucrats all accepted the argument that low prices were the most important goal, meatpacking would thereafter be regulated in a way that ensured cheap beef at the same time that it promoted centralization and tolerated both rancher precariousness and worker exploitation. The only other relevant imperative was also in the interest of consumers; namely, sanitation, a story examined in the final chapter.

Conclusion

In 1906, Upton Sinclair published *The Jungle*, which would become the most famous protest novel of the twentieth century. Hailed as a twentieth-century *Uncle Tom's Cabin*, Sinclair's book spurred passage of the 1906 Pure Food and Drug Act.[116] But Sinclair's heart-wrenching portrayal of the brutal labor conditions on which industrial capitalism rested was lost on readers more concerned about rat feces in their sausage. Sinclair later observed, "I aimed at the public's heart, and by accident I hit it in the stomach."[117] He had hoped for socialist revolution, but had to settle for accurate food labeling.

The struggles in this chapter have explained the public acclaim as well as political failure of Sinclair's book. Readers may have empathized with Jurgis and his family as people, but not as workers. Sinclair's polemic would do little to change that. Industry's defense against striking workers, angry butchers, and bankrupt ranchers—namely, that the new system of industrial production served a higher good—squared with public reaction to *The Jungle*. Readers wanted cheap meat, as long as it was sanitary.

Though this chapter has shown that the story of big meatpacking was fundamentally political, the story of industrial food that privileges markets, railroads, and refrigeration—the story evident in Armour's Senate testimony and the earliest histories of meatpacking—remains popular. From the 1880s through the present, the idea that the beef industry had entered a new phase has justified the industry's status quo. But this does not explain the story's popularity. The truth is that there is a lot that is logical about this account that emphasizes refrigeration and market expansion. Part of its appeal is that it is easier to analyze a large industrial system with a bird's eye view. Butcher infighting, worker struggles, and the Joint Executive Committee's plotting occurred on the ground, and it is difficult to maintain this vantage when examining the system as a whole.

The "refrigerator and railroad" framing is a subjective way of simplifying a complicated historical narrative. It tells us where to look and what processes to investigate, the same way a sky view provides a general idea about life on the ground. But the specifics are flattened into an amorphous mass. Likewise, a ground-level view provides particular insights, but is insufficient for understanding the broader system. One can as easily lose the trees for the forest as the forest for the trees.

In the case of meatpacking, the story is one of centralization of markets, changing legal environments, and the refrigerator car, but only to the extent that they were important parts of a human struggle about how food would be produced. As long as one keeps the subjective nature and ideological effects of these narratives in view, they can answer big historical questions without reducing them to impersonal forces or the kind of self-justifying platitude that allowed Armour to explain strikebreaking as merely a consequence of the "greatest possible economy" the new food production regime necessitated.[118]

Over a relatively brief period of about fifteen years, four firms came to control the majority of the United States' beef. Attention to labor, transportation, and the sale of meat helps explain not only how meatpacking was regulated and why, but also how a set of relationships that once appeared unnatural—whether in the slaughterhouse, on the range, or at the store—began to appear inevitable. Intense de-skilling in slaughterhouse labor only became accepted once organized labor was thwarted, leaving packinghouse labor largely invisible to this day. The refrigerator car, a technological marvel, could only supplant live-cattle shipping thanks to a circuitous route through Canada. The slaughter of meat in one place for consumption and sale elsewhere only ceased to appear "artificial and abnormal" once butchers' protective associations disbanded and lawmakers and the public—not unreasonably—accepted that this centralized industrial system was needed to provide cheap beef to the people. Each of these developments is taken for granted today, but they were the product of struggles that could have resulted in radically different ways of producing beef. Seemingly ideologically neutral processes— the spread of a new technology, a new organizational form, or a shift in constitutional interpretation—were inseparable from a much more ambivalent story.

5

Table

WASHINGTON MARKET, nineteenth-century New York City's largest meat and produce market, occupied the same dreary block for decades. Always a bit dingy, the market hummed with a timeless routine. According to one account, "neither darkness, rest, nor quiet ever soothes into calmness this giant provision store."[1] It was only ever really cleaned once, for the market's centenary celebration, when bunting, flags, and streamers adorned its aging stalls.[2]

Most days at the market were the same as any other. Restaurateurs and high-end purchasers arrived before dawn and servants to New York City's elite arrived shortly thereafter. As the sun rose and the heat took its toll, prices dropped. By late afternoon, butchers were trimming "muggy" pieces of meat to keep their cuts looking fresh. At the end of the day, the poorest customers sought deals on graying meat.

Though beef prices dropped throughout the late nineteenth century, meaning customers were enjoying larger, higher-quality steaks at lower prices, the process of buying food remained largely the same. You found reliable providers and, beyond occasionally shopping around or haggling for better prices, you went with what you knew. Washington Market

TABLE 219

ultimately became a kind of wholesale clearinghouse for produce and meat in the New York region, but individual customers continued to frequent its stalls. In 1912, the Housewives' League held a parade complete with white shopping baskets in order to display support for more public markets in New York.[3] By then some customers had begun shopping at specialized butcher's stores, but, even in these establishments, food buying was the same familiar process of buying cuts of meat from a retail butcher you knew and, ideally, trusted.

Yet the familiarity of food buying concealed a radical change behind the scenes. In 1870, retail butchers bought from local slaughterers and were able to negotiate on prices and the kinds of cuts they wanted. By 1900, the average retail butchers purchased what they could from Chicago suppliers. Retail butchers had once been skilled tradesmen, but by the early twentieth century were "simply handlers or selling agents for the Meat Trusts."[4] This started in the early 1880s, when the Chicago houses began to build large refrigeration facilities in New York and other eastern cities. When Swift & Company moved into New York City in 1882, a "panicky feeling seized" the city's wholesale butchers, whose business would never recover.[5] The entire business of butchering changed, even if customers mostly saw tranquility.

This chapter looks at both the invisibility of industrial production and the democratization of beef. Industrial production's invisibility depended on meatpacker machinations, lack of customer interest, and, to some extent, the nature of food as a commodity. As with any culinary ingredient, consumers purchase beef in some sense half made; in preparing meals, in restaurants, or at home, cooks and diners imbue beef with flavor and meaning.[6] In fact, it was the flexibility of beef as an ingredient, whether drizzled with an elaborate sauce at a restaurant or simply grilled at home, that underpinned the enormous demand for Chicago beef. With food products, the element of preparation often obscures the story of the ingredient before it reaches the kitchen.

Meatpackers encouraged this tendency. Dressed beef entered the supply chain at the wholesale level, sold to local retail butchers. Consumers saw the same retail butcher they had always had. Unlike most industrial products, the meat was also sold unbranded. Even with products whose industrial origins were impossible to conceal, such as canned beef, the meatpackers tried to downplay their industrial aspect. The Chicago packers naturalized canned meat through advertisements and recommended that home cooks unpack canned meat out of diners' view.

This chapter also focuses on the democratization of beef.[7] Poor Americans celebrated abundant beef as a symbol of economic progress. Immigrants wrote home celebrating the United States' culinary bounty.[8] For nineteenth-century Americans, positive associations with beef stretched back centuries to a variety of places: from Italian beef consumption on religious holidays to the Anglo-Saxon connection between beef and liberty.[9] The rise of the cattle-beef complex, then, was about fulfilling aspirational eating.

This new abundance spurred elites and the emerging middle class to develop increasingly creative ways of consuming their meat. Elites dined in elaborate restaurants and steakhouses. Upwardly mobile young men staged "beefsteaks" in which they ate vast quantities of meat, washed down with beer. Middle-class Americans demanded variety in their culinary options, leading to an explosion of cookbooks and recipes. Women were now expected to provide these varied recipes at home. Food was, as ever, an important marker of identity, and the

TABLE   221

democratization of beef consumption brought new burdens and expectations.

Moments that threatened the democratization of beef, or pulled back the curtain that overlaid industrial production, were moments that most powerfully shaped the cattle-beef complex. If a steak were contaminated, or an affordable piece of meat became out of reach, consumers lose an integral part of their culinary world, sparking outcry. The quest to prevent or mitigate this outcry explains why beef producers eagerly embraced regulations that kept meat cheap and sanitary. The nature of this outcry also explains why consumers are less engaged with issues such as labor exploitation, since addressing this concern would likely increase prices. If meat was abundant and sanitary, consumers were happy, and for the Chicago meatpackers, the less consumers thought about beef production the better.

This discussion will highlight the limits of consumer politics. Addressing issues that might ultimately increase the cost of meat—such as labor exploitation or animal abuse—require a high bar of consumer sacrifice. This sacrifice becomes correspondingly greater as an ingredient gains importance in consumers' lives, as was the case with the democratization of beef. Lastly, as the varied uses of beef will suggest, people have limited conscious choice about what foods (or goods) make them happy. Beef was an important social marker; it could not simply be replaced by chicken, fish, or, worst of all, a potato.

Whereas cost once meant that high-end cuts of steak were nearly exclusively available to elites, the new abundance of meat sparked discussions about who should eat what and how. Consumption was a way of asserting hierarchy, whether of men over women, American-born over immigrant, or colonizer over colonized. Late nineteenth-century elites abstractly embraced the idea that through social advancement a high-end porterhouse steak was universally available, but also lamented the fact that immigrants and workers sought fancy cuts of meat when the humble round steak was more appropriate.

Elite interest, bordering on obsession, with the dietary habits of the poor ultimately influenced the rise of nutrition science. For the wealthy as well as the middle classes, there was a distinction between consumption as cultural practice and consumption as a means of staying alive. Eating habits among the poor were treated as a scientific or economic question ("nutrition"), whereas richer Americans treated their own consumption as an aesthetic concern. This difference persists today.

In this chapter, an opening section discusses how people purchased and prepared beef. In the case of fresh beef, the production changes industrial beef brought were largely behind the scenes; people bought beef in much the same way they always had, just at better prices. Though the rise of the cattle-beef complex was a violent process for many, for consumers the democratization of beef was a rapid, widely lauded process. This will set the stage for examining flashes of consumer anger, particularly over prices and contamination.

Consumers were at times suspicious of industrial beef, particularly when it came to new, unnatural-seeming production methods. They were particularly worried when confronted with canned beef, a product whose packaging meant it was regarded with universal suspicion. Yet canned meat fed soldiers worldwide, and the shipment of millions of pounds of canned beef from the Chicago packinghouses to the American, English, and French armies underpinned military ambitions and imperial projects. Less likely to spoil than refrigerated beef, canned meat worked especially well in tropical areas.

Despite its utility, canned meat was a periodic source of scandal, particularly during the Spanish-American War, when

TABLE   223

General Nelson Miles accused low-quality meat of weakening US forces. The ensuing public outcry was ostensibly about canned beef, but it would become about industrial food production as a whole. It reveals that in an age of distant mass production of food, sanitation fears became central to food politics.[10] Further, the resolution of the scandal reveals how industrial production and packaging became naturalized, or at least tolerated.

This discussion underscores the importance of cultural meaning and sanitation to commodification.[11] When contamination fears or rising costs spark consumer outrage, they promote regulatory changes that prevent similar explosions in the future. As consumer fears become more and more remote, consumers become complacent about the system that produces their commodities. This tendency contributes to the ongoing resilience of the cattle-beef complex.

Discussions of beef and diet were always infused with assumptions about race, class, and gender, which a discussion of fresh beef in general, and the porterhouse steak in particular, will highlight.[12] The porterhouse, considered the first truly American cut of meat, could dress for a variety of occasions. The wealthy loved the cut, and home economists lamented that even the poorest laborers believed they deserved a porterhouse steak. When meatpacker and beef shipper T. C. Eastman faced questions about rising beef costs, he lamented that "if the poorer consumers would only consent to confine themselves to the cheaper cuts the price of the others would come down. They won't though."[13] Meanwhile, working-class Americans countered with their own understandings of the relationship between beef and status. Workers framed the Chinese exclusion debate in terms of the civilizational conflict between meat and rice.

Consumption played a vital role in shaping the cattle-beef complex. Taste—such as the predilection for fresh beef or the preference for one cut of meat over another—shaped what the Chicago meatpackers could sell and at what price. Consumer demand for low prices and fears of contamination shaped production around these twin imperatives. Meanwhile, the democratization of beef would have far-reaching social effects. Food was now a source of aesthetic enjoyment as never before, but this also brought new burdens for home cooks and set the stage for twentieth-century discussions about the health and environmental burdens of widely available, delicious food.

Buying Beef

Urban customers generally purchased their meat directly from retail butchers or placed delivery orders. In the case of deliveries, a clerk would often stop by the house in the morning and, in major cities, customers could receive their order that day.[14] Though many likely ordered meat for reasons of convenience or time, the method was not without drawbacks. One critic warned that "if the shopper at home orders 'round steak' she will get round steak cut off anywhere, and tough enough it is likely to be."[15] Visiting a shop or market allowed one to select one's own cuts as well as find deals.[16]

When customers entered a butcher's shop, the cuts of meat they found were reasonably consistent across major urban centers. Nevertheless, there were slight variations. The cut known as a "rump steak" in Boston and Philadelphia was called a "sirloin" in New York. National buying guides occasionally produced diagrams showing regional variations in cut and name.[17] This variety reveals one of the advantages of the meatpackers moving into wholesaling. Meat was shipped from Chicago in

TABLE   225

"quarters," or sections of a quarter carcass. Arriving at one of the meatpackers' branch houses (wholesale distribution points), retail butchers purchased these quarters and divided them for sale. The Chicago meatpackers left local variation to retail butchers. Therefore, centralization in meatpacking and distribution did not necessarily mean homogenization.

To return to the retail butcher, consumers found there was always room for negotiation on cost. *Good Housekeeping* explained that "no self-respecting woman will descend to haggling, but a discreet way of making a bargain, will frequently enable the housekeeper to save a neat sum."[18] Furthermore, "a real lady will be a lady under all circumstances, but she should not hesitate whenever she thinks 60 seconds of conversation with a butcher or grocer will very likely make a saving of several cents a pound."[19] For home economists, the market economy's imperatives trumped expectations about gender.

Trust was at the heart of food buying. The trick for customers was to find a reputable merchant and rely on that merchant's expertise. Yet this approach was also the source of unease. One buying guide warned of "transient and irresponsible parties" and cautioned that "apparent 'bargains' frequently turn out the worst possible investments."[20] Nevertheless, *Miss Parloa's New Cook Book* took a rosy view, noting that "many think the market not a pleasant or proper place for ladies. That idea is erroneous. My experience has been that there are as many gentlemen among marketmen as are to be found engaged in any other business." The same guide even suggested deferring to the butcher's authority "if not a judge of meat."[21] From the merchant's perspective, regular customers were preferable, and it was even worth offering good deals to secure reliable business.[22]

In a family, the ideal was that women would perform the shopping and food preparation. Beef buying guides and home-economics books were often geared toward middle-class women. *Good Housekeeping*, for example, included a guide for "the wife of a young business man."[23] Many guides suggested mothers teach their daughters to shop. According to *The Home, How to Make and Keep It*, when it came to food buying, "knowledge must be acquired in girlhood."[24] In this world, smart shopping was a wifely duty, and instruction had to begin early.

This situation did vary by class and family circumstance. The wealthy had servants to purchase and prepare food for them. Single men purchased many, if not most, meals in bars or restaurants. Some poorer residents bought meat from roving street peddlers. In more rural areas, meat was at times purchased from traveling sales carts.

Late nineteenth-century food buying was not fundamentally different from the period before the rise of Chicago dressed beef. Trust had been a concern since the early nineteenth century, when improvements in transportation and distribution created large, impersonal urban markets in what was known as the market revolution.[25] Gendered expectations about food preparation were comparable prior to the Civil War. This meant that the food-production revolution discussed throughout this book fit neatly behind the scenes of food purchasing and consumption. Over time, however, the dropping price of quality meat would amount to a revolution in consumer expectations.

In terms of production, the question of trust never disappeared; relationships established the reliability of food in consumers' minds. When meat was produced far from where it was consumed, there was risk. As long as the public could trust its food was sanitary, this was not a problem. From the big meatpackers' perspective, as long as trust was chiefly about the relationship between customer and retail butcher, all was well. Yet

TABLE 227

this was not always possible, particularly when it came to selling meat in a can.

Canned Beef and Its Critics

Though a victory abroad, the 1898 Spanish-American War was very nearly a defeat at home. Although there were only five hundred combat-related casualties, there were more than five thousand due to disease, accidents, or food poisoning. Faced with public scrutiny, the commanding general of the United States Army, Nelson Miles, blamed the army's food supply. He alleged that the canned corned beef rations were contaminated and that the limited supplies of refrigerated dressed beef were so full of chemical preservatives as to be "embalmed." Despite a near-total lack of evidence, Miles's charges resonated with a public already suspicious of canned meat.[26] The scandal intensified when the army quartermaster, Charles Eagan, called Nelson a liar and threatened him, spurring a court-martial. A series of investigations in the military and US Senate followed.[27] The scandal would reveal public fears about the new world of industrial food production and the increasing centrality of questions of contamination to mass food politics.

Appreciating the intensity of the scandal first requires understanding the fears surrounding canned meat.[28] Consumers celebrated a new era of cheap beef, but were wary of its production. Canned beef, a product with an innovative new production and storage method, was especially unsettling. The beef scandal exposed these latent fears of industrial meat production.

Even before the scandal, there was simmering concern about the quality and safety of canned beef. Newspapers printed dramatic tales of families poisoned at the dinner table. For a

Mrs. Smith, spoiled meat "seemed to take a hold of her with a death grip, and her suffering and agony for several hours was beyond description." Picnickers in Oregon "nearly escaped death" after eating some contaminated canned meat.[29] Though people consumed canned meat in large quantities—owing to its low price—poisoning stories, many of which were far from conclusive that canned meat was to blame, made them uneasy.

The meatpackers, for whom canned beef was a profitable business, tried to assuage consumer fears with clever marketing. Advertisements either emphasized quality or made the product more exciting by emphasizing its connections to exploration or the American West. Libby, McNeill & Libby, a Chicago firm, produced some of the most striking advertisements, ranging from the truly bizarre—a cow with a can of beef for a body whose "bosom swells with pride when . . . put inside a can"—to simple western scenes of cattle drinking at a watering hole.

Advertising alone could not break the association between canned meat and poverty, but advertisements' use of satire and the juxtaposition of refinement and canned meat could help destigmatize the product. A Paragon Dried Beef advertisement depicts a well-dressed man and woman who apparently "when asked what they'd have, they each of them / gave as the result of their honest belief / that if the restaurant man would bring them a can / they'd try the Paragon Dried Beef."[30] A similar piece depicts a well-dressed lady and her daughter with the caption "that tho' she was on pleasure bent she had a frugal mind, and therefore bought Libby, McNeill & Libby's Cooked Corned Beef."[31] In a quantity-over-quality approach, yet another of the company's advertisements depicted a man personally delivering a ship full of canned beef to a queen.[32]

Romanticizing canned beef was the other major approach to advertising. Libby, McNeill & Libby emphasized canned meat's

FIGURE 9. Libby, McNeill & Libby corned beef trade card (late nineteenth century). Reproduced by permission from the Advertising Ephemera Collection, Baker Library, Harvard Business School (olvwork80631).

FIGURE 10. Libby, McNeill & Libby corned beef trade card (late nineteenth century). Reproduced by permission from the Advertising Ephemera Collection, Baker Library, Harvard Business School (olvwork80658).

TABLE   231

role in exploration and travel. Apparently, "cooked corned beef saves the shipwrecked mariner."[33] Another advertisement shows an explorer gazing off the right-hand side of the page.[34] Advertisements also highlighted canned beef's global distribution and its association with militaries. One advertisement showed Uncle Sam, hat in hand, flanked by a bald eagle holding a can of corned beef, facing a rotund British gentleman flanked by a lion. The caption: "America's offering to England."[35] A related advertisement boasted that "the only thing that keeps the British lion quiet" is the company's canned beef.[36] Beyond allusions to military contracts, a Paragon Dried Beef advertisement referenced the product's ease of distribution and low cost in an advertisement of Uncle Sam offering canned beef to a starving peasant with the caption, "to cure the Chinese famine he acknowledges the 'fame in' Paragon Dried Beef."[37]

Despite marketers' efforts, these advertisements could not avoid revealing that the product was an outgrowth of the industrial production regime. Only in a world in which a single company could distribute a food product far and wide would targeted—and, increasingly, branded—advertising be worthwhile. The trick was keeping this out of consumers' minds as much as possible. Advertisements, then, naturalized canned meat as a commodity. Rather than referencing the production method directly, these advertisements appealed to the broader cultural association of beef to persuade consumers that canned beef was palatable.

The largest canned-beef customers—militaries—were not swayed by advertisements. Military interest in canned beef stretched back to the product's development. Napoleon had offered a large reward for low-cost canning technology during the early nineteenth century. Nicolas Appert rose to the challenge with some early designs, and the practice took off quickly.

Canned food proved vital during the Civil War, when it was an important component of Union rations. As the nineteenth century progressed, military sizes swelled and demand for canned meat increased as European militaries fueled their countries' imperial ambitions.[38]

Meeting this demand had to wait until the rise of the big Chicago meatpacking houses allowed production to meet militaries' insatiable demand for beef. Order sizes swelled in the 1880s. In 1885, a packing company associated with Morris & Company received orders for nearly two million pounds of canned beef from the French and another four million pounds from the British.[39] Armour & Company received comparable orders, including one for more than six hundred thousand pounds of canned meat.[40] By the late nineteenth century, soldiers could have beef with nearly every meal. Though it was widely dismissed as poor tasting, it provided protein and, according to the day's food standards, beef was central to a successful military.

This reflected the fact that the link between beef and imperialism was pervasive. Pieces like "Credit It to Beefsteak" explained that "the old saying that 'beefsteak is better medicine than quinine' is receiving able support from many white men on the Congo." At the European settlement in Boma, Congo, "[cattle] multiplied until [residents] are able to have fresh meat on their table every day, which they think is a great improvement on the tinned meats and canned vegetables upon which Stanley and his followers relied for the strength to lay the foundations of the Congo enterprise."[41] Just as colonial troops pacified a society before colonial officials could remake it, canned beef ensured the colonial regime's food security until live cattle could increase its food quality.

The US Army beef scandal reflected the public's simultaneous fear of, and fascination with, canned meat. Suspicions

TABLE   233

about the quality of canned meat and its general lack of desirability gave General Miles's charges explosive potential. Not only was the public already suspicious of canned beef, but the accusation suggested this spoiled meat threatened health and, by extension, American strength and manhood. Miles charged that the canned roast beef given to soldiers "was nothing more than the pulp left after making extract of beef."[42]

The first investigation yielded little concrete evidence beyond signs that poor planning had allowed meat to spoil in the tropical sun. In February of 1899, President McKinley ordered a military court of inquiry to investigate Miles's charges. Without concrete evidence, however, the scandal threatened to disgrace Miles.[43] The inquiry could not reach any clear conclusions. By March, the press had drawn its own conclusions, agreeing with Miles and again calling for the court-martial of Charles Eagan, commissary general of subsistence.[44] Nevertheless, formal inquiries into the scandal found Miles's evidence inconclusive.

Consumer unease with new industrial production methods and packaging drove the scandal more than actual evidence. It seems likely that Miles was vastly exaggerating the problem, but whether the beef itself was bad, had spoiled, or was prepared inappropriately could not be known. Evidence of contamination was vague. Both a doctor and a funeral-home worker claimed they had smelled embalming fluid in some of the meat.[45] But the military investigation concluded that Miles's claims were unfounded. The scandal would, however, have serious consequences for Miles, who would never reach his ultimate career goal: the Oval Office.

Reactions to the scandal were inseparable from the cultural assumptions, positive and negative, that suffused people's beliefs about industrial beef production. Furthermore, there seems to be little to clearly delineate contamination fears and concerns about health consequences from fears more squarely rooted in the displacement of slaughter and butchering from sites of consumption. In the same breath that expressed concerns about contamination, consumers could note rumors of "equine beefsteak" masquerading as canned beef.[46]

Though officially inconclusive, the investigation did expose the strange new world of industrial beef production. For instance, when beef was boiled before canning, the leftover liquid was used to make beef extract, a product akin to beef bouillon that was touted as a "remedy for disease and exhaustion."[47] Advertisements claimed medical respectability and even suggested that the extract was condensed food.[48] These claims raised questions verging on the metaphysical. How could both the extract and the boiled beef be actual food? When an investigator produced an Armour advertisement for beef extract that explained "Armour's extract is the only meat extract retaining the nutritious properties of beef," he asked how canned meat and beef extract could both contain the nutrition of the same piece of meat. A sheepish employee of Armour & Company could only respond that extract production methods had changed since the advertisement.[49]

Despite this weak defense, the public was disgusted. A medical article channeled public outrage when it observed that "the beef-extract contains no nutriment, the canned beef indigestible, and yet the one is put on the market as a great invigorator, while the other is offered as a food to soldiers, who need all the vigor they can get." The author concluded that "as between canned 'roast-beef' and 'beef-extract' one is a fraud and the other a sham."[50] It was a rare moment of vulnerability of the new industrial meat production regime.

The question, however, is why this unease did not translate into a more fundamental critique of industrial food production.

TABLE 235

The answer is that the army beef scandal may actually have contributed to the naturalization of industrial beef. By focusing concerns on contamination, consumers fixated on an issue on which the meatpackers could take tangible action. Media outrage could then function as a kind of catharsis and the subsequent investigation and regulation of meatpacking would restore public trust in the new production regime and elide other concerns, such as monopoly fears or labor exploitation.[51]

Beef and Hierarchy

There's an old army joke about steak. A young captain, like all ambitious men, wants a porterhouse steak. But his butcher is all out. Apparently, "all the Porterhouse goes to Colonel so-and-so. The Sirloin is reserved for Lieutenant Colonel this-or-that, all but the first cut; that goes to Major Somebody-or-other." All that is left for the captain is a round steak, the staple of the working poor. The young officer complains, "I've been buying beefsteak by rank all my life and I am tired of it."[52]

The democratization of beef sparked new debates about the meaning of beef consumption. Heightened expectations of quality and lower prices, for instance, sparked public conversations about the relationship between gender and food preparation. Elites began studying working-class eating habits. Union leaders celebrated beef consumption as a tangible marker of the labor movement's success. The hapless captain above began to wonder when rank and meat consumption would uncouple. Though in many ways eating is fundamentally about taste, one's dietary choices are always inseparable from broader questions of race, class, gender, and hierarchy.

In the United States, the story of beef and hierarchy really takes shape with the rise of the porterhouse steak. As with all good food legends, the porterhouse's birth story is a mixture of myth, cliché, and truth. Martin Morrison, the owner of a ship pilot's bar in the early nineteenth century, was short of meat, and decided to repurpose the cut at the end of the sirloin, then primarily used for roasting, to provide a steak. It took off. According to the story, Morrison's butcher eventually grew tired of ordering "cut steaks for the porter-house," and eventually dubbed the cut "porterhouse steak."[53] Soon it was famous on both sides of the Atlantic.[54]

When it came to beef, English culinary traditions loomed large. The sirloin was the most famous of all, with centuries of anecdotes about kings who had loved a once-obscure cut of meat so much that they dubbed it Sir Loin.[55] Young Englishmen attended "beefsteaks," ritualized dinners in which they consumed disgusting quantities of meat, and the rallying cry "beef and liberty" had its origins in seventeenth-century England. There were no better known cooks of roast beef than the English. With the porterhouse, American beef eaters forged a new culinary identity that was only validated once the cut became popular across the Atlantic.

Though women were expected to purchase and prepare meat for home consumption, beef was nevertheless a man's domain, as evident in the variety of stories mocking women's purchases, cooking, and even dietary choices. In "The Masculine Way," a man instructs a woman buying beef. He boasts that "a man can buy and sell a cargo of wheat while a woman is ordering a pound of steak," and explains that she "ought to hear me give an order for meat, and profit thereby."[56] Elsewhere, a doctor chastises a woman for her "absurd" breakfast choices. He condemns new foods like "oatmeal . . . though it is said to be healthful, it has caused more dyspepsia than all the candy, pastry, and hot rolls ever made." Rather, "the best breakfast in the world for an

TABLE 237

ordinary healthy person is a steak or a chop, with good coffee, hot rolls, and eggs."[57] With regard to food, women were caught in a condescending trap: expected to purchase and prepare beef as well as mocked for being incapable of doing so.

A barrage of articles attacked women's inability to cook a good steak. A *New York Herald* article, reprinted in the *Philadelphia Inquirer* and elsewhere, wondered "that while there are plenty of men, professional and amateur, who can cook a beefsteak, it is an accomplishment which can be claimed by but few women." Apparently, the secret to a good beefsteak was the butcher, and "women have no taste for butchery and the science evolved from blood."[58] Women were nevertheless expected to provide high-quality meat. In "Beefsteak as a Home Breaker," a widow laments that "a man may be a cherub about everything else; but I never knew one who didn't row about the steak." She observed that this is rooted in elevated expectations, for "taking into account the limited part of a beef's anatomy that is adapted to a Porterhouse, it is mathematically impossible that every man in the country should have the best cut of steak every day." There was a good deal of truth in the observation, though the widow also noted that her deceased husband "always lost his temper over it, and said he didn't care what other men had, he wouldn't chew sole leather and I must change my butcher at once."[59] The rise of dressed beef was changing expectations.

By the day's thinking, if beef was for men, the best beef was for educated white men. In the late 1860s, Dr. George Miller Beard, better known for his study of neurasthenia, penned a lengthy analysis of "the diet of brain workers," that combined social Darwinism (thoughts on the "barbarous races" are sprinkled liberally), quack nutritional analysis (fish is "pre-eminently adapted to nourish the brain"), and rambling monologue ("restaurants are an abomination").[60] The essay, first published in a self-help magazine called *Hours at Home*, placed food at the center of its racial theories, noting that "race, climate, and diet are the chief agencies which give character and development to a people." Addressing the world's "brain workers," the piece is an extended refutation of the idea that "brain-workers— especially literary men—needed less food and less sleep than those who handle the shovel and spade."

Following a vigorous defense of the idea that "even the most secluded book-worm" has greater dietary needs than "the uneducated and laboring classes," the author enters into an argument about the dietary needs of various historical civilizations. Apparently "the ruling people of the world, who have from time to time shaped the destiny of humanity, have always, so far as can be ascertained, been liberal feeders." He contrasts the diets of the powerful English and Germans with those of the Italians and Spaniards, whose "brains are less active and original." The author is even more dismissive of "the rice-eating Hindoos" and other non–Northern European people and diets. Following a dig at the Irish, the author wonders "what have the natives of South America, the savages of Africa, the stupid Greenlander, the peasantry of Europe, all combined, done for civilization, in comparison with any single beef-eating class of Europe?" The essay oscillates between a discussion of classes and occupations and the discussion of race or nationality.[61]

As may be clear by now, Beard believed that meat is the key, for "experience tells us that the diet of brain-workers should consist largely of meat, with, of course, an agreeable variety of fruits and cereals." Fresh meat is to be preferred, since "it contains those substances that are best adapted to feed the brain." While recognizing the appeal of a fish diet, the author dissects several defenses of fish before concluding that "civilization is very little more indebted to fish-eaters than to vegetarians."

TABLE   239

A variety of newspapers and periodicals published excerpts of the essay with added editorial comments. Mostly supportive, republishers recapitulated the author's central conclusions.[62] However, the *Manufacturers' and Farmers' Journal* was skeptical, attacking the author's evidence as limited and impressionistic, before concluding that "we are unable to see the truth of the argument."[63] Read by the laboring classes, the journal resented the author's contempt for those who do "muscular labor."

Discussions about diet often started with the assumption that a beef-heavy diet was essential to success. An 1887 article in the *Kansas City Star* and republished elsewhere mentioned several "brainworkers"—Goethe, Johnson, and Wordsworth—who were "tremendous feeders," and provided a list of "best foods," at the top of which was beef.[64] This list could be compared with a much later article criticizing thinkers like Benjamin Franklin and Thomas Jefferson who had tried vegetarianism and failed. Tolstoy had become vegetarian late in life, but apparently his greatest works were behind him.[65]

This kind of social Darwinian thinking about food reflected the singular importance of meat, and particularly beef, to nineteenth-century consumers. Its importance ensured abundant demand for beef and explained why Americans rich and poor wanted ever-larger steaks at ever-lower prices. Further, the emphasis on the relationship between diet and social status would inform attitudes about food and class in the twentieth century. Although few thought about diet in these crude terms in the twentieth century, the general belief that some people have less need for certain kinds of food is evident even today in the simultaneous aestheticization of elite food and obsession with reforming the eating habits of the poor.[66]

To return to the nineteenth century, the obsession with diet and civilizational accounts of carnivorousness was a reaction to the period's surging immigration. For many of these immi-grants, fresh meat may only have been consumed a few times per year.[67] The abundance of fresh beef in the United States meant that a food for special occasions—generally, religious holidays—became daily fare. While many of these poorer immigrants initially ate cheap cuts like the round steak, they, too, eventually sought choicer cuts.[68]

The class tensions over meat consumption and immigration were most obvious in *Meat vs. Rice*, an American Federation of Labor pamphlet calling for Chinese exclusion.[69] The pamphlet's subtitle expressed the close linkage between meat consump-tion and identity: *American Manhood against Asiatic Coolieism: Which Shall Survive?* Though the pamphlet contained a rela-tively broad analysis of cost-of-living and labor questions, meat was the ultimate symbol of the successful American worker, while rice represented the threat of persistently low wages and the victory of capital. The pamphlet links Chinese labor to the effects of slave labor throughout, and relies on racist tropes of Chinese docility but also hard work and ability to "live on noth-ing" to build concern about the American worker's ability to compete.[70]

The pamphlet closes by quoting James G. Blaine, a supporter of Chinese exclusion, who argues that the effect of immigration will be the further impoverishment of the American worker. Blaine argues "in all such conflicts, and all such struggles, the result is not to bring up the man who lives on rice to the beef-and-bread standard, but it is to bring down the beef-and-bread man to the rice standard."[71] Though *Meat vs. Rice* was a partic-ularly egregious example, the connection between meat and the manhood of American laborers was one that workers and reformers reproduced again and again. Workers connected eco-nomic success with increased meat consumption and meat was

TABLE 241

(and often still is) one of the few products for which consumption increases directly with income.[72]

This tendency was cause for alarm among elites, since they worried workers expected too much meat. An emerging literature argued the poor should be eating less beef. An 1875 article, for example, observed that though "men love meat as cats love fish," they must "listen to the logic of events." The strongest athletes in the world, the Chinese, "eat more rice than roast beef." In the same article, an English professor argued that "the potato-fed Irishman was stronger of muscle than the Scotchman fed mainly on oat-meal, and that the latter was stronger than the Englishman, fed mainly on bread and meat."[73] It was no coincidence that early studies of nutrition focused on workers' diets, rather than elite practices. For Americans rich and poor, beef was both tasty and a marker of success, but elites treated workers' food as an input to be scientifically optimized.

Reformers planned new diets for the poor. In the 1880s, the American Public Health Association organized an essay prize for authors who provided recipes and cooking instructions for people of modest means as well as "those who may be called poor." This assistance would function through women, since entries provided information for the "housewife."[74] The winning submission was a "useful and valuable contribution to the needs of [a] great army of working people, made possible through the humanitarian benevolence of a private citizen."[75] The essay prize constituted an early example of a long tradition of elite reformers instructing poorer Americans in what they should be eating.

The unanimous winner, Mary Hinman Abel, developed sample diets based on the day's nutrition science.[76] Abel begins her essay with an analysis of the five "nutritive ingredients": water, proteins, fats, carbohydrates, and salts or mineral constituents.[77] Regarding flavor, Abel observed that "if [the housewife] does not understand how to 'make the mouth water,' her labor is largely lost. Especially if she has but little money, should she pay great attention to this subject, for it is the only way to induce the body to take up plain food with relish."[78] Taste mattered insofar as it encouraged economical and healthful eating.

Central to this obsession with poor diets was a persistent belief, related to the "everyone wants a porterhouse" lament, that the working classes ate more beef than they needed, unnecessarily raising the cost of living.[79] Abel gestures at this idea throughout her essay, observing that "many workingmen in America would be surprised to learn how well health and strength can be maintained on what is, after all, not such a very large amount of meat, provided the rest of the diet contains enough vegetable protein and fat."[80] However, this also depended on the housewife learning "self-denial and saving, . . . [as] we indulge ourselves and our children too much in what tastes good, while all the time we know we have not money enough to buy necessaries."[81] According to Abel, the poor were enjoying their meals more than necessary.

Reformers worked to persuade workers and the poor to eat less desirable cuts of meat, particularly the round steak. Food scientists of the day emphasized that cheaper cuts—like round steak—were tougher, but equally nutritious. Reporting on this work, the *Kalamazoo Gazette* explained to readers that "Round steak [is] just as good as Tenderloin."[82] Others added that the cheaper, coarser cuts merely requiring longer cooking.[83]

Reformers considered that the poor were not missing much without finer cuts; poorer people supposedly lacked the refinement to appreciate the differences between various cuts of steak. Coverage of a Cleveland butcher's shop theft joked that

TABLE   243

the burglar took "nice juicy round steak in preference to Porterhouse hanging near."[84] In this case, "preference" was shorthand
for either ignorance or lack of refinement.

Perhaps the most visible proponent of the belief that the
poor ate beyond their means was Secretary of Agriculture Julius
Morton. A onetime farmer, Morton had long been a skeptic
of populism and had been associated with several railroads.[85]
Responding to a consumer complaint about high beef prices,
which carried an implicit criticism of the broader production
system, Morton blamed consumption. A housewife had asked
if Morton "could do something to help her and thousands of
other poor people to get meat for their dinner tables at a more
moderate price." Morton answered that "in this country even
the poor man, the day laborer, thinks he must have his Sirloin
steak for dinner. Round steak is not good enough for him."
He closed with an anecdote about a foolish woman to whom
a charity gave money to buy her family food, and the woman
"went out to buy . . . and chancing to see some canned lobsters
spent all her money on lobsters." Apparently "our housekeep-
ers . . . must learn how to get more for their money."[86]

Criticism of poor diets often relied on clichés about thrift
and success. Professor W. O. Atwater addressed "the food of the
poor" in just these terms. He began with the cliché that the rich
grow richer through saving and the poor poorer through wast-
ing. Regarding food, "it is the poor man's money that is the most
uneconomically spent in the market, and the poor man's food
that is worst cooked and served at home." He quotes a butcher
who observes that "I am told that the people in the poorer parts
of New York City buy the highest-priced groceries, and that
the meat-men say they can sell the coarser cuts of meat to the
rich, but that people of moderate means refuse them."[87] While
the butcher's argument seems too clichéd to be true, the idea

is not entirely implausible. The wealthy bought a large quantity of the finer cuts of meat, but it also seems possible that wealthy customers would at times buy cheaper cuts, in part because they would feel less social pressure to buy high-quality cuts. Status markers are easier to ignore when one's status is never in doubt. People of moderate means would have more reason to seek better cuts of meat as a tangible expression of their success.[88] Overall, rich and poor, immigrant and native born: all viewed beef consumption as a marker of superiority, ensuring abundant demand for beef.

Beyond obsessing about poor diets, elites as well as middle-class Americans embraced new culinary practices to differentiate their beef consumption. Wealthier Americans began to eat and socialize more out of the home; the word "restaurant" entered common usage during the period, and high-end restaurants spread in the nation's cities.[89] French-style cooking and elaborate dinner parties became crucial to the consolidation of the elite social world. According to Abram Dayton, "to lunch, dine, or sup at [New York restaurant] Delmonico's is the crowning ambition of those who aspire at notoriety."[90] Meanwhile, middle-class Americans ate out in their own restaurants as well.[91] Beef was not the only driver of these processes, but it was certainly an important part of them.

At the same time that eating was becoming more refined, there was also a tendency, particularly among upwardly mobile men, toward simplicity and recapturing the primal aspect of eating. In "an incident that recalls both George Washington and Primeval Man," roughly a dozen men met in New York one night in March 1881 to discuss the day's politics and eat vast quantities of steak washed down with beer.[92] This was only one of many late-nineteenth-century "beefsteaks," which amounted to rowdy bonding meals for elite and upper-middle-class men.

TABLE 245

FIGURE 11. 1908 photograph of a beefsteak dinner. Library of Congress.

Though the beefsteak was rooted in eighteenth-century practice, its revival in the late nineteenth century was a reaction to
changing culinary practices. By the 1880s and 1890s, steaks were
cheaper and more abundant than ever before, and men across
the country could participate in the same tradition in which
"old New Yorkers were wont to drop in, eat their beefsteaks,
[and] discuss the politics of Adams, Jefferson, Madison." Eating
with one's fingers was a prerequisite; "*sans* knives, forks, table,
or any other of the paraphernalia of the conventional dining
room," boasted one account of a beefsteak.[93] According to a
popular joke, dessert was a lamb chop.

This embrace of the primitive fit into the broader evolution of
the period's gender ideals, away from restrained manliness and
toward an aggressive and sometimes violent masculinity. The
ideal man could switch between primitive and refined contexts

with ease, and kept some of each with him at all times.[94] What mattered, then, was not only the beefsteak's simplicity—the unrefined could just as easily eat a simply prepared steak off an overturned box—but that beefsteak participants could comfortably eat at a place like Delmonico's the next night.

The drive to distinguish one's eating habits in novel ways is evident in the period's cookbooks as well. Recipes, often gathered in what were known as "receipt books," or buried in women's "home guides," grew more elaborate in the late nineteenth century. During the first half of the century, American cookbooks were largely derivative of British ones, but by mid-century cookbooks looked distinctly American. Once simple guides to preparing food now held hundreds of recipes with varied ingredients. Home diners also began to expect novel meals regularly, rather than simply on special occasions. The 1890 book *The Table* featured "menus for every day of the year," with varied options for every meal. Beef preparations included "Beefsteak with anchovy butter" and "braised beef à la flamande."[95] Though the book was for skilled chefs—Delmonico's head chef Alexander Filippini was the author—it was designed for home use. Except in the case of those rich enough to employ home cooks, elaborate new recipes heavily burdened women, who were expected to be doing the home cooking.[96]

The democratization of beef had far-reaching effects on culinary practice as well as sparking new conversations about the relationship between food and identity. For rich and poor Americans, affordable beef allowed them to turn the aspirational into the everyday. For wealthier people, this meant dining out and elaborate, European-style recipes. For the working classes, this meant a daily portion of beef and the occasional porterhouse. These changes forced conversations about identity that reflected the racial and social thinking of the time, and

TABLE 247

would spur the kinds of investigations into, and discussions of, eating practices that would anticipate twentieth-century nutrition science.

Concluding with a Meat Riot

In March 1902, meat prices were rising fast. The Chicago packers blamed cattle shortages and spiking western grain prices, but retail butchers suspected a meatpacker plot to increase profits now that they controlled the nation's meat supply.[97] This had been an ongoing debate since the mid-1880s, when the Vest Committee—discussed in the section "Early Regulatory Approaches" in the previous chapter—began studying long-term beef and cattle prices. Short-term price spikes always caused consumer grumbling, but in 1902 they were bad enough to spark a riot.

The fight was over kosher meat. In early 1902, wholesalers—owned by or in concert with the Chicago packinghouses—had begun charging retail butchers more and more.[98] New York's sixteen hundred eastside kosher butchers had initially resisted, shuttering their doors. The measure earned public support, but when the struggling butchers reopened with increased prices on May 15, the public turned. "Maddened women" smashed windows and poured "water, kerosene oil, and, according to some of the butchers, carbolic acid" on meat. They seized meat from customers and threw it to the ground, stomping on it. More than five hundred police were needed to disperse the crowd.[99]

Neither the prices nor the unrest abated. On May 24, 1902, a crowd assembled outside the United Beef Company's shops, threatening customers and smashing windows. A Brooklyn crowd attacked kosher butcher George Davis for refusing to close his shop and "selling meat to Italians." Davis found himself at the mercy of somewhere from several hundred to nearly one thousand men, women, and children.[100]

During these disturbances, butchers and protesters traded rival explanations. The protesters claimed retailers were motivated by greed, whereas butchers blamed the meatpackers or surging prices in the Midwest.[101] Price was always the central consideration. The president of the Hebrew Retail Butchers' Kosher Guarantee and Benevolent Association "attribute[d] the disturbances to two causes: first, the presence in the affected district of large number of socialists and anarchists, and second, to the fact that housewives want cheap meat."[102] Customers, however, replied that they simply wanted the prices to which they were accustomed.

Scholars since E. P. Thompson have studied angry crowds and mass protests around prices.[103] In this case, though there were cheaper options—bread, chicken, etc.—customers wanted beef. Fishmongers "vowed they would assist the poor women of the east side by selling them all the fish they wanted," but red meat was king. During a 1906 price spike, a frustrated woman explained that "what fools we are to buy meat when fish is cheaper. Fish is better than meat. It is more nourishing. If you don't know how to make fancy dishes out of fish I will teach you . . . when you have it cooked in different styles you can't tell the difference from meat."[104]

But the riot was not a simple question of calories. Learning new ways to prepare and enjoy fish was not something that could happen overnight. And even if it could, people did not want fish, they wanted beef. Nobody wrote back to the old country about the United States' abundance of fish.

The late nineteenth century brought the democratization of beef. Prices declined over the last decades of that century and

TABLE   249

wages rose, allowing poor laborers and immigrants to eat beef daily. Meanwhile, for elites these changes meant the ability to import high-end European cuisine and the increasing refinement of the dinner party, even as men reconnected with their primal side through the beefsteak. Democratization, however, was not the same thing as equality. Beef was widely available, but distinctions of race, class, and gender remained as important as ever.

Whether consuming a porterhouse or a round steak, consumption was inseparable from what it said about who you were and what you thought about your fellow Americans. Men and women alike consumed beef, but its meaning was highly gendered, as seen in the all-male beefsteak and the constant lament that women could not cook a good steak. Meanwhile, elite obsessions with workers' diets were rooted in a belief that expectations exceeded status. These complicated questions and debates about beef and self ensured that the commodity was always in demand and irreplaceable.

Changes in consumption supported the rise of the cattle-beef complex. Industrial beef producers stayed behind the scenes as consumers purchased beef in familiar ways and maintained gendered expectations about its purchase and preparation. The familiarity of beef purchasing, with few changes other than dropping prices, allowed revolutionary change in production to hide within continuity. In the case of a product like canned meat, this was much more complicated, as the US Army beef scandal suggests. Taking meat out of a tin can instantly reminded people that this was a new, highly industrial product. This was why soldiers were wary of canned beef and quartermasters stressed that canned meats should be removed from their containers out of soldiers' sight. Further, through sanitary reforms and advertising strategies, producers tried to assuage similar fears among consumers.

At moments of crisis, beef's production history is inescapable, since the inability to purchase beef, fear of becoming sick, or contact with a new distribution method threatens the varied meanings beef holds for consumers. Reforms that minimize these moments of friction will gain traction over alternatives that do not. This is especially obvious in light of the two chief ways the meatpacking industry was regulated during the early twentieth century: the Federal Meat Inspection Act (FMIA) of 1906 and the Packers and Stockyards Act of 1921. Where the FMIA was meant to address the public outcry over sanitation sparked by *The Jungle's* publication, the Packers and Stockyards Act was intended to address increasing beef prices by breaking up the Beef Trust.[105] What is important about the role of consumers in this story is that they drove not *how* beef products would be regulated but that they would be regulated toward two goals—purity and low prices. As long as producers could meet these goals, the public was uninterested in whether local butchers were able to keep their jobs or whether slaughterhouse labor conditions were safe. This reality underscores the core strength and fatal weakness of consumer politics.

The flexibility of beef as a commodity was crucial to the growth of the cattle-beef complex. It was the fact that Chicago beef could be on a dinner plate in Little Italy, at a military camp in Puerto Rico, on a restaurant table in San Francisco, and at a dinner party in Boston that ensured the incredible demand for beef that fueled the ranching and meatpacking industries. Further, the centralization of the food production process accompanied the rise of increasingly varied diets and types of cuisine. This was no coincidence. As desirable foods become more widely available, they become central to increasingly varied culinary contexts. For beef, homogeneity in production depended on heterogeneity in consumption.

TABLE   251

When consumers fear that their food might be contaminated or that it is getting too expensive, they push for reform. Once consumers are satisfied, the end result is a system that produces sanitary and affordable meat, but is otherwise invisible. Beef became a blank slate on which one could project one's own tastes. Beyond enabling ongoing human and animal exploitation, this invisibility explains the contemporary lament that beef comes to us shrink-wrapped or in a taped bundle of butcher paper, long divorced from a living, breathing, bleeding animal.[106]

Conclusion

TEDDY ROOSEVELT was briefly a rancher. After his wife died in 1884, he moved west to recover. In three books, *Ranch Life and the Hunting Trail, Hunting Trips of a Ranchman,* and *The Wilderness Hunter,* Roosevelt detailed life at his Elkhorn ranch in North Dakota. Spurning the "emasculated, milk-and-water moralities" of softer men, Roosevelt celebrated the aggressive masculinity and self-reliance of the cowboy.[1] A member of the elite by all measures, Roosevelt found peace hunting game, wrangling cattle, and eating the cowboy's simple fare. Yet he remained equally comfortable at society dinners back east. Like the attendees of chapter 5's beefsteaks, Roosevelt celebrated a strength found in the coexistence of savagery and refinement. In his case, however, this coexistence would be inflected with western American values, particularly a kind of self-reliance.

Roosevelt's emphasis on a western-inflected individualism informed his thinking about economic development. According to Roosevelt, "the welfare of the aggregate of citizens which makes the nation, must rest upon individual thrift and energy, resolution, and intelligence. Nothing can take the place of this individual capacity." The role of the state was to use "honest and intelligent administration" to ensure the "opportunity" for this individual capacity to flourish.[2]

This individualism made Roosevelt suspicious of big business. If individuals were the cornerstone of a successful society, massive corporations with thousands of replaceable employees could be agents of social decay. This was particularly true if these businesses bankrupted small producers. As a result, Roosevelt railed against the trusts that dominated business in his day, and the Beef Trust made a natural target. The Chicago meatpackers had bankrupted thousands of local butchers scattered across the country. Moreover, they squeezed their profits from the same cattle ranchers Roosevelt admired. Early in his presidency, he made an investigation of the meatpacking industry one of the first major projects of his newly created Bureau of Corporations. Though the investigation was ill managed and largely unsuccessful, it was emblematic of Roosevelt's suspicion of unchecked corporate interests. Business was to be subservient to the individual.

Though he was sharply critical of big business, this individualism meant Roosevelt was no socialist. In fact he saw unfettered commerce and state socialism as two extremes. In *History as Literature*, he explained that "the very reason why we object to state ownership, that it puts a stop to individual initiative and to the healthy development of personal responsibility, is the reason why we object to an unsupervised, unchecked monopolistic control in private hands. We urge control and supervision by the nation as an antidote to the movement for state socialism."[3] He described Upton Sinclair as "hysterical, unbalanced, and untruthful," though this did not stop Sinclair's *The Jungle* from spurring Roosevelt to call for a fresh investigation of the Chicago packers.

The Beef Trust—Don't shoot, I'll come down.

FIGURE 12. An early twentieth-century newspaper cartoon by Charles Lewis Bartholomew showing Theodore Roosevelt hunting a cow labeled "Beef Trust." The newspaper headline reads "beef is way up," which explains why the animal is sitting on the moon. Library of Congress.

The difference between Roosevelt's attitudes about big business and his attitudes about socialism was that he accepted modern industry as inevitable. In 1902, Roosevelt described big corporations as an "inevitable development of modern industrialism," and noted that efforts to destroy them would be "futile."[4] A year earlier, he had explained that he understood that "combination of capital in the effort to accomplish great things is necessary," and that, therefore, "combination and concentration should be, not prohibited, but supervised and within reasonable limits controlled."[5] The job of government was to tame business and make it a tool for individual advancement. This view made Roosevelt the ideal capitalist reformer.

Roosevelt's reformist views were not alone, but rather part of a broader regulatory context that saw the state as a tool for taming, rather than remaking, capitalism.[6] Prosperity and collective benefit were central to the period's politics, as seen in the Vest Committee testimony of chapter 4. At the heart of the reform climate over which Roosevelt presided was the simultaneous embrace and regulation of big business.

In 1906, this regulatory climate culminated in the passage of both the Pure Food and Drug Act and the Federal Meat Inspection Act. Revolutionary pieces of legislation, their nature is still debated by scholars—were they instances of corporate regulatory capture or consumer victory? The answer is probably both. In terms of the cattle-beef complex, these acts accepted the state of the meatpacking industry as of 1906. In looking to regulate centralized food production, they took its existence as a baseline assumption. Though assembled through a violently contested process, big meatpacking was no longer questioned, it was regulated.

The embrace of regulated centralization did not silence the deep tensions, anxieties, and contradictions in this system, but it did mute them. Land expropriation was largely finished and traditional butchers had long since been driven out of business. Slaughterhouse labor remained brutal, low-paid work, and, despite Upton Sinclair's best efforts, few cared. Ranching would be decentralized, weak, and so dependent on beef processing that ranchers had to accept a subordinate role in the industry.

The cattle-beef complex would evolve over the twentieth century. Thanks to trucking, beef processing moved out of midwestern cities and into rural areas closer to ranches and feedlots.[7] The rise of the fast-food industry, particularly McDonald's, would revolutionize how people ate. Beef consumption crested in the 1970s and began a slow decline in the wake of health concerns. Nevertheless, the persistent association of red meat with manliness explains the continued popularity of eating regimes like the beef-heavy Atkins diet or the paradoxically industrial-agriculture friendly caveman/paleo diet.

Despite these changes, the system's broad strokes remain the same. The nineteenth century's four largest beef processors remained in business well into the twentieth century and survive in some form today.[8] A small number of companies still dominate global beef production.[9] Ranching remains decentralized and subordinate to meat processing. Slaughterhouse labor remains largely invisible immigrant labor, though now these workers are generally from Latin America, rather than Central or Eastern Europe.[10]

Contemporary food politics still reflects its nineteenth-century origins. The obesity epidemic and the "foodie" cultural phenomenon suggest that food debates remain inflected with class and gender concerns. Similarly, the willingness to celebrate the aesthetic qualities of one's own food choices and neglect them when considering the diets of the poor or heavy continues. Vegetarianism—eschewing animal flesh—and veganism—rejecting animal products altogether—are popular for reasons ranging from health to animal rights. While these perspectives embrace concern about the production process, contra the argument developed in chapter 5, supporters of these practices too often remain unaware of the class implications of their choices.

Today, as in 1900, the cattle-beef complex's resilience remains a result of the narratives that naturalized it and the spatial and economic changes examined throughout this book. People remain uneasy with modern industrial production, as illustrated by the panic following the 2013 revelation that a number of European beef products actually contained horsemeat. But public response generally frames these scandals as a consequence of individual actions—a shady processing plant or a dubious regulatory regime—rather than structural factors, such as labor exploitation, animal abuse, or cost reduction.[11] Meanwhile, structural critiques often emphasize only one piece of the overall story, whether environment, labor, public health, or another factor.[12]

Both ways of understanding industrial meat production are flawed. The focus on individual bad actors or businesses obscures structural problems. Well-publicized investigations into food contamination or illegal labor practices can be distractions from deeper problems for which it is impossible to assign blame, but which nevertheless have serious consequences. Similarly, structural critiques must accept both the gains and costs of industrial agriculture as well as think holistically about the many facets of the food system. Rather than breaking into rival camps—whether animal-rights crusaders, labor organizers, or others—that sometimes treat reform as a zero-sum game, critics must build political coalitions that allow conversations about the industry as a whole.

To return to the history of the cattle-beef complex, its rise shaped processes well beyond food production. As chapter 1 argues, American power in Texas and across significant stretches of the West rested on cattle ranching and its role in American Indian land dispossession. Similarly, the expansion of the regulatory state was rooted in its engagement not merely with meatpackers and ranchers, but also with the railroads, whose transport revolution was founded on the delivery of agricultural products. From cotton to wheat to beef, the American economy was built on agricultural commodities, suggesting that the rise of American economic power is as much an ecological story as an industrial one.

In the late nineteenth century, quality fresh beef became daily fare. A multiplicity of regional food markets became a single national one; ranches in the rural West could now feed the urban East. Butchers became slaughterhouse workers, turning animal processing into factory work. Four processes enabled these changes: (1) the reorientation of the Plains ecosystem from grass-bison-nomad to grass-cattle-rancher through the violent expropriation of Indian land; (2) the standardization of spaces across the West and the rise of regulatory mechanisms to promote mobility; (3) the outcome of conflicts around beef processing, distribution, and sale; and (4) the dynamics of a consumer politics inextricably linked to beef's cultural meanings. Driving each of these processes were human struggles over economic, political, and social power.

The remaking of the Plains ecosystem had consequences that persist today, though the rancher has been replaced by the farmer (as boosters once predicted) and, more recently, by the suburb. Yet the early story of the American West made the cattle-beef complex possible. If, as historian Alfred Chandler agues, the key achievement of the modern corporation was that it developed the internal management of supply, there would have been no incentive to do so without the overabundance of commodities that began with ranchers like Susan Newcomb.[13]

Integrating the Great Plains into commodity markets was not simply a process of rationalizing nature. As argued in chapter 1, the unpredictability of nature was a vital source of profit. Through a combination of deliberate maneuvering and historical accident, food processors came to dominate a production system founded

on natural processes. This allowed the supply chain not to rationalize nature, but to manage it. Ranchers absorbed the risks, and
meatpackers could reap profits in good times and bad. It was a
system that would serve as a model for twentieth-century agriculture. In modern agricultural production, value comes from the
human and animal relationship with the land, but profit comes
from displacing the unpredictability of weather, animals, and
microorganisms onto ranchers and farmers.[14]

The integration of a national beef market was a story of
technological change paired with political and economic struggles over the movement of goods and people. These struggles
resulted in the proliferation of standardized spaces—cattle
towns, livestock exchanges, rail routes—through which goods
moved, as well as regulation to ensure trust and stability across
vast distances. Local fights would lead to regional, and later
national, regulatory solutions. Though often driven by local
actors, whether town boosters or struggling cattle merchants,
this standardization and regulation would ultimately favor the
biggest meatpackers, who needed less and less local knowledge
about communities to do business.

This is not to suggest that the Chicago meatpackers did not
depend for their existence on ranchers or the particular con-
figurations of local power on the Plains. In fact, the speed with
which commodities could move is what produced an integrated cattle-beef complex in which dietary changes or micro-
level ranching practices could have far-reaching effects. Born in
particular places, the cattle-beef complex would become larger
than any of them. Even Chicago, the nerve center of this system,
and in many ways nineteenth-century America, would fade in
importance during the twentieth century.[15]

One should not underestimate the traditional story of
the rise of big meatpacking. The refrigerator car was a great

technological achievement and its utilization drove far-reaching business changes. The aim has not been to overturn this narrative, but to suggest it is an incomplete story and one oft repeated to justify the state of the food production system. Centralized production was as much the consequence of institutional developments and social conflict as of technological change.

Further, this is not merely a production story; the democratization of beef mattered. As it does today, beef held special importance for Americans and this importance justified a system that left consumers largely satisfied with those factors they found most salient—taste and sanitation—even if it did not address other factors of periodic concern, such as labor conditions or environmental degradation. Consumers reconciled themselves to industrial meat products by distancing themselves from industrial meat production.

Red Meat Republic examines the origins of industrial beef production and explains why, despite widespread criticism, the industry has persisted in roughly the same shape for over a century. Yet it is also a reminder that this method of producing our food is a question of politics and political economy, rather than technology and demographics. Alternate possibilities remain unclear, but as long as this story is understood as one of political economy, we may be able to fulfill Armour & Company's credo—"We feed the world"—using a more equitable system.

NOTES

Introduction

1. Sinclair, *Jungle*.

2. Russell, *Greatest Trust*, 2.

3. Armour, *Packers*, vi.

4. William Cronon's *Nature's Metropolis* is the path-breaking work in this regard, particularly regarding Chicago. However, there is a tendency in the book to attribute too much agency to markets and capital. In the book's section discussing meatpacking, Cronon discusses butchers' struggles, but more as an example of the human effects of structural changes, rather than treating the conflict between wholesale butchers and the big meatpackers as a meaningful part of the story. This tendency to downplay the human side of the story is Peter Coclanis's major criticism of the book: Coclanis, "Urbs in Horto," 14. Recent works on agricultural production and capitalist transformation include Beckert, *Empire of Cotton*; Clark, "Agrarian Context"; Giesen, *Boll Weevil Blues*; Johnson, *River of Dark Dreams*.

5. The fact that no single word captures the totality of meatpacking, ranching, and consumption reflects both the difficulty and importance of treating this subject holistically.

6. The Federal Meat Inspection Act and Pure Food and Drug Act were signed on the same day in 1906, partly in response to the consumer outcry following the publication of Sinclair's and Russell's works.

7. For an overview, see Nimmo et al., *Range and Ranch Cattle*. For detailed statistics, see the Chicago Board of Trade Annual Reports.

8. By democratization, I mean widespread beef consumption and a pervasive belief that beef was something everyone should be able to eat.

9. The exact extent of beef consumption's increase in the nineteenth century is a complicated question, in part because there are almost no precise statistics. Meat consumption rose slightly during the late nineteenth century, but the evidence suggests that beef consumption, in particular, rose more strongly. There is also a great

deal of qualitative evidence, as examined in chapters 4 and 5. The best sources on the subject are Horowitz, *Putting Meat*, 11–13, and Warren, *Great Packing Machine*.

10. This is explored in chapter 5.

11. Clemen, *American Livestock*. The book received a glowing review in the *American Historical Review*. The review provides a clear statement of the technological inevitability argument: "the national railroad net was fundamental. The city residents, collected by the factory, created the indispensable market. The ice machine and the refrigerator car were *sine qua non*." See F. Paxson, "Review," 360.

12. Armour, *Packers*, 38. Armour was discussing the pioneering efforts of his father, Philip Danforth Armour, to distribute meat using the refrigerator car and then his efforts to promote (and dominate) fresh fruit distribution.

13. McCoy, *Historic Sketches*. For a discussion of McCoy's influence and a critique of using him as a source, see D. Walker, *Clio's Cowboys*. Nevertheless, McCoy is still useful (if often problematic) for some of the early history, and you will find him cited a few times throughout this book.

14. I have used the term "car" throughout for clarity. Other, more common usages from the time, such as "railcar" or "stock," have been avoided in the interests of preventing confusion.

15. US Bureau of Corporations, *Report of the Commissioner*, xviii.

16. On the financial end of things, Armour was intimately involved in the wheat industry, having profited from a corner on the market in the late 1870s. He prevented a rival from doing the same in 1897–98.

17. Armour and Company, "Armour's Food Source Map."

18. The word "agribusiness" has a fascinating and politically charged history. See Hamilton, "Agribusiness."

19. Discussed at length in Christopher Leonard, *Meat Racket*. For a historical look at the displacement of risk and costs onto poultry farmers through producer contracts, see Gisolfi, *Takeover*.

20. For an overview, see McTavish et al., "New World Cattle." On the domestication of the aurochs (cattle's ancestor), see Ajmone-Marsan et al., "Origin of Cattle."

21. I explore this in Specht, "Rise, Fall, and Rebirth."

22. "The Longhorn Strikes His Last Trail," *New York Times*, March 27, 1927.

23. This is a simplification of an enormously complicated story of cultural interaction. The best take on this, and on the origins of ranching in general, is Jordan, *Cattle-Ranching Frontiers*. The takeaway is that despite local claims, cattle ranching was not invented in Texas, but rather was the product of imported traditions.

24. See Sluyter, *Black Ranching Frontiers*.

25. American beef in Latin America has its own global story. British firms pioneered meat processing in Argentina, but the Chicago houses eventually got involved. See Hanson, *Argentine Meat*. For a history of ranching in South America,

particularly one that balances local context with how it connects to regional and global processes, see R. Wilcox, *Cattle in the Backlands*.

26. There was also a significant Australasian beef (and mutton) trade. This was relatively independent of the American trade. For a fascinating look at this story, see Woods, *Herds*.

27. This book participates in a cross-fertilization of the fields of the history of capitalism and environmental history. Key recent books in this trend include Andrews, *Killing for Coal*; Cushman, *Guano*; J. W. Moore, *Capitalism*; Soluri, *Banana Cultures*. There are also a number of thorough essays on the topic, such as Barca, "Laboring the Earth"; Brown and Klubock, "Environment and Labor"; J. W. Moore, "Modern World-System"; Peck, "Nature of Labor." *Red Meat Republic* builds on this work by emphasizing and theorizing the importance of breadth—the story of ecological change is as important as that of industrial production—as well as exploring the role of conflict in producing structural change. This latter point helps introduce contingency into processes that in environmental history and histories of capitalism often seem like an inevitable consequence of the working out of forces of capital or markets.

28. With a few noteworthy exceptions, business histories and histories of capitalism underemphasize questions of space and economic development. (Notable exceptions being Beckert, *Empire of Cotton*; Cronon, *Nature's Metropolis*; R. White, *Railroaded*). Even works that emphasize circulation tend to consider the broadest level of interconnection, rather than the way in which mobility reshaped (and was enabled by) the spaces through which it moved.

29. A burgeoning literature suggests that consumer choice happens at the pre- or nonrational level. This is the focus of the field of consumer psychology. For an accessible overview of these kinds of concerns, see Kahneman, *Thinking, Fast and Slow*.

30. There is a lengthy scientific literature. For example, see Loftus et al., "Two Independent Domestications," and Beja-Pereira et al., "Origin of European Cattle."

31. David Nibert refers to animal domestication as "domesecration," in order to connect the domestication of animals with subsequent violence against humans, animals, and environments. While I have a slightly more rosy perspective on the historical relationship between humans and cattle, this book does explore similar themes: how the rise of large-scale beef production was connected to exploitation not only of animals, but also of ecosystems and human communities. See Nibert, *Animal Oppression*. For recent anthropological work on human-animal relationships see Govindrajan, *Animal Intimacies*, and Vitebsky, *Reindeer People*.

Chapter One: War

1. The proper name for the large, woolly creatures that once roamed much of the United States is "bison" or, in more formal company, "American bison" (*Bison*

bison). However, nineteenth-century Americans mostly used the term "buffalo," and today both names are used. I will generally use the word bison, but occasionally for context surrounding a quote using the word "buffalo," I will use that term.

2. The image is ambiguous. Is Wo-Haw suggesting that his people embrace cattle and settled agriculture? Is he protecting the buffalo from encroachment? For more on the painting, see Rand, *Kiowa Humanity*, 104–5.

3. Generally, I will be examining the stories of the Kiowa, Comanche, Cheyenne, Lakota, and the Sioux more broadly. However, these are only some of the largest and most well known of the Plains Indian polities. Because I am largely working with Euro-American sources that were not often sensitive to distinctions in Indian political systems or culture, it is often difficult to precisely identify the appropriate polity or nation. I often use "Indian" as an umbrella term, but where possible I will be more specific.

4. There is debate about the extent to which the US military directly supported the bison hunt. I agree with historian David Smits that the military was intimately connected with the destruction of the bison, employing tactics focused on destroying the enemy supply base (in this case, bison herds) that the Union army had pioneered during the Civil War. For an overview of the debate, see Smits, "Frontier Army."

5. Madley, "California's Yuki Indians," 315. On the same page, Madley quotes one observer: "the Indians were killing stock, and the whites were killing Indians." See also his book on the subject: *American Genocide*.

6. What exactly was meant by "Great American Desert" and the pervasiveness of this view are the subject of some debate. See Morris, "Notion," and, more recently, Bowden, "Great American Desert."

7. Nimmo et al., *Range and Ranch Cattle*, 49.

8. "The Brutal Beef Issue," *Columbus Daily Enquirer*, July 30, 1886. These handouts, referred to as "beef issues," were often compared to Spanish bullfights in their savagery, presumably to draw a connection between two different enemies at the time. See the aforementioned article as well as "Scout Shave Head," *Grand Forks Daily Herald*, February 19, 1885.

9. I use the word "paternalism" with the recognition of David Sim's objection that it is a flawed paradigm in part because of the incoherence of late nineteenth-century federal policy. Sim, "Peace Policy." Despite this objection, I do see a pervasive belief on the part of state actors that Indian policy should be crafted in the interests of an abstracted (and not fully competent) Indian rather than in consultation with the people themselves. "Paternalism" is a useful, if flawed, shorthand for this idea. The classic work on federal policy is Prucha, *Great Father*. For a recent overview of scholarship on federal Indian policy, see Carter, "U.S. Federal Indian Policy."

10. Nimmo, *Range and Ranch Cattle*, 18–19. For an interesting comparison between this process in the United States and central Asia, see Sabol, "American and Russian Internal Colonization."

11. Slotkin, *Fatal Environment*, particularly ch. 1–3.

12. For a powerful example of this process, see G. Anderson, *Conquest of Texas*, which characterizes small-scale violence, paramilitary activity, and the violence on the southern Plains as ethnic cleansing.

13. Ostler, *Plains Sioux*, 40.

14. Jacki Thompson Rand describes settlers as a "constant source of conflict." Rand, *Kiowa Humanity*, 39.

15. Despite being published back in 1931, the most influential book on the Great Plains remains Webb, *Great Plains*. Though largely persuasive, at times Webb risks a kind of environmental determinism in his emphatic claim that "the Great Plains have bent and molded Anglo-American life" (8). While Webb's position is extreme, a key argument of this chapter is that while Anglo-Americans imposed a social, legal, and political regime radically different from that of the Plains Indians, the resulting system was ecologically quite similar, illustrating the ways in which environmental history brings out deep similarities between apparently radically different ways of organizing a society.

16. "Report of Major General John Pope." Though Pope's views were clear, not all Americans believed in this "barren country" account. Some recognized the abundance of the Plains and realized ranching's possibilities quite early. That said, many, like Pope, were initially quite skeptical. For some detail on these different views, see Morris, "Notion," and Bowden, "Great American Desert."

17. For a good summary of human societies on the Plains and how they changed over the centuries following the arrival of horses, see Sherow, *Grasslands of the United States*, particularly ch. 2.

18. The pioneering works on this subject are Flores, "Bison Ecology," and Sherow, "Workings of the Geodialectic." More recently, see E. West, *Contested Plains*, and Hämäläinen, *Comanche Empire*. Despite their power, horses did have limits and posed new challenges for their riders. Sherow, "Workings of the Geodialectic," describes horses as both an "innovative addition, and a vexation" (81).

19. Isenberg, *Destruction of the Bison*, 16.

20. Ibid. See also Flores, "Bison Ecology," 482.

21. For an overview of this lengthy debate, see Isenberg, *Destruction of the Bison*, ch. 1, especially 24–25. Dan Flores makes a similar estimate of 28–30 million with roughly 8 million on the southern Plains. For a treatment of this subject and the ecology of the bison hunt in Canada, see Dobak, "Killing the Canadian Buffalo."

22. E. West, *Way to the West*, ch. 2.

23. This periodization for the spread of horses appears in many works; see E. West, *Contested Plains*; Isenberg, *Destruction of the Bison*; Hämäläinen, *Comanche Empire*.

24. These trade networks were quite elaborate and have been the focus of extensive study. See Jablow, *Cheyenne*; Lecompte, *Pueblo, Hardscrabble, Greenhorn*; Hämäläinen, "Western Comanche Trade Center."

25. See Hämäläinen, *Comanche Empire*.

26. The best examination and discussion of this story is Flores, "Bison Ecology."

27. Recent scholarship has studied the effect European commodities such as horses and guns had on indigenous trade networks. These goods caused incredible violence and often created social and political instability long before white Americans first reached parts of the West. See Blackhawk, *Violence over the Land*. Other commodity flows—such as the whiskey trade—continued into the reservation period and were the source of ongoing violence and conflict. See Unrau, *White Man's Wicked Water*. See also Lecompte, *Pueblo, Hardscrabble, Greenhorn*, ch. 9 and 10.

28. E. West, *Way to the West*, 62.

29. As Elliott West has put it, "peace, in a sense, was killing the bison": E. West, *Way to the West*, 63. Of course, the key was that peace among humans and growing demand for buffalo robes were together leading to dramatically expanded hunting. One could say that peace and capitalism were killing the bison.

30. Nimmo et al., *Range and Ranch Cattle*, 73. Boosters often told a similar story. Walter Baron von Richthofen explained that, "[settlers] had seen herds of buffalo living on the plains without shelter, and getting fat. What was more natural than to conclude that, under such favorable circumstances, the business of raising cattle must be a profitable one?": von Richthofen, *Cattle Raising*, 4.

31. This claim echoes Elliot West's argument in *Contested Plains* about the importance of gold to changing Americans' desire to occupy western lands.

32. From their arrival in North America, colonists had an uneasy relationship with the animals they found. For an expansive look at this relationship, as well as how individual animals occasionally got the best of people, see Smalley, *Wild by Nature*.

33. Susan Newcomb, undated diary entry, between September 27 and October 20, 1866, Wallet 2, Anne Watts Baker Collection, Southwest Collection.

34. These accounts also come from Susan Newcomb's diary.

35. Samuel Newcomb, diary entry, January 17, 1866, Wallet 1, Anne Watts Baker Collection. Susan Newcomb's description of the same event: "Nothing happened to day except a little fun we had with a buffalo Mich Anderson drove one up late this evening and put him in pa's cowpen the boys roped his head and heels and threw him down, and men women and children all crowded around to take a peep at the wild wooly monster of the west. The boys after cuting him up pretty severly let him

out and he took his course right strait into the fort and came very near going into M. McCartys house and McCarty shot he turned then and went to the river the boys thought then they had seen enough fun and they killed him in the bed of the river." Diary entry, January 17, 1866.

36. Susan Newcomb, diary entry, June 22, 1867.

37. Ibid., September 27, 1866.

38. Samuel Newcomb, diary entry, July 30, 1865.

39. Ibid., February 12, 1864.

40. Susan Newcomb, diary entry, April 6, 1867.

41. Ibid., April 1, 1867.

42. Samuel Newcomb, diary entry, date unclear [likely 1864].

43. Susan Newcomb, diary entry, October 19, 1866.

44. Ibid., November 18, 1866.

45. There is a persistent popular myth that there were few women in Texas during this period. For an illuminating and empirically rich study of women and the ranching industry, see Maret, *Women of the Range.*

46. Susan Newcomb, diary entry, September 27, 1866.

47. The role of the bison herds' decline (and its extent) is a matter of some debate. For one perspective, see Flores, "Bison Ecology."

48. For background on immigration to Texas and war with American Indians, see G. Anderson, *Conquest of Texas.* Anderson's book puts struggles with Indians at the forefront of our understanding of the Mexican-American War.

49. G. Anderson, *Conquest of Texas,* 3.

50. The centrality of the Plains Indians to this story is the focus of DeLay, *War of a Thousand Deserts.* This also forms an important part of Hämäläinen, *Comanche Empire.* Another name for the war is the "US war with Mexico." See Chavez, *U.S. War with Mexico.*

51. DeLay, *War of a Thousand Deserts,* xiii.

52. G. Anderson, *Ethnic Cleansing,* as well as *Conquest of Texas.*

53. Mason Maxon correspondence, May 19, 1878, Box 11, Folder 2, Benjamin H. Grierson papers, Southwest Collection.

54. Affidavit of Witness [Richard Francklyn Tankersley], Box 2, File 1, Coggin Brothers and Associates Records, Southwest Collection.

55. Letter from Lieutenant of 10th Cavalry, Box 2, File 1, Coggin Brothers and Associates Records.

56. Special Orders No. 106, HQ department of Texas, May 31, 1875, Wallet 1, William Rufus Shafter papers, Southwest Collection.

57. Scholars have long argued that property is not an inherent quality of an object, but rather a bundle of rights attached to one. Yet this academic understanding of property bears little relation to the popular understanding, and it was this

understanding—one that saw cattle as inherently a rancher's property even far out-side the authority of the federal, state, or local government—that was key.

58. For a study of similar processes in early America, see V. Anderson, *Creatures of Empire*.

59. "Treaty with the Kiowa and Comanche," October 21, 1867, in Kappler, *Indian Affairs*, 977–82. For an overview of the framing of the treaty, its problems, and the conflict that precipitated it, see Chalfant, *Hancock's War*, particularly pp. 465–522.

60. Kappler, *Indian Affairs*, 978.

61. These rations were specifically stipulated in the agreement. As will be dis-cussed later in the chapter, white Americans would later view rations as a kind of handout or act of charity, when the reality was that they were actually part of a contract.

62. Ibid., 981.

63. Sherman to Sheridan, September 26, 1872, quoted in Athearn, "General Sherman," 45.

64. Kappler, *Indian Affairs*, 980–81.

65. For an overview of how the buffalo hunt worked, see M. Schultz, "Anatomy." According to Schultz (154), a commercial buffalo hunting operation was "highly efficient," with a complex division of labor (cook, hunter, skinner, etc.).

66. For the international trade angle, see M. Taylor, "Buffalo Hunt." Apparently because it was thicker and tougher than cattle leather, bison leather was especially well suited for shoe-sole leather as well as industrial belts for machinery. Ibid., 3169. On uses of hides and the state's role in the trade, see also Hanner, "Government Response."

67. Hämäläinen, *Comanche Empire*, 329.

68. For more information on Parker and Isatai, see Hämäläinen, *Comanche Empire*, 337. On army size, see J. Taylor, "Indian Campaign," 3.

69. G. West "Battle of Adobe Walls," 11–16.

70. Ibid., 18.

71. John Wesley Mooar, letter, July 7, 1874, John Wesley Mooar papers, South-west Collection.

72. Smits, "Frontier Army," 323.

73. For an overview of the battle and war from an archaeological perspective, see Cruse, *Battles*. For an engaging narrative of the war, see J. L. Haley, *Buffalo War*.

74. "Records of Events, 4th Cavalry, 1874," filed under Archambeau, Panhandle-Plains Historical Museum. This record of events is a copy of from Regimental Returns, September 1874, Record Group 94, National Archives and Records Administration.

75. Kiowa and Comanche Agency letters, January 17, 1878, Agency Letters, Office of Indian Affairs, Southwest Collection microfilm.

76. Ibid. It is important to note that this quotation is based on a translation, and hyperbolic language was part of the political process.

77. Cook, *Border and the Buffalo*, 115.

78. M. Schultz, "Anatomy," 142.

79. This quote is popular with the employees of Palo Duro State Park. I had my doubts about its veracity, but it appears everywhere, including biographies of O'Keeffe. See Reilly, *Georgia O'Keeffe*, 237.

80. For an interesting set of perspectives on the war, see Greene, *Battles and Skirmishes*, and *Lakota and Cheyenne*.

81. Sturgis, *Common Sense*, and *Ute War of 1879*.

82. Sturgis, *Common Sense*, 52.

83. Sheridan's wording, from Cook, *Border and the Buffalo*, 113. Cook relates the story as a first-hand account, though scholars have questioned its veracity. For my purposes, however, this is beside the point. More important than who said it is the underlying sentiment.

84. Mooar to his mother, March 5, 1879, Folder 2, John Wesley Mooar papers.

85. "Beef to Braves," *Aberdeen Daily News*, October 30, 1889.

86. C. C. French, quoted in Hunter and Price, *Trail Drivers of Texas*, 742.

87. "Standing Rock Agency: Scenes at the Distribution of Beef among the Indians," *Bismarck Daily Tribune*, January 11, 1888.

88. Ned Blackhawk makes a similar point that "native peoples were not relics of an ancient past but products of the most rapid territorial expansion in world history. Racial and cultural difference, however, more easily explained Indian misery." Blackhawk, *Violence over the Land*, 11.

89. F. Walker, *Indian Question*, 14–15.

90. Though these two camps roughly explain approaches to Indian policy, policies in general were quite muddled and contradictory. According to David Sim, "deep incoherence and dissonance" characterized the Peace Policy. Sim, "Peace Policy," 244.

91. Even President Grover Cleveland recognized this: "In these days when white agriculturalists and stock raisers of experience and intelligence find their lot a hard one, we ought not to expect Indians . . . to support themselves on the small tracts of land usually allotted them." Quoted in Hagan, "Private Property," 135.

92. Senate Select Committee, *Condition of the Indian Tribes*, 87.

93. Ibid., 59.

94. Ibid., 63.

95. Ibid., 261.

96. Letter dated September 26, 1877, from Superintendent William Nicholson, Kiowa and Comanche Agency Letters.

97. Hagan, "Kiowas, Comanches, and Cattlemen," 334. For a study of how cattlemen manipulated the reservation system on the northern Plains, see Sanderson, "We Were All Trespassers."

98. Contracts to supply the US Army were quite lucrative and a vital source of business for ranchers and other westerners. For a perspective on military contracts that finds far less corruption, see Miller, "Civilians and Military Supply."

99. The winning contracts for several South Dakota agencies for beef supply in 1885 ranged from $3.45 to $3.57 per hundred pounds, when prices in Chicago ranged from roughly a high of $5.50 to a low of $3.00 ("Indian Beef Contracts," *Aberdeen Weekly News*, June 19, 1885). For an example contract, see Senate Select Committee, *Condition of the Indian Tribes*, 300–301.

100. Abner Taylor to A. G. Boyce, October 18, 1889, Book 4, Letters Sent, Chicago Office, XIT Ranch collection, Panhandle-Plains Historical Museum. This is the only hard evidence I found of this practice, but ranchers were unlikely to discuss it openly. Based on letters about corruption and other more abstract discussions about disposing of difficult-to-sell cattle, my sense is that this was more common than it appears.

101. Stuart, *Forty Years*, 153.

102. Sanderson, "We Were All Trespassers," 62.

103. John Thayer, Letter dated [probably October 17], 1870, Box 882, Ayer Manuscript Collection, Newberry Library.

104. Sanderson, "We Were All Trespassers," 61. Teddy Roosevelt, a knowledgeable cattleman in his own right, commented on this problem when he visited the Pine Ridge Reservation. See Roosevelt, *Report*, 6.

105. For a detailed analysis of late-winter supply contracts, see Senate Select Committee, Condition of the Indian Tribes, 171–73.

106. Ibid., 159.

107. Ibid., 139.

108. Congress and Senate Committee on Indian Affairs, *Leases of Lands*, 20.

109. Ostler, *Plains Sioux*, 140.

110. Sanderson, "We Were All Trespassers," 56.

111. Hagan, "Kiowas, Comanches, and Cattlemen," 338–39.

112. Sanderson, "We Were All Trespassers," 60.

113. Teller explained to Senate investigators, "the privilege to graze cattle is but a license and not a lease. It conveys no interest in the lands occupied. It is true that the Indians did attempt to make leases with a fixed period during which the parties would, if the power existed, have all the rights of lessees, but doubting the power to make as well as the policy of such leasing, I declined to approve the same as a lease, but did treat them as amounting to a license to be revoked by the Indians at will." Congress and Senate Committee on Indian Affairs, *Leases of Lands*, 542.

114. For more detail on the Cherokee Strip, also known as the Cherokee Outlet, see Savage, *Cherokee Strip*. Savage provides a good account of the Cherokee Strip and the federal government's involvement in the issue. He emphasizes the inefficiency and incompetence of a federal bureaucracy that tried to manage or interfere with the informal leases between cattlemen and the Cherokee. While I agree with much of this, I believe Savage is too celebratory of these arrangements between cattlemen and Cherokee, ignoring the wider context of these leases as well as their effects on individual Cherokee residents (as opposed to the Cherokee political elite).

115. Congress and Senate Committee on Indian Affairs, *Leases of Lands*, 61.

116. Like much of the testimony surrounding the leasing controversy, the ranchers were evasive, but this claim (that low prices are in part a consequence of the leases' unclear legal status) seems to be the defense of Hunter and others, even as Hunter claims he believed he had tacit approval from the federal government. See testimony of R. D. Hunter, ibid., 61–65.

117. Ibid., 108–9.

118. Richard White makes an analogous argument in "Information, Markets, and Corruption." White argues that some business leaders believed that what today looks like corruption was considered acceptable by late nineteenth-century businessmen if they were doing something dubious that was ultimately for a common interest, like that of shareholders.

119. Congress and Senate Committee on Indian Affairs, *Leases of Lands*, 114.

120. Ibid., 119.

121. Ibid., 6–7.

122. Ibid., 505.

123. In a letter, Armstrong claimed his innocence and resigned in disgust with his treatment. It is hard to say whether or not he was guilty. See ibid., 507. Claims about pressure from Indian agents appeared elsewhere as well. A special agent investigating the situation in the Kiowa, Comanche, and Wichita Agency described the Indian agent there as "petty, distant, and repelling in his intercourse with the Indians." Ibid., 670.

124. The incident is recounted in ibid., 632–33.

125. Ibid., 654.

126. Ibid., 655–56.

127. In one case that was actually in favor of leasing, a man named Dick Rice appeared on a note purporting to express Pottawatomie opposition to one agreement, but told Indian Inspector Robert S. Gardner that he not only did not sign the document, but had supported the lease. See ibid., 733–34.

128. Nimmo et al., *Range and Ranch Cattle*, 19.

129. The belief that private property was the key to solving the Indian question has a lengthy history. See Hagan, "Private Property."

130. Though the area and its residents were initially exempted from the Dawes Act, a special measure later passed Congress (the Curtis Act of 1898).

131. Hagan, "Kiowas, Comanches, and Cattlemen." For more on rancher opposition to the Dawes Severalty Act, see Sanderson, "We Were All Trespassers," 65–69. On the struggles over severalty and, more broadly, the transformation of the area that became Oklahoma, see Lynn-Sherow, *Red Earth*.

132. For an analysis of the Plains Sioux reservation system and its relationship to US colonialism, see Ostler, *Plains Sioux*.

133. *Goodnight v. Comanche Nation*, US Justice Department Record of Indian Depredation Case No. 9133, Southwest Collection microfilm.

134. For an overview of the cases, see Skogen, *Indian Depredation Claims*.

135. Ibid.

136. See deposition of Jose Pieda Tafoya in *Goodnight v. Comanche Nation*.

137. Charles Goodnight, deposition in *Goodnight v. Comanche Nation*, [3].

138. In a letter to a client making a depredation claim, Isaac Hitt emphasizes the amity point. See Isaac Hitt, letter to client, May 1893, Box 2, File 1, Coggin Brothers and Associates Records.

139. Skogen, *Indian Depredation Claims*.

140. Isaac Hitt, letter to client, May 1893, Box 2, File 1, Coggin Brothers and Associates Records.

141. Deposition of Frank Collinson, Box 2, File 1, Coggin Brothers and Associates Records.

142. Charles Goodnight, deposition in *Goodnight v. Comanche Nation*.

143. Deposition notes, Box 2, File 1, Coggin Brothers and Associates Records.

144. Charles Goodnight, deposition in *Goodnight v. Comanche Nation*.

145. Manuel Gonzales, deposition in *Goodnight v. Comanche Nation*.

146. Court of Claims Testimony, Depredation Case Nos. 2996, 2997, and 3000, Southwest Collection microfilm.

147. Isaac Hitt, letter on evidence, Box 2, File 1, Coggin Brothers and Associates Records.

148. "Report of Agent Charles Adams," in "John Hittson Indian Depredation Suit," Southwest Collection microfilm.

149. Isaac Hitt, letter to client, May 1893, Box 2, File 1, Coggin Brothers and Associates Records.

150. This rewriting of the narrative is part of a broader struggle over the memory of conflict between American Indians and the US government and white Americans. See Cothran, *Remembering the Modoc War*; Grua, *Surviving Wounded Knee*; Kelman, *Misplaced Massacre*.

151. See Skogen, *Indian Depredation Claims*, 152, for detailed analysis.

152. Deposition notes, Box 2, File 1, Coggin Brothers and Associates Records.

153. In a sense, this chapter has looked at the role of human-animal relationships in the process of western expansion. For a look at the role of animals in overland travel during an earlier period, see Ahmad, *Success*.

154. Heather Cox Richardson explores this subject (which she refers to as a "paradox") in *West from Appomattox*. Her emphasis on an understanding of "true Americans" and the kind of pursuits that warrant government support explains this mind-set and is a perspective I share. It is also an example of how narratives and self-understandings drive the material settlement of the West, a process I also examine. Similarly, highlighting the centrality of the federal government to the history of the West is a central goal of Richard White in *It's Your Misfortune*.

155. On Fort Davis and the military's role in expansion in the Southwest, see Wooster, *Frontier Crossroads*.

156. The role of the frontier myth throughout American history is the focus of Richard Slotkin's work. See Slotkin, *Fatal Environment*, as well as *Regeneration through Violence*. A key figure in placing the cowboy and cattle ranching at the heart of the new Western myth was the author Zane Grey, popularizer of the Western as a genre. See Blake, "Zane Grey."

157. Sturgis, *Ute War of 1879*, 25. He also makes a similar point in *Common Sense*, when he notes that westerners are largely "of Yankee extraction" (3).

158. Violence as a central theme of western (and American) history is a position with which this chapter agrees. For the most emphatic defense of this view, see Blackhawk, *Violence over the Land*. I agree with Blackhawk and build on his point to suggest the centrality of these violent processes not just to the establishment of the American state, but also to industrial agriculture and animal husbandry.

159. The line "The red man was pressed . . ." is taken from the 1910 John Lomax version of the song. See Lomax, *Cowboy Songs*. The incredibly popular song has a strange history that includes a $500,000 lawsuit on the part of two Arizonans who claimed to have penned the song in 1905, despite Lomax's claims that it is much older (and strong evidence to that fact). See Mechem, "Home on the Range." Lomax's account in light of the lawsuit is also interesting, in "Half-Million Dollar Song." Finally, it is important to note that the theme of this part of the song, of the disappearing American Indian, was a popular trope that helped justify dispossession and ongoing exploitation. Despite these claims, American Indians did not disappear but remained an active and important part of western society.

Chapter Two: Range

1. Von Richthofen, *Cattle-Raising*, ix, 11. Von Richthofen wanted to sell books, but he also probably held a genuine desire to promote western American business interests. He was an important businessman in Denver, Colorado, and even helped

found that city's chamber of commerce. He was also the uncle of the famous German "Red Baron" flying ace, Manfred von Richthofen.

2. Ibid., 104.

3. Brisbin, *Beef Bonanza*, 194.

4. Von Richthofen, *Cattle-Raising*, 70–71.

5. Brisbin gives a comparably optimistic herd growth rate of 25 percent per year, assuming "good business management was displayed." See Brisbin, *Beef Bonanza*, 36. Optimistic math appears in Brisbin's book as well as (the aptly titled) B. C. Keeler's *Where to Go to Become Rich*. There is more on booster math in Gressley, *Bankers and Cattlemen*, 47–49.

6. Von Richthofen, *Cattle-Raising*, 7.

7. Brisbin, *Beef Bonanza*, 48.

8. Gressley, *Bankers and Cattlemen*, 63.

9. It is quite a story. See Gressley, "Teschemacher and deBillier."

10. Brayer, "Influence of British Capital," 92. According to J. Fred Rippy, the 1880s was one of the most significant periods of British capital investment abroad. He provides estimates comparable to those of Brayer for the extent and amount of British investment. See Rippy, "British Investments."

11. This is essentially the account in Stuart, *Forty Years*.

12. "Cattle Ranches in America," *Economist*, May 12, 1888.

13. Barnes, *Story of the Range*, 7.

14. McFerrin and Wills, "Who Said the Ranges," and their follow-up, "Big Die-Off."

15. On the land and cattle boom, specifically, there are several histories that emphasize the overstocking of the ranges; e.g., Osgood, *Day of the Cattleman*, and Mitchell and Hart, "Winter of 1886–1887." More broadly, works like Cronon, *Changes in the Land*, and R. White, *Roots of Dependency*, emphasize how landscapes and economic systems are intertwined, leading to ecological disaster as landscapes are incorporated into commodity markets. Regarding White and Cronon, their accounts are accurate, but sometimes the extent of the intertwinement of landscapes and economic systems, especially during the early phase of an area's integration into commodity markets, is overstated.

16. Or, to put it another way, certainty cost too much.

17. Skaggs, *Prime Cut*, 70.

18. Skaggs observes that "it is eminently arguable that the historical cattle ranch in America has received undue attention, then and now" (ibid., 69). While Skaggs is right, I still think analysis of the corporate ranching boom is necessary to understanding the rise of industrial beef production. Three reasons: first, as will be discussed in chapter 3, cattle markets were thoroughly integrated by the mid-1880s, and the rise and fall of corporate ranches reverberated across the nation's cattle mar-

kets. Midwestern ranchers and feeders not only competed with them, but they also bought many of their feeder cattle from the West. Similarly, while small stockholders controlled the majority of the cattle in the West, the large ranchers had much of the political power, and the conflict between large and small drove the development of the industry. Second, I emphasize the role of narratives in enabling and justifying industrial animal husbandry, and the struggle over corporate ranching produced some of the central myths of cattle ranching and the West. Following the boom, criticism of corporate ranching would be key to connecting ranching to the themes of independence, manhood, and authenticity. Finally, this chapter tells a story of alternate possibility for the cattle-beef complex. When large ranching, which was becoming increasingly common in the 1880s, failed, the meatpackers gained control over the supply chain in a way that small ranchers could never match. The large ranchers held sway not only over production but also over western political power, which represented a kind of property regime that could have challenged the Chicago meatpackers.

19. Brayer, "Influence of British Capital," 90.

20. Gressley, "Teschemacher and deBillier," 127. In addition to receiving money from Teschemacher's father, which was mentioned earlier in this chapter, the company secured investment from a number of the founders' Harvard classmates, including Teddy Roosevelt.

21. This account applies particularly to the period before widespread fencing. The spread of barbed wire and its effect on the industry is discussed later in this chapter.

22. Prairie Cattle Company, "Notice for Extraordinary General Meeting of Company on 12th June 1884; and statement by the board of directors," 7, Folder 15, Box 26, Dundee Records, Matador Land and Cattle Company Records, Southwest Collection.

23. Moreton Frewen, "Free Grazing: A Report to the Shareholders of the Powder River Cattle Co. Limited," 11, Folder 24, Box 23, Dundee Records.

24. This question was on investors' minds when the Prairie Cattle Company nearly went bankrupt. In an address to shareholders, J. Guthrie Smith asked "what constitutes a Cattle Company's 'profits'?" and entered a discussion of how revenue should be calculated relative to herd size. "The Prairie Cattle Company Limited to the Shareholders," 1, Folder 15, Box 26, Dundee Records.

25. Prairie Cattle Company, "Extraordinary General Meeting."

26. "American Cattle Companies in 1885," Economist, March 20, 1886.

27. Sommerville to Mackay, January 16, 1888, Folder 1, Box 2, Dundee Records. This concern appears in many of Sommerville's letters; e.g., Sommerville to Mackay, April 6, 1888, Folder 2, Box 2, Dundee Records, in which he suggests that proper counting methods for bulls must be adopted and the book count revised.

28. See, e.g., Sommerville to H. H. Campbell, December 4, 1883, Folder 8, Box 13, Headquarters Collection, Matador Land and Cattle Company Records. Here, Sommerville put a great deal of emphasis on the herd book: "I wait your official report + hope you will keep in mind to bring or send the Branding book itself which is, in reality, our only official record. I have to remind you also that I have not yet received your classification of the herd so often promised. It is hardly creditable to us that, twelve months after commencing business, we are still without a stock book; and I hope you will provide me with the data on which to base it."

29. "Land and Cattle Companies," letter to editor, *Economist*, April 7, 1883.

30. "Land and Cattle Companies," letter to editor, *Economist*, April 14, 1883.

31. Ibid.

32. John Clay, quoted in Mitchell and Hart, "Winter of 1886–1887," 4.

33. Frewen, "Free Grazing," 8.

34. Stuart, *Forty Years*, 144.

35. Michael D. Wise has used the history of human-wolf relations to rethink the remaking of the northern Rockies. His story raises and answers many important questions about industrial agriculture and human-animal relationships, as well as providing a fascinating account of the (often failed) attempts of people to eradicate wolves. See Wise, *Producing Predators*.

36. Tyng to Foster, April 1, 1887, Box 4, Francklyn Land and Cattle Company Records, Panhandle-Plains Historical Museum.

37. Ibid.

38. Managers were dubious about the wolf claims. See letter to Farwell, January 13, 1891, XIT Annual Reports—1889, Panhandle-Plains Historical Museum [misfiled].

39. Quoted in Nimmo et al., *Range and Ranch Cattle*, 103.

40. Ibid., 133.

41. *Breeder's Gazette* 7 (May 28, 1885): 819.

42. Nimmo, *Range and Ranch Cattle*, 43.

43. This was especially the case in southern Texas; see *Breeder's Gazette* 4 (August 30, 1883): 264: "dying in large numbers, because all of the water holes and most of the streams are dry."

44. Windmills were a frequent topic in the *Breeder's Gazette*; e.g., 4 (July 12, 1883): 42; 7 (March 19, 1885): 433. Regarding the Hansfield company's efforts, *Breeder's Gazette* 3 (June 21, 1883): 794.

45. Lomax, *Cowboy Songs*, 24.

46. H. H. Campbell to John Farwell, November 1, 1886, XIT Annual Reports—1886.

47. Mellars, "Fire Ecology"; Pyne, *Fire in America*, ch. 2; *Fire: A Brief History*.

48. Specht, "Rise, Fall, and Rebirth." Timothy LeCain takes a similar approach in *Matter of History*. For a different animal, see Boyd, "Making Meat." Regarding animal breeding, Gabriel Rosenberg argues breeding is informed by a variety of racial and political ideas. See Rosenberg, "Race Suicide."

49. H. H. Campbell to John Farwell, November 1, 1886, 18, XIT Annual Reports—1886.

50. Mercer, *Banditti of the Plains*, 13.

51. Sommerville to Mackay, June 24, 1887, Folder 10, Box 1, Dundee Records.

52. *Breeder's Gazette* 7 (March 12, 1885): 392. Today, calving season generally starts a bit earlier and the period from January to March is often considered ideal.

53. Tyng to de P. Foster, February 17, 1887, Box 4, Francklyn Land and Cattle Company Records.

54. "Report by Mr. John Stuart Smith 17 August 1889," 5, Folder 15, Box 26, Dundee Records.

55. Underwood to Fleming, November 4, 1882, Folder 1, Box 1, Dundee Records.

56. [Illegible, probably Mackay] to Robert Fleming, November 16, 1882, Folder 1, Box 1, Dundee Records.

57. Dave Weir to Sommerville, March 5, 1887, Folder 9, Box 1, Dundee Records.

58. "Proceedings at the Fourth Annual General Meeting 1889," 4, XIT Shareholder Proceedings, Panhandle-Plains Historical Museum.

59. Aztec Land & Cattle Company pamphlet, January 5, 1885, 5, Folder 24, Box 23, Dundee Records.

60. Ibid., 10.

61. "Report by Mr. John Stuart Smith 17 August 1889," 8, Folder 15, Box 26, Dundee Records.

62. Ibid., 6.

63. Manager's letter, September 30, 1886, Folder 1, Box 4, Espuela Land and Cattle Company (Spur Ranch) Records, Southwest Collection.

64. What constituted "established trailing routes," was of course a matter of sharp disagreement.

65. Lomax to Matthews & Reynolds, July 15, 1885, Folder 6, Box 5, Espuela Land and Cattle Company (Spur Ranch) Records.

66. Lomax to Mooar bros., February 1, 1886, Folder 6, Box 5, Espuela Land and Cattle Company (Spur Ranch) Records.

67. Lomax to Messrs Cage, Ladd & Small, June 5, 1886, Folder 6, Box 5, Espuela Land and Cattle Company (Spur Ranch) Records.

68. Abner Taylor to W. L. Wand, April 5, 1887, Book 1, 168, XIT Letters to Chicago, Panhandle-Plains Historical Museum.

69. *Breeder's Gazette* 9 (January 21, 1886): 75.

70. "Proceedings of the Stock Raisers Convention of Northwestern Texas Held at Graham on 15th and 16th of Feb, 1877," Wallet 1, Stock-Raisers Association of Northwestern Texas, Southwest Collection.

71. Conger, "Fencing in McLennan County," 219.

72. For an economist's take on the effect of barbed wire on agricultural development, see Hornbeck, "Barbed Wire." Hornbeck argues that barbed wire was vital to a world in which "states' inability to protect this full bundle of property rights on the frontier, beyond providing formal land titles, might have otherwise restricted agricultural development" (767). He concludes that "institutional failure was resolved not by legal reform but by technological change: the introduction of barbed wire fencing" (807). While I agree to an extent, the following pages of this chapter show that Hornbeck underestimates the extent to which state power and barbed wire were mutually reliant for establishing property rights.

73. *Breeder's Gazette* 4 (August 9, 1883): 169.

74. From the *Montana Live-Stock Journal*, quoted in *Breeder's Gazette* 10 (September 9, 1886): 370. Opposition to fencing, particularly on a kind of moral ground, is reminiscent of Karl Jacoby's study of local people's resistance to conservation laws and practices. Particularly Jacoby's use of "moral ecology" to describe rural people's historically-situated sense of the proper (and justifiable) organization of land, animals, and people. See Jacoby, *Crimes against Nature*.

75. For a study about barbed wire tensions as they relate to drought, see Gard, "Fence-Cutters." I largely agree with Gard, though he embraces the idea of barbed wire as a technological fix that only sparked momentary disruption. I emphasize the property regime that barbed wire helped enable, rather than simply the technology.

76. Gard, "Fence-Cutters," 7–10.

77. *Breeder's Gazette* 5 (March 6, 1884): 348.

78. Quoted in ibid., 4 (October 11, 1883): 490, and 4 (October 18, 1883): 525.

79. Gard, "Fence-Cutters," 4.

80. Ibid., 13–14.

81. William H. Kittrell, foreword to Mercer, *Banditti of the Plains*, xlvii.

82. Skaggs, *Prime Cut*, 65.

83. This strange story is described in Conger, "Fencing in McLennan County," 221.

84. For a good narrative of the war alongside a discussion of the property rights implications of the struggle, see McFerrin and Wills, "High Noon." For an environmental historian's perspective, see Belgrad, "Power's Larger Meaning."

85. For an (admittedly biased) overview of the relationship between Wyoming stock raising and political power in the state, see Mercer, *Banditti of the Plains*.

86. These two were the only deaths in the conflict, though there had been two infamous lynchings connected with the tensions in the years prior. For an excellent study of western violence, see Dykstra, "Quantifying the Wild West." Dykstra provides

a powerful critique of studies that claim high homicide rates in the nineteenth-century West. He explicitly leaves out war with American Indians, however, which was absolutely central to western expansion and a large part of the cultural idea that the West was a violent place. I would argue that the West was not particularly violent, in large part because of how successful the creation of a white-supremacist regime had been through forcible Indian land expropriation. Furthermore, Dykstra underestimates the cultural power of the violence mythology, which was not merely a twentieth-century phenomenon, but one present at the time as well. Nevertheless, his work on this subject has been an important corrective. See also Dykstra, "Overdosing on Dodge City."

87. *New York Times*, April 14, 1892, front page.

88. Mercer, *Banditti of the Plains*, 76.

89. Ibid., ch. 7–8.

90. Randy McFerrin and Douglas Wills see the fight as one over rival property regimes, though I think this might overemphasize homesteaders' role in the fight. Small ranchers would accept individual ownership of land to oppose the big ranches, but I am not sure it was their primary concern. For the property-rights perspective, see McFerrin and Wills, "High Noon."

91. Sommerville to Mackay, February 26, 1886, Vol. 1, Office Letter Press Book, Box 1, Headquarters Collection, Matador Land and Cattle Company Records.

92. Gressley, *Bankers and Cattlemen*, 54. Gressley argues that eastern investors often relied on family connections.

93. Murdo Mackenzie to Alexander Mackay, August 16, 1890, Folder 5, Box 2, Dundee Records.

94. Alexander Mackay to Matador board, October 9, 1888, Folder 3, Box 2, Dundee Records.

95. Sommerville to Mackay, March 25, 1884, Folder 3, Box 1, Dundee Records.

96. Sommerville to Mackay, December 11, 1884, Folder 6, Box 1, Dundee Records.

97. It is unclear how the dispute with Campbell was eventually resolved. See Johnstone to Mackay, January 6, 1892 [1893?], Folder 8, Box 2, Dundee Records, as well as Mackay to Ross, Chapman & Ross, Folder 2, Box 11, Dundee Records. Foreign ownership of lands was a hotly contested issue, with endless examples of political outrage, but it is unclear how much it actually affected businesses. For an overview of the outrage, see Rippy, "British Investments."

98. Prairie Cattle Company, "Report of Proceedings at Fifth Annual General Meeting," 13–14, Folder 15, Box 26, Dundee Records.

99. "Report of Committee of Investigation to the Shareholders," 1, Folder 15, Box 26, Dundee Records.

100. Ibid., 11.

101. Updegraff to family, November 6, 1885, File 1, Way Hamlin Updegraff papers, Southwest Collection.

102. Updegraff to mother, September 24, 1886, File 2, Way Hamlin Updegraff papers.

103. Updegraff to mother, January 12, 1887, File 3, Way Hamlin Updegraff papers.

104. Updegraff to mother, September 24, 1886, File 2, Way Hamlin Updegraff papers.

105. Updegraff to mother, March 5, 1886, File 1, Way Hamlin Updegraff papers.

106. Sheriff East, quoted in Allen, *Organized Labor in Texas*, 37. According to Gene Gressley, $25–$40/month was typical for the period; *Bankers and Cattlemen*, 151.

107. See Clayton et al., *Vaqueros, Cowboys, and Buckaroos*; Glasrud and Searles, *Black Cowboys*; Iverson, *When Indians Became Cowboys*; Massey, *Black Cowboys of Texas*. For an expansive synthetic social history of the cowboy, see Dary, *Cowboy Culture*.

108. N. Love, *Life and Adventures*.

109. "The Lone Star Trail"; Lomax, *Cowboy Songs*, 311.

110. "John Garner's Trail Herd"; ibid., 114.

111. "The Bull-Whacker"; ibid., 69.

112. "The Melancholy Cowboy"; ibid., 263.

113. "The Cowboy's Meditation"; ibid., 297.

114. "A Fragment"; ibid., 306.

115. "A Cowboy Toast"; Lomax, *Songs of the Cattle Trail*, 176.

116. "The Camp Fire Has Gone Out"; ibid., 322.

117. "The Old Cowman"; ibid., 165.

118. Lomax, *Cowboy Songs*, xxii.

119. "The Last Longhorn"; ibid., 199.

120. The longhorn declined as ranchers embraced more profitable, but less independent, breeds. This was part of a broader transition away from the hands-off approach to ranching described in this chapter and toward more hands-on (and smaller-scale) production.

121. "To Hear Him Tell It"; Lomax, *Songs of the Cattle Trail*, 39.

122. "The Disappointed Tenderfoot"; ibid., 183.

123. "The Dreary, Dreary Life"; Lomax, *Cowboy Songs*, 233.

124. There is a lengthy literature on John Lomax as well as his ethnomusicologist son, Alan Lomax. For John, see Allred, "Needle"; Filene, "Our Singing Country"; Mullen, "Representation in Folklore Studies"; Porterfield, *Last Cavalier*. On cowboy songs more broadly, see Slowik, "Capturing the American Past."

125. William Haywood, quoted in Allen, *Organized Labor in Texas*, 34.

126. For a book-length study of the strike and its context and consequences, see Lause, *Great Cowboy Strike*.

127. Some of these accounts rely on biased (against the strikers) newspaper reports, though the idea that the workers would oppose strike breakers is plausible. It

turns out the strike was picked up nationally. See: "Cowboys on a Strike," *Chicago Daily Tribune*, April 19, 1883; "Strike of the Cowboys," *New York Herald*, April 20, 1883.

128. See Allen, *Organized Labor in Texas*, and "Labor Troubles: A Good Place for 'Tenderfeet' to Steer Clear of," *Detroit Free Press*, April 20, 1883.

129. Allen, *Organized Labor in Texas*, 38–39.

130. *Breeder's Gazette* 5 (April 17, 1884): 592.

131. Allen, *Organized Labor in Texas*, 33–42.

132. Regarding small-scale ranching, the key was to present it as traditional and noncapitalist. That is to say, these ranchers made money, but they emphasized values greater than money (values like localism, family, and tradition). This made the later ideology of ranching noncapitalist, but, significantly, not anti-capitalist, since there was no critique of the broader economic system. With cattle labor, the public liked to imagine cowboys as noncapitalist and this public became uneasy when the strike revealed at least some cowboys to be anti-capitalist.

133. Perhaps the best example is "Cowboys on a Strike," *Chicago Daily Tribune*, April 19, 1883.

134. "Panhandle; Efficient," *Las Vegas Daily Gazette*, March 28, 1883.

135. See "Cowboys on a Strike," *Chicago Daily Tribune*, and "Labor Troubles," *Detroit Free Press*.

136. "Preparing for the Strike of the Cowboys," *Chicago Daily Tribune*, April 25, 1883.

137. Nimmo et al., *Range and Ranch Cattle*, 133.

138. Allen, *Organized Labor in Texas*, 40–41.

139. Jacqueline Moore has explored the interaction between class and gender on the cattle ranch. What was at stake in these conflicts were not merely questions of class, but also competing beliefs about the nature of manhood. See J. M. Moore, *Cow Boys*.

140. This observation is inspired by Gunter Peck's emphasis on considering "geographies of labor" in "Nature of Labor." See also Barca, "Laboring the Earth."

141. Campbell to Sommerville, January 27, 1886, Folder 8, Box 1, Dundee Records.

142. Sommerville to Mackay, April 30, 1888, Folder 2, Box 2, Dundee Records.

143. Sommerville to Mackay, June 5, 1888, Folder 2, Box 2, Dundee Records.

144. Though these were not the only bad winters. In the winter of 1884–85, Texas experienced "the heaviest [loss] ever known in Texas for some length of time and will probably not occur again for many years"; Nimmo et al., *Range and Ranch Cattle*, 132. Montana also saw heavy losses in the winter of 1881–82 (ibid., appendix 25).

145. Updegraff to family, July 9, 1886, File 1, Way Hamlin Updegraff papers.

146. Wheeler, "Blizzard of 1886," 422. For the following year, see Mitchell and Hart, "Winter of 1886–1887."

147. Bahre and Shelton, "Rangeland Destruction."

148. Wheeler, "Blizzard of 1886," 426.

149. For lengthy descriptions of the winters, see Mitchell and Hart, "Winter of 1886–1887."

150. Wheeler, "Blizzard of 1886," 426.

151. Matador manager Sommerville had to explain this to nervous investors following a tough winter in 1883; Sommerville to Mackay, February 9, 1883, Folder 1, Box 1, Dundee Records.

152. "Cattle Ranches in America," *Economist.*

153. See Stuart, *Forty Years*, 236. Also quoted in Mitchell and Hart, "Winter of 1886–1887."

154. Osgood, *Day of the Cattleman*, and Dale, *Range Cattle Industry*. Regarding the oversimplified narrative, the purpose here is not to celebrate (or condemn) either corporate ranching or small-scale ranching. Both are business types for good and ill, but the idea that they are radically different (or that the industry learned from its successes) can help elide ongoing problems of environmental degradation or labor exploitation. Further, it can inadvertently serve the purposes of meatpackers who trade on the ideology of small-scale ranching to market their products even as they exploit ranchers themselves. The real difference between the two periods was ranchers' potential for market power relative to the meatpackers, more than anti-corporate values such as localism, tradition, or independence.

155. Wheeler, "Blizzard of 1886," 416.

156. McFerrin and Wills, "Who Said the Ranges."

157. On the Southwest, see Sayre and Fernandez-Gimenez, "Genesis of Range Science."

158. For an overview of the origins of range management science, see Sayre and Fernandez-Gimenez, "The Genesis of Range Science." For a treatment of the entire history of rangeland science, see Sayre, *Politics of Scale.*

159. For an argument that ranchers understood almost nothing about the carrying capacity of ranges and the Plains climate, see Todd, "Discouraging Word." Todd is more convinced of the scale of the blizzards, but attributes the disaster less to investor greed and more to ignorance.

160. *Breeder's Gazette* 10 (July 29, 1886): 108.

161. Salmon, *Beef Supply*, 5.

162. Nimmo et al., *Range and Ranch Cattle*, 102. Unsurprisingly, Loving never clarifies whether he is on the list of tax-evading ranchmen. McFerrin and Wills, "Who Said the Ranges," explore tax evasion as well (17–18 in particular).

163. *Breeder's Gazette* 7 (February 19, 1886): 274. There are, however, reasons why this person could be lying as well.

164. By rationalize, I mean to make predictable, controlled, and nonthreatening. Profitability, then, depended on a landscape being in some sense "wild."

165. Osgood, *Day of the Cattleman*, 222.

166. George Tyng to Mr. F. de P. Foster, February 17, 1887, Box 4, Francklyn Land and Cattle Company Records.

167. Tyng's pessimism was well founded. While there were a variety of prices and significant variance by the day and carload, some general statistics are useful. By one metric, Chicago cattle prices (per 100 lb) in February 1887 were down nearly 16% over the previous year ($3.85 to $3.24) and down nearly 36% from two years previously ($5.03). Based on Chicago Board of Trade reports, this is a running average of market prices. Data from National Bureau of Economic Research, "Wholesale Price of Cattle."

168. Telegram received by Sommerville, September 1, 1887, Folder 10, Box 1, Dundee Records.

169. Tyng to Foster, February 17, 1887, Box 4, Francklyn Land and Cattle Company Records.

170. For an overview of the ranch's history, see Sheffy, *Francklyn Land & Cattle*.

171. Tyng to Foster, September 24, 1886, Box 4, Francklyn Land and Cattle Company Records.

172. Tyng, letter, June 1887, Box 4, Francklyn Land and Cattle Company Records.

173. Sommerville to Mackay, November 25, 1885, Folder 7, Box 1, Dundee Records.

174. "American Cattle companies in 1885," *Economist*.

175. On "unprecedentedly low," see Prairie Cattle Company, "Fifth Annual General Meeting," 6–7. Regarding prices, Chicago Board of Trade, *Twenty-Ninth Annual Report*, 31.

176. Mitchell and Hart, "Winter of 1886–1887," 5, n. 9.

177. Sommerville to Mackay, May 4, 1888, Folder 2, Box 2, Dundee Records.

178. Chicago Board of Trade, *Thirty-Fourth Annual Report*, 56.

179. From an unsigned/undated draft of a letter, probably by John Farwell. "Letter to the Chairman and Board of Directors," 4–5, XIT Annual Reports—1887.

180. "Report by Mr. John Stuart Smith 17 August 1889," 4, Folder 15, Box 26, Dundee Records.

181. Osgood, *Day of the Cattleman*, 222–24.

182. Brayer, "Influence of British Capital," 98.

183. This is similarly a conclusion of Gressley, "Teschemacher and deBillier."

184. Osgood explores the rivalry between big and small ranchers as well as the spread of farming onto ranges as crucial trends at the time of the disastrous winters of the 1880s. These winters greatly weakened the largest stock owners, to the benefit

of these latter parties. For more, see Osgood, *Day of the Cattleman*, "Disaster and Transition." Osgood concludes his narrative of the decline of large-scale ranching with the observation that "isolated ranches, where small cattlemen maintain themselves by combining winter feeding and a partial utilization of the range for summer pasturage . . . these have succeeded the great range outfits of other days"; Osgood, *Day of the Cattleman*, 258. More evidence comes from Peter Simpson's social history of ranching in Oregon. He makes one of his central claims that "the modern cattleman descended from victorious would-be farmers and small cattle growers who won the classic feud between sodbusters and cattle barons"; Simpson, "Social Side," 42. Edward Everett Dale traces a similar trajectory from larger to smaller ranches, though emphasizes settlement and land prices. I would argue that the failure of the boom (and its dynamics) explains all of these processes. For Dale's discussion, see *Range Cattle Industry*.

185. For an example in the Pacific Northwest, see Simpson, "Social Side."

186. As Osgood explains, "those who still remained in the business found the margin of profit so small that a winter loss that had been but an average one in the old days would now prove ruinous"; *Day of the Cattleman*, 224. A similar claim is made in Simpson, "Social Side."

187. *Breeder's Gazette* 9 (January 7, 1886): 3.

188. Raish and McSweeney, "Livestock Ranching"; J. Schultz, *Sociocultural Factors*; Simpson, "Social Side."

189. H. H. Campbell to John Farwell, November 1, 1886, 18, XIT Annual reports—1886.

190. This myth of ranching coexisted awkwardly with the claim that a certain kind of authentic frontier lifestyle had passed away with the decline of the open range. See Osgood, *Day of the Cattleman*, 229. This mythology was not only believed by people outside the West, but also was important for ranchers themselves moving into the twentieth century. This explained some of their reluctance to embrace more market-oriented practices. For an argument about the role of culture and traditional practices in the course of the industry, see Simpson, "Social Side," 47–48.

191. Despite the collapse of the boom, a few corporate ranches did survive this period (though generally just barely). One example is the Cherokee Strip Live Stock Association, which survived until 1893. The association was hurt badly by the end of the boom, but perhaps it survived because it was an agglomeration of a number of smaller locally owned ranches, as opposed to the multinational behemoths that comprise the primary focus of this chapter. The most famous survivor in this category is the Matador ranch, which despite major setbacks in the late 1880s survived under Scottish ownership until 1951. It then was liquidated, though significant portions of the ranch were ultimately sold to Fred Koch, one of the cofounders of Koch Industries. It still operates as part of that company. Though corporate ranches

still survive, they are not on anything like the scale (relatively) of the 1880s. Further, their relative importance to the beef supply chain is much diminished.

Chapter Three: Market

1. Chicago Board of Trade, *Thirty-Fifth Annual Report*, 26.

2. Despite Chicago's importance as a commodity center, it was a clearinghouse rather than final destination. Cities like New York and London were much larger local markets, but it was the fact that Chicago was the great aggregator and processor of western commodities before distributing them across the country (and world) that made it so important as a market.

3. This is a study of the cattle marketing system that emphasizes space, place, and questions of scale. For a similar study of the beef commodity chain and questions of space, see Hoganson, "Meat in the Middle." Hoganson observes that "all too often, local histories begin with maps rather than ending with them, filling in predetermined outlines rather than following the threads that have bound particular places and communities to wider webs" (1026). This is a powerful way of understanding the issue. My chapter develops a framework for understanding these webs. Hoganson's key suggestion is pairing an examination of a particular commodity with a local history of place, allowing the two to tease out questions of scale and the relationship between places. While my focus is on much of the United States, particular moments in this chapter (such as on the rise and fall of cattle towns), take just this approach.

4. This does leave out finance, which was a vital part of the industry (as with any industry). I think of finance as (in a sense) fitting with the moving-cattle part of the system. Capital keeps the wheels of the entire system turning. See Gressley, *Bankers and Cattlemen*.

5. While this system was basically national, California was an important exception. The state contained its own hoof-to-table cattle system that was largely separate from the industry in the rest of the country. It was also dominated (unusually) by a ranching corporation. See Igler, *Industrial Cowboys*. On pp. 160–67, Igler tells a fascinating story of the fight between Miller & Lux and the Chicago packers for control of the San Francisco market. Finally, the American South was a different case as well. Rates of beef consumption were much lower in the South, making the system far less important there until into the twentieth century. Poultry production, however, was important in the region, and that industry's story shares some of the dynamics examined throughout this book. See Gisolfi, *Takeover*.

6. Feedlots are animal feeding operations that confine cattle to a relatively small area and fatten them on grain for a period of roughly three to six months before sale.

7. A very large percentage of the nation's cattle were in these regions, though it is important to note that feeders often bought and fattened western (particularly Texan)

cattle. See Hoganson, "Meat in the Middle." When it came to high-end cattle, there were also parallel operations around other major cities, such as New York and Boston.

8. On pigs as urbanites, see Hartog, "Pigs and Positivism." Pigs were also city dwellers in the medieval period; see Jørgensen, "Running Amuck?"

9. For discussion of these difficulties and some of the ways government bureaucrats tried to overcome them, see Salmon, *Beef Supply*. The number of beef cattle per thousand people did decrease dramatically during the Civil War from 542 in 1860 to 386 in 1870. In 1889, there were 523 beef cattle per thousand people. For more, see ibid., 6. On increasing animal weights and the general improvement in quality leading to more available meat, see ibid., 7.

10. US Bureau of Corporations, *Report of the Commissioner*, 3.

11. Dale, *Range Cattle Industry*, 101.

12. Ibid., 109.

13. Dale places the relationship between western cattle raising and corn-belt fattening at the center of his analysis. See ibid., ch. 8.

14. Frank Stillman, letter, September 16 [year illegible], Folder 16, Box 24, Dundee Records. Ernest Osgood makes a similar point in his work on the cattle-raising industry: "From the outset the market for Texas cattle had been a threefold one: first, the Northern grazing grounds of Colorado, Dakota, Wyoming, and Montana . . . second, the eastern stock centers, which each year received the beef steers . . . and third, the feeders of the middle west." Osgood, *Day of the Cattleman*, 90.

15. On the difficulty Texas ranchers had in fattening cattle and improving breeding (as opposed to simply making the skeleton), see Prairie Cattle Company, "Fifth Annual General Meeting," 8.

16. Frank Stillman, letter, September 8, 1886, Folder 16, Box 24, Dundee Records.

17. See C. Love, "Cattle Industry."

18. Igler, *Industrial Cowboys*.

19. C. Love, "Cattle Industry," 382.

20. See Henlein, *Cattle Kingdom*. The Ohio River Valley cattle area roughly encompasses Illinois, Indiana, Kentucky, and parts of Ohio. Henlein's book is one of the best on the early cattle-raising and meatpacking industries.

21. Clemen, "Cattle Trails," 428.

22. Clemen, *American Livestock*, 72.

23. These contests amount to a "spatial politics," along the lines explored by Richard White, who emphasizes how political contestation shapes infrastructural development, quite literally changing relationships of distance and mobility between places; see R. White, *Railroaded*.

24. During the 1880s, $10 in corn could fatten an animal by three to four hundred pounds. Some information about prices is discussed in Frank Stillman, letter, August 30, 1886, Folder 16, Box 24, Dundee Records.

25. Hogs waste less corn and fatten more efficiently, so there was less risk involved; Henlein, *Cattle Kingdom*, 72–73. Henlein describes corn farmers' flexibility colorfully: "Corn was king, but that did not necessarily make the steer prime minister" (72).

26. Pate, *America's Historic Stockyards*, 94.

27. Sommerville to managers, August 15, 1890, Folder 5, Box 2, Dundee Records.

28. Some of this backstory is discussed in Clemen, *American Livestock*, ch. 2.

29. Ibid., 69–70.

30. For more, see ibid., 85.

31. For a nineteenth-century overview of Kansas City as a livestock market, see Powell, *Twenty Years*.

32. For Armour's involvement in Kansas City, see Pate, *America's Historic Stockyards*, 85–89.

33. Ibid., 73.

34. To deal with the large volume, railroads require expensive loading and unloading facilities. This makes the economies of scale considerable. Truck distribution facilities are relatively cheaper to build, allowing for distribution points to be widely dispersed.

35. "Report by Mr. John Stuart Smith," 15.

36. "The American Cattle and Dead Meat Industry," *Economist*, February 21, 1885.

37. This suspicion was euphemistically referred to as European "prejudices," in Chicago Board of Trade, *Twentieth Annual Report*, 15.

38. Ibid., 16–17. For more details on shipments, see "The Cattle Interest in the United States," *Economist*, September 12, 1885.

39. Frank Stillman, letter, October 4, 1886, Folder 16, Box 24, Dundee Records, quoting "Mr. Walker of Victoria," a large stockholder.

40. Sommerville to Mackay, January 19, 1883, Folder 1, Box 1, Dundee Records.

41. A "dogie" was a motherless calf that straggled at the back of a herd out of fear or desire to return to its mother. Even in the nineteenth century the term was obscure outside of cowboy circles. In his memoir of his time as a cattleman, Teddy Roosevelt spells it "doughgies" and adds that it is "a name I have never seen written; it applies to young immigrant cattle." His definition is not quite the same as the more popular meaning, but the term was perhaps used flexibly. See Roosevelt, *Ranch Life*, 89. These lyrics copied from Lomax, *Cowboy Songs*, 87. Lomax actually dedicated the volume to Theodore Roosevelt.

42. McCoy, *Historic Sketches*, 20.

43. Ibid., 29.

44. Bailey, *Texas Cowboy's Journal*, 67.

45. "Jayhawker" was originally a term to refer to free-soil guerrillas who fought against pro-slavery groups during the period before the American Civil War. Here, Daugherty is using the term pejoratively to refer to essentially anti-southern bandits.

46. Hunter and Price, *Trail Drivers of Texas*, 699. The meaning of this story is hard to know for certain. Texas fever, as will be explored later in this chapter, was a serious problem, so the men could have been honestly upset about the threat. More than the veracity of Daugherty's account is how it reflects the tensions of the early days of the cattle trade.

47. McCoy, *Historic Sketches*, 56.

48. Both Skaggs, *Cattle-Trailing Industry* (3), and Worcester, *Chisholm Trail* (137), provide the same estimate.

49. Skaggs, *Cattle-Trailing Industry*, 88.

50. Worcester, *Chisholm Trail*, 137. Worcester makes the important point, though, that by retaining ownership and assuming risk, the rancher stood to gain more if prices were good at the time of final sale.

51. Jimmy Skaggs has referred to trailers as "hip-pocket businessmen." See Skaggs, *Cattle-Trailing Industry*, 10.

52. Pryor figure is from Worcester, *Chisholm Trail* (139); 57,000 figure is from Hunter and Price, *Trail Drivers of Texas* (510).

53. Worcester, *Chisholm Trail*, 138–39.

54. Sam Neill, quoted in Hunter and Price, *Trail Drivers of Texas*, 256.

55. G. W. Scott, quoted in ibid., 116. Scott describes a time when "range was dry and water scarce, and many of our cattle gave out and had to be left on the trail."

56. John James Haynes, quoted in ibid., 246. Another account talks about local farmers asking for the excess calves, since outfits often simply killed them anyway (860).

57. This was also an issue when mothers were separated from their yearlings at cattle markets. R. J. Rennings described trying to get a herd away from a bunch of recently sold yearlings as particularly difficult because the mothers would often try to return to their offspring, reversing the herd's progress. Rennings used a particularly colorful comparison to make his point: "I was two or three days getting away from where we cut the cows from their yearlings; we moved like a snail climbing a slick log, so far up in daytime, slipping back at night"; ibid., 535.

58. John James Haynes, quoted in ibid., 246.

59. John M. Sharpe writing about D. H. Snyder, in ibid., 724.

60. James Marion Garner, quoted in ibid., 585.

61. W. M. Shannon, quoted in ibid., 607.

62. Bailey, *Texas Cowboy's Journal*, 5.

63. John Jacobs, quoted in Hunter and Price, *Trail Drivers of Texas*, 663.

64. John Sharpe describes using two "lead steers" that were "trained swimmers" to get a herd across a river. See ibid., 724.

65. Tom Welder, quoted in ibid., 293.

66. John C. Jacobs, quoted in ibid., 663.

67. Regarding the "slowest drag," see Stuart, *Forty Years*, 232.

68. McCoy, *Historic Sketches*, 82.

69. Ike T. Pryor, quoted in Hunter and Price, *Trail Drivers of Texas*, 367.

70. W. T. Jackman, quoted in ibid., 859.

71. Jim Ellison explains that on his first drive in 1868, they brought only a hundred cattle, which at the time "was considered a large herd"; ibid., 538.

72. Fletcher and Gard, *Up the Trail*, 7.

73. Ike T. Pryor in Hunter and Price, *Trail Drivers of Texas*, 367.

74. McCoy, *Historic Sketches*, 95.

75. Fletcher and Gard, *Up the Trail*, 10.

76. McCoy, *Historic Sketches*, 81.

77. Almost every narrative is organized around river crossings and the search for water. Good examples are G. H. Mohle's account in Hunter and Price, *Trail Drivers of Texas*, 43, as well Sam Dunn Houston's narrative in the same volume (71–88). But this is true of most narratives.

78. Stuart, *Forty Years*, 192.

79. McCoy, *Historic Sketches*, 160.

80. Addressed in Fletcher, *Up the Trail*, 45, and elsewhere.

81. Shaw, *North from Texas*, 39–40. The point about cattle smelling water is a strange, but fairly common claim. Since water is odorless, they are probably describing the ability of cattle to smell the kinds of things that exist near water (vegetation, etc.).

82. Richard Withers, quoted in Hunter and Price, *Trail Drivers of Texas*, 312.

83. Adams, *Log of a Cowboy*, 60.

84. Ibid., 62.

85. Joseph Spaugh says that it is "well known" that extremely dehydrated cattle go blind; quoted in Hunter and Price, *Trail Drivers of Texas*, 945.

86. Sam Garner, quoted in ibid., 522.

87. Ibid., 523.

88. Fletcher and Gard, *Up the Trail*, 40.

89. Ibid., 41.

90. Blevins, *Dictionary*, 309.

91. A. Huffmeyer, quoted in Hunter and Price, *Trail Drivers of Texas*, 263: "every one of them showed fight when we pulled him out of the quicksand, and took right after us, and we had to hustle to keep out of reach." See also Shaw, *North from Texas*, 38. A fictionalized account of bogged cattle also appears in Adams, *Log of a Cowboy*, ch. 11, "A Boggy Ford," 158–76. There was also the expression to "pull bog"; see Blevins, *Dictionary*, 296.

92. G. H. Mohle, quoted in Hunter and Price, *Trail Drivers of Texas*, 43.

93. Shaw, *North from Texas*, 37.

94. McCoy, *Historic Sketches*, 97.

95. On the buffalo concern, see Shaw, *North from Texas*, 58. Yet stampedes could also occur for no reason at all. W.D.H. Saunders claimed that, while grazing in a field, "the cattle became frightened at [a] haystack and stampeded"; quoted in Hunter and Price, *Trail Drivers of Texas*, 267.

96. McCoy, *Historic Sketches*, 99–100: "during rainy, stormy season, herds of cattle are apt to form the habit of stampeding every cloudy or stormy night."

97. Bailey, *Texas Cowboy's Journal*, 11.

98. Ibid., 15.

99. Ibid., 16.

100. Shaw, *North from Texas*, 47.

101. George W. Brock, quoted in Hunter and Price, *Trail Drivers of Texas*, 221.

102. Fletcher and Gard, *Up the Trail*, 33.

103. Ibid., 16.

104. Ibid., 16–17.

105. Ibid., 48.

106. All of these trails have been written about extensively, perhaps most famously the Chisholm trail. Wayne Gard's book on the subject includes a bibliography of 300+ items. See Gard, *Chisholm Trail*. Even in the decade following the first publication of Gard's book in 1954, there was further interest in the subject. See Jager, "Mountain of Words."

107. M. J. Ripps, quoted in Hunter and Price, *Trail Drivers of Texas*, 470.

108. V. M. Carvajal, quoted in ibid., 549.

109. A. M. Gildea, quoted in ibid., 982. He is reporting information he received from Chisum and his men, and using it to explain why his outfit was particularly alert while moving through the reservation.

110. A. Huffmeyer, quoted in ibid., 265.

111. Thomas Welder, quoted in ibid., 294.

112. "Spanish Fever Scare," *Western Recorder*, August 8, 1884.

113. "Texas Fever among Cattle," *New York Times*, July 30, 1884. See also "The Texas Cattle Fever," *New York Times*, July 29, 1873. "Droop" or "droopy" were common adjectives for describing the affects of Texas fever.

114. Skaggs, *Cattle-Trailing Industry*, 106.

115. National Cattle Growers' Association, *Proceedings*, 108.

116. For an overview of the origins of the Bureau of Animal Industry as well as conflicts over diseases, state power, and scientific authority, see Olmstead and Rohde, *Arresting Contagion*.

117. Salmon, "Texas Fever," 293.

118. National Cattle Growers' Association, *Proceedings*, 105.

119. Ibid., 112. This disagreement over the scientific understanding of Texas fever was not pure opportunism on the part of Texas ranching interests; skepticism existed on both sides. When a Dr. Wozancraft presented his own account of the disease—one that saw quarantine legislation as misguided—quarantine supporters described him as "one of the great army of cranks"; *Breeder's Gazette* 9 (April 15, 1886): 532.

120. McCoy, *Historic Sketches*, 151.

121. For more on the confusion about the nature of Texas fever, see Havins, "Texas Fever."

122. "More of the Cattle Fever," *New York Times*, September 8, 1884.

123. Galenson, "Cattle Trailing," 461.

124. McCoy, *Historic Sketches*, 188.

125. "Texas Cattlemen Aroused," *New York Times*, November 29, 1885.

126. There had been a convention on the issue of Texas fever as far back as 1868, and although participants established a basic understanding of the disease, their conclusions were far from common knowledge. See Snow, *Convention of Cattle Commissioners*.

127. J. E. Haley, "Texas Fever."

128. Letter from Charles Goodnight to the ranch, quoted in ibid., 42. Goodnight was, of course, in northern Texas (just outside Texas fever's endemic area), where official quarantines were not a real political issue, but his attitude was indicative of a broader sentiment.

129. The role of pleuropneumonia is stressed in Osgood, *Day of the Cattleman*, 165–70.

130. National Cattle Growers' Association, *Proceedings*, 41.

131. Ibid., 45.

132. Ibid., 50.

133. Ibid., 84.

134. In addition to railing against those who opposed Texas fever restrictions, the *Breeder's Gazette* was obsessed with the vexatiousness of the system of irregular and often unenforced quarantines. See "vexatious and embarrassing" state-based solutions in " 'Regulating' Texas Fever," *Breeder's Gazette* 5 (May 22, 1884): 788.

135. 49 Cong. Rec. 17, pt. 4, 3936 (April 28, 1886).

136. Skaggs, *Cattle-Trailing Industry*, 120.

137. Galenson, "Cattle Trailing," 463.

138. Strom, "Texas Fever," 55.

139. The dispossession argument is Strom's central assertion in "Texas Fever." Small ranchers hated government-stipulated cattle dipping vats so much that they

would often vandalize them and threaten government veterinarians; ibid., 49–74. See also Strom, *Making Catfish Bait*.

140. The definitive book on Joseph McCoy and the Chisholm trail is Sherow, *Chisholm Trail*.

141. Small-town merchants in the American West have been understudied in recent years. For some of the earliest work, see Atherton, "Frontier Merchant," and *Pioneer Merchant*. For a more recent look (and one that suggests there is a lot more to be found and written on this subject), see English, *By All Accounts*.

142. On the names and theme, see Dykstra, *Cattle Towns*, 87.

143. For an overview, see Carol Leonard and Walliman, "Prostitution and Changing Morality."

144. For an early account of Ellsworth, see Streeter, "Ellsworth." I explore the story of Ellsworth in more detail in Specht, "Future in the Distance." Thanks are due to an anonymous reader of that article, who disagreed with some of my claims about Ellsworth and provided some useful information about the town.

145. Dykstra, *Cattle Towns*, 31–34.

146. Ibid., 34–35.

147. William Sigerson & Company, *To Cattle Owners and Dealers* (St. Louis, 1869), Everett D. Graff Collection, Newberry Library.

148. Gard, *Chisholm Trail*, 100.

149. McCoy, *Historic Sketches*, 57.

150. Dykstra, *Cattle Towns*, 38.

151. Kansas Pacific Railway Company, "Guide to the Kansas Pacific Railway" (map) (1872), call no. K Port 385 Un3 W528, Folder 9, Kansas Historical Society, Topeka.

152. Ibid., 41.

153. This is a possibly apocryphal tale that has been told many times. See, e.g., Gard, *Chisholm Trail*, 187.

154. Dykstra, *Cattle Towns*, 41.

155. The sidewalk claim is amusing, if dubious. Presumably this meant the only sidewalk in Kansas west of Kansas City. It seems likely there was a sidewalk in Denver in 1870 and almost certainly in California.

156. Ibid., 163–68.

157. Worcester, *Chisholm Trail*, 127.

158. McCoy, *Historic Sketches*, 57.

159. It only seems fair to note that it was more likely the promoters of the Kansas Pacific than the residents of Ellsworth who perpetrated this fraud.

160. For an excellent overview of cattle shipping technology and concerns, see J. White, "Riding in Style" (on the point about injuries, 266).

161. Ibid., 267.

162. Clemen, *American Livestock*, 197.

163. Ibid., 200.

164. White, "Riding in Style," 269, provides a good overview and image.

165. This was a finding of a Senate committee investigating the livestock industry. For more details, see Clemen, *American Livestock*, 200.

166. Relatively simple cars for transporting livestock—known as "stock cars"— did eventually become popular in the late nineteenth century, but these looked like a standard boxcar with slats for increased ventilation. Elaborate stock cars, such as the ones discussed above, never entered general use.

167. Rhode Island Railroad Commissioner, *Annual Report*, 105.

168. 25 cents/head was the charge in Kansas City. For a good overview of the Kansas City yards, see the Vest Committee testimony of Harry P. Child, superintendent of the Kansas City Stock Yards, in Select Committee, *Transportation and Sale*, 376.

169. For a lengthy description of the prod and cattle deaths, see Clemen, *American Livestock*, 195–97.

170. Sommerville to Mackay, January 19, 1883, Folder 1, Box 1, Dundee Records.

171. "General intelligence office" observation made by commission merchant quoted in Skaggs, *Cattle-Trailing Industry*, 76. This might be an optimistic reading or best-case scenario. Regarding cost estimates, see Select Committee, *Transportation and Sale*, 497. On the 5%–10% pricing, see Skaggs, *Cattle-Trailing Industry*, 76.

172. American Live Stock Commission Company to Sommerville, July 18, 1889, Folder 8, Box 13, Headquarters Collection, Matador Land and Cattle Company Records.

173. Sommerville to Hunter, Evans & Company, November 1, 1888, Letter Press Book, Box 13, Headquarters Collection, Matador Land and Cattle Company Records.

174. Hunter was politically very active and turns up in the transcripts of many cattleman's association meetings, and even testified to the Vest Committee: Select Committee, *Transportation and Sale*, 178. For an account of Hunter and his company, see Skaggs, *Cattle-Trailing Industry*, 78–84.

175. Sommerville to Mackay, January 19, 1883, Folder 1, Box 1, Dundee Records.

176. Letter to Espuela chairman, February 12, 1888, Folder 3, Box 5, Espuela Land and Cattle Company (Spur Ranch) Records.

177. For specifics, see Hazlett, "Chaos and Conspiracy," and Olson, "Regulation."

178. Hazlett, "Chaos and Conspiracy," 134.

179. Ibid., 137.

180. Ibid., 140.

181. Ibid., 144.

182. Cuyler to Mackay, July 3, 1891, Folder 7, Box 2, Dundee Records.

183. Alexander McNab, letter, July 1, 1889, Folder 3, Box 5, Espuela Land and Cattle Company (Spur Ranch) Records.

184. Telegram to Sommerville, September 1, 1887, Folder 10, Box 1, Dundee Records.

185. Sommerville to Mackay, December 6, 1887, Folder 11, Box 1, Dundee Records.

186. Select Committee, *Transportation and Sale*, 6.

187. Ibid., 183.

188. Ibid., 299.

189. Ibid., 376.

190. Ibid., 212.

191. Ibid., 4.

192. Ibid., 268.

193. Meeting transcript from Texas Cattle Raiser's Association materials [document may predate the association], Wallet 1, Stock-Raiser's Association of Northwestern Texas, Southwest Collection.

194. Scott, *Seeing like a State*.

195. Tsing, "Supply Chains."

196. For details, see Condra and Leib, *Cottage Food Laws*, introduction. This is not to attack the idea of government regulation of food products (though this exact argument is often used to do so). Rather, it is to indicate that a conversation about the contours and scale of American food production is necessary.

Chapter 4: Slaughterhouse

1. To be precise, the Big Four were alleged to operate as an oligopsony-oligopoly. That is to say, the claim was that they functioned as a small number of collusive buyers of cattle on one end of the supply chain and a small number of collusive sellers of beef on the other.

2. "Both ends of the string" was a phrase that appeared multiple times in the testimony; see, e.g., Select Committee, *Transportation and Sale*, 267. The other quote is taken from ibid., 455. The biggest meatpacking companies during the late nineteenth century were popularly known as the Big Four. The term would be expanded to the Big Five and then the Big Six in the early twentieth century.

3. Ibid., 477.

4. This quotation appears in a written statement in defense of what Armour refers to as "different rules" by which one must now evaluate his industry. Ibid., 434.

5. Clemen, *American Livestock*, 6–7.

6. Ibid., 9.

7. Ibid., 243.

8. The literature on meatpacking has existed within an organizational-technological frame. See the pioneering work of Mary Yeager in *Competition and Regulation*. This is also a theme of her earlier article on the subject; see Yeager Kujovich, "Refrigerator Car." Yeager traces social conflict, but only as it was precipitated by the refrigerator car. Though I largely agree with her analysis, there is a question of emphasis: she connects success in the conflict between the meatpackers and their rivals to the use of the technology. I would place the emphasis on the opposite; the technology was only more efficient because of the success of certain practices and legal reforms and the failure of others. This technological/organizational approach was also evident in Alfred Chandler's coverage of Swift & Company in *Visible Hand*, ch. 12. More recently, see Perren, *Taste, Trade and Technology*. Perren is exactly right when he asserts in the introduction that much of the literature on meatpacking is overly invested in criticism of business practices, sanitation, etc. Yet he treats these criticisms as minor issues, whereas I believe it is essential to explore these debates to understand the ultimate shape of the meat industry. That said, Perren's book provides much-needed global coverage and a strong analysis of taste preferences, class, and market segmentation. Similarly, Roger Horowitz in *Putting Meat* is quite strong on the linkages between consumption and production, but in that book underemphasizes the role of social conflict in shaping the food production regime. His book does, however, cover the production of a variety of meats, which provides important context for the present story. Horowitz does explore conflict (within the slaughterhouse) in *Negro and White*.

9. For an overview of the incident discussed here, see Illinois Supreme Court, *Reports of Cases*, 156–61, *Swift & Company v. Rutkowski* (1897).

10. Child labor was quite common during the period and mostly unproblematic. Workers' concerns were more with safety issues (such as the one outlined here) rather than blanket concern for child workers. The late nineteenth century was the moment when child labor became a social problem, in part (according to James Schmidt) as families sought compensation for industrial accidents. See Schmidt, *Industrial Violence*.

11. Illinois Supreme Court, *Reports of Cases*, 157.

12. Ibid., 159–60. The Supreme Court's ruling overturned the lower court's decision, but did not preclude retrying the case. Years after his injury, Rutkowski went on to receive a paltry sum. For information on the final developments of the case, see Illinois Appellate Court, *Reports of Cases*, 108–16.

13. Finding archival records of Vincentz Rutkowski has proved difficult. It appears that he was born around 1879 in Poland and lived most of his life in Chicago after presumably immigrating at a young age. He apparently died in 1901, at the age of 22. It's unclear if his early death had any connection to his injury. Some of these

facts could also be inaccurate, but this is based on a 1901 death record for a Vincent Rutkowski, born in 1879 in Poland, who lived in Chicago and would have been roughly the correct age in 1892. This biographical information was found through www.ancestry.com.

14. Giedion, *Mechanization Takes Command*, 93–94.

15. Ford and Crowther, *My Life and Work*, 81.

16. Armour & Company, souvenir pamphlet. For great detail on the evolution of killing techniques, see Clemen, *American Livestock*.

17. "Beef, Blood, and Bones," *Scientific American* 58, no. 24 (June 1888): 376; as well as Clemen, *American Livestock*, and Commons, "Labor Conditions." The exact specifics of this process varied between 1880 and 1920, but this should give a rough idea of how it worked. The key change over time was an increase in speed and further division into more and more steps.

18. Examples of this postcard can be found on my personal website, http://www.joshuaspecht.com/blog/wordpress/2018/03/22/round-goes-the-wheel-to-the-music-of-the-squeal/

19. Cudahy Packing Company, *From the Ranch*.

20. This is related to the practice of using a "Judas goat," the name for a goat used to lead sheep to slaughter.

21. Armour & Company, souvenir pamphlet.

22. This is not totally surprising, since readers found more novelty in the slaughterhouse's innovations than the people making it run. To the extent workers are addressed, they are described as robotic or insect-like. See, for instance, the usage of "human bees" in "Beef, Blood, and Bones."

23. Barrett, *Work and Community*, 30.

24. Margaret Walsh, in *Midwestern Meat Packing Industry*, makes the defeat of the seasons a central part of her argument. This is absolutely correct, though seasonal fluctuations remained important in terms of labor marginalization.

25. The crowds outside meatpacking plants are addressed further in Barrett, *Work and Community*. See also Bushnell, "Social Problem," 26. For two interesting examinations of the relationship between the communities around the stockyards and what happened inside the slaughterhouses, see Pacyga, *Slaughterhouse*, and Wade, *Chicago's Pride*.

26. "Doubts and Fears," *Daily Inter-Ocean*, November 15, 1886.

27. Commons, "Labor Conditions," 14.

28. Barrett, *Work and Community*, 27. The one-in-ten estimate comes from Commons, "Labor Conditions," 7.

29. Foreman Ernest Poole, quoted in Barrett, *Work and Community*, 28.

30. The benefits of these highly paid men are discussed at length in Commons, "Labor Conditions," particularly p. 7: "If the company makes a few of these partic-

ular jobs desirable to the men and attaches them to its service, it can become independent of the hundreds who work at the jobs where they can do but little damage; and their low wage brings down the average to 21 cents, where, if all were all-round butchers, the average would be 35 cents."

31. Splitters cut the animal into separately processed halves or quarters. This work was not only grueling, but extremely delicate; poor cutting meant lost value.

32. Commons, "Labor Conditions," 7.

33. Wade, *Chicago's Pride*, 235.

34. Ibid., 241. For a narrative overview of the Haymarket incident, see Green, *Death in the Haymarket*.

35. Knights of Labor General Assembly, *Proceedings*, 1479.

36. See Wade, *Chicago's Pride*, 253, for the claim that they were National Guard troops.

37. "Ready for Conflict," *Daily Inter-Ocean*, November 9, 1886.

38. Knights of Labor General Assembly, *Proceedings*, 1481.

39. "Stock Yards Strike," *Daily Inter-Ocean*, October 15, 1886.

40. "The Stock Yards Strike," *Daily Inter-Ocean*, October 14, 1886. "Paper" refers to a short-term loan system businesses used to meet immediate cash needs. Paper could be purchased from a business creating a loan that would be repaid after a set period of time. The conspiracy claimed that Armour was essentially making a series of short-term loans to smaller packinghouses to ensure they would do his bidding.

41. "Ready for Conflict," *Daily Inter-Ocean*.

42. Wade, *Chicago's Pride*, 253–54.

43. For information on the relationship between the Haymarket violence and perceptions of labor, see Painter, *Standing at Armageddon*, particularly ch. 2. For specific information on the relationship between the Haymarket incident and packinghouse workers, see Wade, *Chicago's Pride*, 257.

44. Smith had concerns about the effects of assembly-line work. Yet his concerns viewed these problems as more of a side effect: simple, repetitive tasks did not challenge workers and would lead to unhappiness. For this reason he advocated a kind of proto-welfare state. For information on Smith's views about social security more generally, see Rothschild, "Social Security." Smith, however, does not emphasize the fact that increased productivity is rooted in more effective worker coercion.

45. For an excellent discussion of these issues today, see Pachirat, *Every Twelve Seconds*. For a popular account, see Schlosser, *Fast Food Nation*.

46. This finding fits broadly with Richard White's argument in *Railroaded*. White argues that railroads were overbuilt, and, as I will argue, it was the abundance of rail lines that made dressed-beef shipment possible.

47. Sutherland received patent #71,423 for a "refrigerator car" design; US Commissioner of Patents, *Annual Report*, 1386. Clemen, *Livestock and Meat Industry*, 218, lists

Sutherland as the first American patent recipient. However, there was clearly a flurry of developments around the refrigerator car at the time. See, for instance, "Lyman's Ventilated Car for the Transportation of Dressed Beef," *New York Times*, June 7, 1867.

48. Over time, improved refrigerator-car designs promoted better ventilation, cooled with slower-melting ice mixtures, and with better insulation. The twentieth century brought mechanical refrigeration, eliminating the need for icing stations along the routes refrigerator cars traveled. See J. White, *Great Yellow Fleet*, and Rees, *Refrigeration Nation*, ch. 4.

49. Gunsaulus, "Philip D. Armour," 172.

50. Yeager Kujovich, "Refrigerator Car," 465–69.

51. Chicago Board of Trade, *Eighteenth Annual Report*, 19.

52. Trunk Line Executive Committee, *Relative Cost*, 5. For another good overview of this struggle, see Yeager Kujovich, "Refrigerator Car."

53. Trunk Line Executive Committee, *Relative Cost*, 38.

54. Ibid., 30.

55. At the end of the conference the participants agreed the livestock rate should be 40 cents and the dressed-beef rate should be somewhere between 70 and 86 cents. A panel was appointed, which ultimately decided on the 40–70 differential. For a full discussion, see Clemen, *American Livestock*, 240–41.

56. Numbers from Grand Trunk Railway, "Verbatim Report of the President's Speech," April 30, 1886, 31, Vol. 13333, Record Group 30, Library and Archives Canada.

57. Ibid.

58. Grand Trunk Railway, "Sixth Annual Report of Directors," 1885, 258, Vol. 13331, Record Group 30.

59. Grand Trunk Railway, "Verbatim Report of the President's Speech" [date unclear, likely 1881], 20, Vol. 13332, Record Group 30.

60. Chicago & Grand Trunk Railway, "Third Annual Report of the Directors to the Shareholders," 1883, in "Chicago and Grand Trunk Railway Minute Book Volume 1," 170, Vol. 860, Record Group 30. For 1885 comment, see "Draft of Report of Directors," 1885, 231, in ibid.

61. Trunk Line Executive Committee, *Relative Cost*, throughout, but see 22 and 24.

62. Grand Trunk Railway, "Verbatim Report of the Proceedings at the Ordinary Half-Yearly General Meeting (Held at the City Terminus Hotel, Cannon Street, London, on 25th October, 1883)," October 25, 1883, 12, Vol. 13332, Record Group 30.

63. Grand Trunk Railway, "Verbatim Report of the President's Speech," October 13, 1887, 10, Vol. 13333, Record Group 30.

64. Grand Trunk Railway, "Verbatim Report of the President's Speech," April 24, 1888, 16, Vol. 13333, Record Group 30.

65. Ibid., 17.

66. Grand Trunk Railway, "Report of Proceedings," June 7, 1888, 29–30, Vol. 13333, Record Group 30.

67. Chicago & Grand Trunk Railway, "Annual Report for the Year Ended December 1891" (Detroit, 1892), 11, Vol. 13331, Record Group 30.

68. Grand Trunk Railway, "Report for the Half-Year Ended 30 June, 1900," 8, Vol. 13332, Record Group 30.

69. Congress, Senate, and Select Committee on the Transportation and Sale of Meat Products, *Transportation and Sale*, 75.

70. Ibid., 577.

71. Ibid., 598.

72. Ibid., 602.

73. "To Protect Minnesota Butchers," *New York Times*, March 10, 1889.

74. For discussion of Barber's case as well as similar legal struggles, see McCurdy, "American Law."

75. Though the overall quote is disingenuous, and the Big Four did often act as retail butchers in the short term, Armour's testimony to the Select Committee helps explain his firm's relationship to retail butchers: "My firm does not do a retail business and has never, except in one instance, come in competition with retail butchers, and then only when it became absolutely necessary in one city to protect our interests against an unwarranted boycott." Select Committee, *Transportation and Sale*, 445.

76. Ibid., 169.

77. Ibid., 171.

78. Ibid., 486.

79. Ibid., 6. This was one of the most incriminating documents the Vest Committee was able to find.

80. These are only a few examples. The Vest Committee found many more. See, for example, testimony of P. F. Morrissey, ibid., 260. Also, Levi Samuels discusses predatory pricing in ibid., 118.

81. Ibid., 446.

82. Ibid., 455.

83. Ibid., 446.

84. Ibid., 169.

85. Ibid., 170.

86. Ibid., 407.

87. Ibid., 444.

88. Ibid., 144–45.

89. Ibid., 152. The Akron story appears in Cronon, *Nature's Metropolis* (242–43) as an illustration of how excited consumers were about cheap dressed beef.

90. Select Committee, *Transportation and Sale*, 150.

91. The quotes "soulless corporations" and "monster monopolies" are taken from association president Thomas Armour's call for a convention, reported in "Butchers to Protect Themselves," *New York Times*, March 9, 1886.

92. Select Committee, *Transportation and Sale*, 150–51.

93. Many of these were at the state level and unfortunately left little or no archival trace. There are references to an Iowa Butchers' Protective Association (see "Southern Ice Exchange," 117). In other nineteenth-century periodicals there are similar brief references to associations in Michigan, Kentucky, and other states. Furthermore, many small local-butchers' committees were formed to agitate for municipal regulations; see, e.g., the testimony of P. F. Morrissey in Select Committee, *Transportation and Sale*, 260.

94. "Butchers Protecting Themselves," *New York Times*, March 16, 1884.

95. "Boycotting a Fellow Butcher," *New York Times*, July 7, 1884.

96. Beyond Minnesota, McCurdy, "American Law" (644) notes that inspection laws also passed in Colorado and Indiana.

97. Select Committee, *Transportation and Sale*, 134.

98. Interestingly, the pioneers in this regard were the Big Four and the Singer Sewing Machine Company. Again, see McCurdy, "American Law." McCurdy's article is a defense of the centrality of a specific legal framework to the emergence of large-scale corporations, placing less emphasis on improvements in transportation to create a continental market, à la Chandler. This approach is one I share, in that it is a critique of the organizational-technological account of the emergence of national markets, instead emphasizing how a national market was pieced together through social conflict, inside the courts as well as on the factory floor, on western ranches, and in stores.

99. The court's decision in the Barber case doubted that the idea local inspection was necessary to ensure public safety was "universally, or even generally entertained." Barber decision, quoted in ibid., 647.

100. Ibid.

101. Select Committee, *Transportation and Sale*, 502.

102. Ibid., 503.

103. Ibid., 504–5.

104. Ibid., 511.

105. Ibid., 88.

106. Ibid., 212.

107. Ibid., 387–88.

108. Ibid., 131.

109. Ibid., 132–33.

110. Legal battles were ongoing at the time of the committee hearings. In fact, there are a few indications that the examiners would have been surprised by the upcoming Supreme Court rulings striking down local inspection measures. Nevertheless, they were more concerned about the consumer consequences of the spread of these measures, rather than their constitutionality.

111. Ibid., 135.

112. Ibid., 140.

113. The Sherman Antitrust Act was a landmark piece of legislation allowing the government to investigate, punish, and prevent anticompetitive business practices. The pioneering work on the law is Letwin, *Law and Economic Policy*. For an economist's more recent overview of antitrust's connection to meatpacking, see Libecap, "Chicago Packers."

114. *Swift & Co. v. United States*, 196 U.S. 375 (1905) (Holmes, O.).

115. *Swift & Co.*, 196 U.S. at 400.

116. In a review, the writer Jack London described it as the "*Uncle Tom's Cabin* of wage slavery." See Mookerjee, "Muckraking and Fame," 72.

117. Upton Sinclair, "What Life Means to Me," *Cosmopolitan* 41, October 31, 1906, 594.

118. Armour testimony in Select Committee, *Transportation and Sale*, 434.

Chapter 5: Table

1. "Washington Market, Scenes by Night and by Day," *New York Times*, July 27, 1874. For works from the time on the early history of Washington Market and nineteenth-century food markets on the east coast more broadly, see de Voe, *Market Book* and *Market Assistant*. For a recent academic perspective, see Baics, *Feeding Gotham*.

2. "Centenary Blush on Washington Market," *New York Times*, October 6, 1912.

3. "Women Descend on Washington Market," *New York Times*, April 4, 1912.

4. "Lamb the Cheapest in Many Years," *New York Times*, November 2, 1911.

5. "A Huge Meat Refrigerator," *New York Times*, October 10, 1882.

6. This "half-made" quality is what makes food such a useful focus for understanding culture more broadly. For an anthropological approach that similarly treats a food product as an "unfinished" commodity, see H. Paxson, *Life of Cheese*.

7. I mean democratization in the sense of making beef widely available. It does not, however, mean that beef was equally available or that it meant the same thing to everyone. As this chapter will show, the democratization of beef brought new gendered expectations as well as new forms of hierarchy.

8. The best source on this is Diner, *Hungering for America*.

9. Gabaccia, *What We Eat*; Rogers, *Beef and Liberty*.

10. Counterfeit food was a major concern as well. For a broad look at contaminated and counterfeit food during the period, see Wilson, *Swindled*.

11. Discussion of the cultural history of beef by-products—soap, candles, etc.—has been intentionally omitted. Soaps and other products derived from tallow were a critical source of profit for the large Chicago meatpackers and were part of a broader cultural moment emphasizing refinement and domesticity that remade the late nineteenth-century home. Yet consumers did not connect these products to cattle slaughter and beef production. That this central aspect of cattle processing was ignored is indicative of how the cultural meanings of beef were key to explaining consumer mobilization and advocacy for reform. By-products were important to the success of the cattle-beef complex (and meatpackers' profits), but how and why the cattle-beef complex was regulated is much more about the consumer politics surrounding beef.

12. The chapter emphasizes that beef is a product that allows people to both create and contest social hierarchy. In examining the role of culture in social hierarchy, the chapter draws from Bourdieu, *Distinction*.

13. "The Cause of Dear Beef," *New York Times*, December 3, 1886.

14. "The Market and the Grocery Store," *Good Housekeeping* 10, no. 10, September 13, 1890.

15. Ibid.

16. This is generally the advice in household manuals. See Parloa, *New Cook Book*, 9

17. Ibid., 12–13, 26–29.

18. "Market and the Grocery Store," *Good Housekeeping*.

19. Ibid.

20. E. Wilcox, *Buckeye Cookery*, 421.

21. Parloa, *New Cook Book*, 9.

22. Beecher, *Home*, 381. See also Parloa, *New Cook Book*, 9.

23. "Market and the Grocery Store," *Good Housekeeping*.

24. Beecher, *Home*, 381.

25. The classic, if pessimistic, analysis of this is Sellers, *Market Revolution*. For a more recent and less pessimistic take, see Howe, *What Hath God Wrought*.

26. The meat's quality inspired widespread skepticism. German officials, for example, claimed that the packers used their lowest quality meat for canning, producing a potentially unhealthy product, something American officials and meatpackers sharply denied. See "American Canned Beef" *Sun*, August 6, 1895.

27. For the best overview of the scandal, see Wade, "Hell Hath No Fury."

28. Canned food is perhaps the key flash point in industrial food producers' battle to win consumer confidence. For a detailed look at this struggle, see Zeide, *Canned*.

29. "Canned Beef Poison," *Morning Olympian,* June 9, 1897.

30. Libby, McNeill & Libby's Cooked Corned Beef [trade card], TC4121.0014, Baker Library.

31. Libby, McNeill & Libby's Cooked Corned Beef [trade card], TC4121.0043, Baker Library.

32. Libby, McNeill & Libby's Cooked Corned Beef [trade card], TC4121.0044, Baker Library.

33. Libby, McNeill & Libby's Cooked Corned Beef [trade card], TC4121.0030, Baker Library. This same card was also produced in French (as presumably, were many of them): Libby, McNeill & Libby's Cooked Corned Beef [trade card], TC4121.0031, Baker Library.

34. Libby, McNeill & Libby's Cooked Corned Beef [trade card], TC4121.0026, Baker Library.

35. Libby, McNeill & Libby's Cooked Corned Beef [trade card], TC4121.0019, Baker Library.

36. Libby, McNeill & Libby's Cooked Corned Beef [trade card], TC4121.0018, Baker Library.

37. Libby, McNeill & Libby's Cooked Corned Beef [trade card], TC4121.0015, Baker Library.

38. For information on canned meat and the British context, see Collingham, *Imperial Bodies.*

39. "Big Meat Contract," *Kalamazoo Gazette,* December 11, 1885; "Canned Beef for the British," *Cleveland Plain Dealer,* March 25, 1885.

40. "Pressed with Orders," *Cleveland Plain Dealer,* March 27, 1885.

41. "Credit It to Beefsteak," *Critic-Record,* May 26, 1888.

42. "The Army Meat Scandal," *New York Times,* February 1, 1899.

43. Miles was recognized as the author of the contamination claims and he risked disgrace if they were exaggerated or false. See "Beef Inquiry Is Ordered," *New York Times,* February 10, 1899.

44. See "The Beef Investigation," *Independent,* March 30, 1899.

45. Wade, "Hell Hath No Fury," 179–81.

46. "Danger of Eating Equine Beefsteak," *Philadelphia Inquirer,* June 1, 1895.

47. "On the Extract of Meat," *Littell's Living Age,* July 23, 1870, republished from *Nature.*

48. "Concentrated Beef."

49. US War Department, *Food Furnished,* 725.

50. "Extractum Carnis," *Medical Era* 17, no. 4 (April 1899): 90.

51. For more on these questions, see Young, "Pig that Fell." See also Law and Libecap, "Progressive Era Reform."

52. "Buying Beefsteak by Rank," *New York Times,* October 13, 1894.

53. "Origin of the Porter-house Steak," *Frank Leslie's Illustrated Newspaper,* November 20, 1869.

54. For an overview of the origin of the porterhouse and other early American foods, see Kurlansky, *Food.* On its esteem, "How to Select Beef," *New York Times,* March 28, 1883: "for ordinary mortals, I suppose porter-house is best."

55. This legend has been applied to a variety of monarchs and historical figures since the early modern period. See Beeton, *Book of Household Management,* 169.

56. "The Masculine Way," *Aberdeen Daily News,* December 25, 1887.

57. "Beefsteak and Rolls," *Aberdeen Daily News,* December 1, 1887.

58. "Can Women Broil Beefsteak?" *Philadelphia Inquirer,* March 29, 1893.

59. "Beefsteak as a Home Breaker," *Philadelphia Inquirer,* February 21, 1900.

60. "The Diet of Brain Workers," *Hours at Home* 9, no. 5, September 1869. The original essay appears unsigned, but when it was republished in the *American Educational Monthly* in 1871, the essay referred to the author as "Dr. Beard." Further investigation revealed George M. Beard as an author of a "popular manual of food and diet," that included a discussion of brain-workers' diets. See Beard, *Eating and Drinking.* Beard, as it turns out, has an important (though dubious) place in medical history as a popularizer of "neurasthenia" as a psychological diagnosis. See Rosenberg, "George M. Beard."

61. "Diet of Brain Workers," *Hours at Home.*

62. "The Diet of Brain Workers," *St. Albans Messenger,* February 11, 1870; Beard, "Diet of Brain Workers"; [Beard], "Diet of Brain Workers."

63. "The Diet of Brain-Workers," *Manufacturers' and Farmers' Journal,* August 26, 1869.

64. Dana, "Special Diets."

65. "Vegetarianism No Diet for Brain Workers," *Salt Lake Telegram,* July 18, 1915.

66. Katharina Vester argues that this obsession with class and diet was initially focused on men, but ultimately gave rise to women's dieting as part of a similar process of establishing superiority over immigrants and the poor. See Vester, "Regime Change." She has also written on another topic relevant to this chapter—how culinary writers used cookbooks and food guides as tools for inscribing social hierarchy—in *Taste of Power.*

67. See Diner, *Hungering for America,* particularly ch. 1. Diner quotes one immigrant writing back to relatives in Italy: "here I eat meat three times a day, not three times a year" (57).

68. Massachusetts Bureau of Statistics of Labor, *Annual Report,* 319.

69. Gompers and Gutstadt, *Meat vs. Rice.*

70. Ibid., 8.

71. Ibid., 22.

72. Discussed in Levenstein, *Revolution at the Table*, ch. 2. Levenstein addresses *Meat vs. Rice* as well.

73. "The Question of Diet," *New York Times*, February 7, 1875.

74. Abel, *Sanitary and Economic Cooking*, iv.

75. Ibid., vii.

76. As an interesting aside, Abel suggests that nutrition science had its origin in "investigations . . . applied with profit to the feeding of cattle"; ibid., 2.

77. Ibid., 5.

78. Ibid., 10.

79. More than a question of worker well-being, the topic of cost of living was intimately connected to the desire of capitalists for lower wages.

80. Ibid., 13.

81. Ibid., 15.

82. "Round Steak as Good as Tenderloin," *Kalamazoo Gazette*, July 1, 1909. Some sources even claimed that tougher cuts were *more* nutritious. See "How to Select Meats," *Washington Post*, August 7, 1898, and "Daily Diet Hints," *Washington Post*, March 4, 1910.

83. See Parloa, *Young Housekeeper*, 345. Abel in *Sanitary and Economic Cooking* makes a similar argument.

84. "Burglar Makes Choice," *Plain Dealer*, December 8, 1907.

85. Morton had a lot of unusual and entertaining ideas about farming and consumption. For his perspective: Morton, *Addresses*.

86. "Secretary Morton's Idea," *Idaho Statesman*, December 31, 1895. NB: the essay is republished, but the original source is unclear.

87. W. O. Atwater, "The Food of the Poor," *Manufacturer and Builder*, March 1888 (stating that the article was originally published in *Century*).

88. There are analogues to this today in how the media or elites often celebrate the frugal rich and criticize the conspicuous consumption of the poor.

89. Dining and socializing outside of the house brought new gendered expectations about public space. See Freedman, "Women and Restaurants," and Remus, "Tippling Ladies."

90. Quoted in McWilliams, "Conspicuous Consumption," 35.

91. A. Haley, *Turning the Tables*.

92. "Hints for the Household: Eating Beefsteaks with One's Fingers," *New York Times*, March 27, 1881.

93. Ibid.

94. This reflected a broad shift in beliefs about how men should act from manly self-restraint to a more assertive (and violent) masculinity. See Bederman, *Manliness and Civilization*.

95. Filippini, *Table*, 25.

96. For a related argument, see Cowan, *More Work for Mother.*

97. "Meat Prices Are Higher," *New York Times*, March 29, 1902. The exact cause of rising meat prices at this specific moment is unclear. Though it seems likely the meatpackers played a role in the rise, fluctuations can happen for all sorts of reasons, ranging from weather to overall economic conditions.

98. The wholesale trade, particularly as regards kosher beef, was increasingly under the control of the Chicago packers and the rapidly expanding New York firm Schwarzchild and Sulzberger (S&S). Though the evidence is slightly unclear and S&S denied it, the company had gone from being rivals with the Chicago packers to allies. Some of these details and more on S&S can be found in Santlofer, *Food City*, ch. 41. For an overview of the viewpoint of the protestors, see Hyman, "Immigrant Women."

99. "Fierce Meat Riot on Lower East Side," *New York Times*, May 16, 1902.

100. "Police Club Meat Rioters," "Two Hurt in a Meat Riot," and "Anti-Beef Trust Conclave," *New York Times*, May 25, 1902.

101. Much of the coverage was tinged with nativism and anti-Semitism, but it was also revealing of the difficulties butchers faced. According to the *New York Times*, one butcher, following a 1906 disturbance, explained the trouble thus: "Ve pay ten cents ind a half for meat, ind a lady comes der shop ind insists on getting' for eleven cents a pound." "East Side Women Riot over High Meat Rates," *New York Times*, November 30, 1906.

102. "Fierce Meat Riot," *New York Times.*

103. Thompson, "Moral Economy." For a recent US example, see Fullilove, "Price of Bread."

104. "East Side Women," *New York Times.*

105. Scholars in law, history, and economics have examined almost every aspect of both laws (as well as the related Pure Food and Drug Act), highlighting how consumers, producers, and bureaucrats all advanced their own interests. For an interdisciplinary study of progressive-era reform broadly using the Pure Food and Drug Act, see Law and Libecap, "Progressive Era Reform."

106. Even critiques of today's food system are inflected with the older cultural meanings of red meat. The new emphasis on self-slaughter and celebration of the bloody process of producing beef reproduces the same logic that embraced the "beefsteak" and celebrated a return to "primeval man." For an example of these new primeval diets, see Wolf, *Paleo Solution.*

Conclusion

1. Roosevelt, *Ranch Life*, 56.

2. Roosevelt, "First Annual Message."

3. Roosevelt, *History as Literature*, ch. 5.

4. Roosevelt, "Second Annual Message." Full quotation: "Our aim is not to do away with corporations; on the contrary, these big aggregations are an inevitable development of modern industrialism, and the effort to destroy them would be futile unless accomplished in ways that would work the utmost mischief to the entire body politic."

5. Roosevelt, "First Annual Message."

6. The best work on this argument is Painter, *Standing at Armageddon*.

7. For the story of trucking and its effect on the American economy in the twentieth century, see Hamilton, *Trucking Country*.

8. Brazilian giant JBS acquired Swift & Company in 2007. After many changes including a brief stint as part of the Greyhound Corporation, Armour & Company became part of ConAgra. None of the other Big Four went bankrupt—they were eventually spun off and sold in parts to different players—and the overall industry structure remains largely the same.

9. The largest meatpackers at the time of writing are Tyson, JBS, Cargill, and National Beef.

10. For a recent study of slaughterhouse work, see Pachirat, *Every Twelve Seconds*. Pachirat's research involved fieldwork in a slaughter facility and provides a first-hand account of the work today (which remains eerily similar to nineteenth-century descriptions). See also Andreas, *Meatpackers and Beef Barons*; Fink, *Meatpacking Line*.

11. Regarding the horsemeat scandal, a report from the UK Parliament explained, "contamination was a result of fraud by elements of the food industry," and suggested, "retailers should have been more vigilant against the risks of adulteration." See UK House of Commons, *Food Contamination*, 3 (summary). Meat processors take a similar approach to revelations about inhumane slaughterhouse conditions, blaming individual workers or supervisors for incidents of animal cruelty while underplaying worker exploitation or labor practices that may have led to cruelty. See, for instance, a case in which a farm associated with Perdue was perpetrating acts of animal cruelty. The worker in question was fired and the company was quick to express outrage. Justin Moyer, "Man Arrested after Undercover Video Reveals Alleged Abuse at Perdue Chicken Supplier," *Washington Post*, December 11, 2015.

12. There have been some popular attempts to address industrial animal husbandry, such as Schlosser, *Fast Food Nation*, and Pollan, *Omnivore's Dilemma*, but even these face a problem when moving to action. It is very difficult to think of a holistic response in terms of consumer/regulatory action, so people address particular issues (labor, animal rights, health) and the larger structure remains resilient.

13. Chandler, *Visible Hand*.

14. See Christopher Leonard, *Meat Racket*; Hauter, *Foodopoly*; Gisolfi, *Takeover*.

15. For information on the Chicago Union Stockyards' twentieth-century decline and (perhaps) subsequent renewal, see Pacyga, *Slaughterhouse*, ch. 5 and 6. Though Chicago is certainly the most important city in this story, I have tried to show it was by no means the only market and that, on balance, other parts of the cattle-beef complex, whether ranches scattered across the American West or restaurants in New York and home kitchens in Boston (or across the United States), mattered as much.

BIBLIOGRAPHY

Archives Consulted

Baker Library (Harvard Business School), Cambridge, MA
    Advertising ephemera collection
Chicago History Museum, Chicago, IL
Kansas Historical Society, Topeka, KS
Library and Archives Canada, Ottawa, ON
    Chicago and Grand Trunk Railway Company records
    Grand Trunk Railway records
National Archives and Records Administration, Washington, DC
    General Records of the Department of Justice
    Records of the Bureau of Indian Affairs
Newberry Library, Chicago, IL
    Ayer Manuscript Collection
    Graff collection
Panhandle-Plains Historical Museum, Canyon, TX
    Francklyn Land and Cattle Company Records
    XIT Ranch collection
Southwest Collection (Texas Tech University), Lubbock, TX
    Baker, Anne Watts, collection
    Coggin Brothers and Associates Records
    Comstock, Henry Griswold, papers
    Espuela Land and Cattle Company (Spur Ranch) Records
    Grierson, Benjamin H., papers
    Mackay, Alexander, papers
    Matador Land and Cattle Company Records
    Mooar, John Wesley, papers
    Mooar, Lydia Louisa, papers
    Powell, I. R., papers

Shafter, William Rufus, papers
Sharps Rifle Company records
Slaughter, C. C., papers
Stockraisers Association of Northwestern Texas records
Updegraff, Way Hamlin, papers

Published Primary Sources

Abel, Mary Hinman. *Practical Sanitary and Economic Cooking Adapted to Persons of Moderate and Small Means*. Washington, DC: American Public Health Association, 1890.

Adams, Andy. *The Log of a Cowboy: A Narrative of the Old Trail Days*. New York: Houghton Mifflin, 1903.

Armour, J. Ogden. *The Packers, the Private Car Lines, and the People*. Philadelphia, PA: H. Altemus, 1906.

Armour & Company. "Armour's Food Source Map" (Chicago, 1922), David Rumsey Historical Map Collection, Stanford University, #9905.002, https://www.davidrumsey.com/luna/servlet/detail/RUMSEY~8~1~278701~90051810:Armour-s-food-source-map.

Armour & Company. Souvenir pamphlet. Chicago: Foster, 1893. Chicago History Museum.

Bailey, Jack. *A Texas Cowboy's Journal: Up the Trail to Kansas in 1868*. Norman, OK: University of Oklahoma Press, 2006.

Beard, [George Miller]. "The Diet of Brain Workers." *American Educational Monthly* 7 (February 1870): 72–73.

[Beard, George Miller]. "The Diet of Brain Workers." *Phrenological Journal* 1 (April 1870): 245–46.

Beard, George Miller. *Eating and Drinking: A Popular Manual of Food and Diet in Health and Disease*. New York: G. P. Putnam and Sons, 1871.

Beecher, H. W. *The Home, How to Make and Keep It*. Minneapolis, MN: Buckeye, 1885. http://catalog.hathitrust.org/Record/100191584.

"Beef, Blood, and Bones," *Scientific American* 58, no. 24 (June 1888): 376.

Beeton, Isabella. *Mrs Beeton's Book of Household Management*. Edited by Nicola Humble. Abridged ed. (Oxford World Classics). Oxford: Oxford University Press, 2008.

Brisbin, James Sanks. *The Beef Bonanza, Or, How to Get Rich on the Plains: Being a Description of Cattle-Growing, Sheep-Farming, Horse-Raising, and Dairying in the West*. Philadelphia, PA: J. B. Lippincott, 1881.

Chicago Board of Trade. *Eighteenth Annual Report of the Trade and Commerce of Chicago, for the Year Ending December 31, 1875*. Chicago: Knight and Leonard, 1876. Consulted at the Newberry Library.

———. *Twentieth Annual Report . . . Year Ending December 31, 1877.* Chicago: Knight and Leonard, 1878. Newberry Library.

———. *Twenty-Ninth Annual Report . . . Year Ended December 31, 1886.* Chicago: Knight and Leonard, 1887. Newberry Library.

———. *Thirty-Fourth Annual Report . . . Year Ended Dec 31, 1891.* Chicago: J.M.W. Jones Stationery and Print, 1892. Newberry Library.

———. *Thirty-Fifth Annual Report . . . Year Ended Dec 31, 1892.* Chicago: J.M.W. Jones Stationery and Print, 1893. Newberry Library.

"Concentrated Beef." *Scientific American* 14, no. 2 (January 1866): 23–24.

Cook, John R. *The Border and the Buffalo.* Topeka, KS: Crane, 1907. https://archive .org/details/borderbuffalount00cook.

Cudahy Packing Company. *From the Ranch to the Table.* Omaha, NE: Cudahy Packing, 1893. Chicago History Museum.

Dana, Charles. "The Special Diets in Various Nervous Diseases." *Scientific American Supplement* 25, no. 649 (June 1888): 10373–74.

de Voe, Thomas. *The Market Assistant.* New York: Hurd and Houghton, 1867.

———. *The Market Book: Containing a Historical Account of the Public Markets in the Cities of New York, Boston, Philadelphia, and Brooklyn, with a Brief Description of Every Article of Human Food Sold Therein.* New York: author, 1862.

"Extractum Carnis." *Medical Era* 17, no. 4 (April 1899): 90.

Filippini, Alexander. *The Table: How to Buy Food, How to Cook It, and How to Serve It.* New York: Webster, 1890.

Fletcher, Baylis John, and Wayne Gard. *Up the Trail in '79.* Norman, OK: University of Oklahoma Press, 1968.

Gompers, Samuel, and Herman Gutstadt. *Meat vs. Rice: American Manhood against Asiatic Coolieism, Which Shall Survive?* San Francisco: American Federation of Labor, 1902.

Gunsaulus, Frank W. "Philip D. Armour: A Character Sketch." *American Monthly Review of Reviews* 23 (January–June 1901): 167–76.

Hunter, J. Marvin, and B. Byron Price. *The Trail Drivers of Texas.* Austin, TX: University of Texas Press, 1985.

Illinois Appellate Court. *Reports of Cases Decided in the Appellate Courts of the State of Illinois,* Volume 82. Chicago: Callaghan, 1899.

Illinois Supreme Court. *Reports of Cases at Law and in Chancery Argued and Determined in the Supreme Court of Illinois,* Volume 167. Chicago: Myers, 1897.

Kappler, Charles Joseph. *Indian Affairs: Laws and Treaties,* volume 2, *Treaties.* Washington, DC: US Government Printing Office, 1904.

Keeler, B[ronson] C. *Where to Go to Become Rich: Farmers', Miners' and Tourists' Guide to Kansas, New Mexico, Arizona and Colorado.* Chicago: Belford, Clarke, 1880. http://archive.org/details/wheretogotobecom00keel.

Knights of Labor General Assembly, eds. *Proceedings of the General Assembly of the Knights of Labor of America, Eleventh Regular Session.* Minneapolis, MN: General Assembly, 1887.

Lomax, John Avery. *Songs of the Cattle Trail and Cow Camp.* New York: Macmillan, 1919.

———. *Cowboy Songs and Other Frontier Ballads.* New York: Sturgis and Walton, 1910. http://archive.org/details/cowboysongsother00loma.

Love, Nat. *Life and Adventures of Nat Love, Better Known in the Cattle Country as "Deadwood Dick," by Himself: A True History of Slavery Days, Life on the Great Cattle Ranges . . . Based on Facts, and Personal Experiences of the Author.* Los Angeles: author, 1907.

Massachusetts Bureau of Statistics of Labor. *Annual Report of the Bureau of Statistics of Labor.* Boston, MA: Wright and Potter, 1886.

McCoy, Joseph G. *Historic Sketches of the Cattle Trade of the West and Southwest.* Kansas City, MO: Ramsey, Millett and Hudson, 1874.

Mercer, A. S. *The Banditti of the Plains; or, The Cattlemen's Invasion of Wyoming in 1892: The Crowning Infamy of the Ages.* Norman, OK: University of Oklahoma Press, 1975.

Morton, J. Sterling. *Addresses of J. Sterling Morton.* Baltimore, MD: Friedenwald, 1893.

National Cattle Growers' Association of America, ed. *Proceedings of the . . . National Convention of Cattle Growers of the United States.* St. Louis, MO: R. P. Studley, 1884.

Nimmo, Joseph. *Report in Regard to Range and Ranch Cattle Business of U.S.* Treasury Department Document No. 690, Bureau of Statistics. Washington, DC: US Government Printing Office, 1885.

Parloa, Maria. *Miss Parloa's New Cook Book and Marketing Guide.* Boston, MA: Estes and Lauriat, 1880.

———. *Miss Parloa's Young Housekeeper.* Boston, MA: Estes and Lauriat, 1894.

Powell, Cuthbert. *Twenty Years of Kansas City's Live Stock Trade and Traders.* Kansas City, MO: Pearl, 1893.

"Report of Major General John Pope of the Condition of the Department of the Missouri, February 25, 1866." House Executive Document No. 39-76, Serial 1263 (n.d.).

Rhode Island Railroad Commissioner. *Annual Report.* Providence, RI: Freeman, 1893.

Roosevelt, Theodore. "First Annual Message to Congress." December 3, 1901. Published online by Gerhard Peters and John T. Woolley, *The American Presidency Project.* http://www.presidency.ucsb.edu/ws/?pid=29542.

———. *History as Literature.* New York: Scriber's Sons, 1913.

———. *Hunting Trips of a Ranchman: Hunting Trips on the Prairie and in the Mountains.* New York: Review of Reviews, 1885. http://archive.org/details /huntingtripsranch04roosrich.

———. *Ranch Life and the Hunting Trail.* Mineola, NY: Dover, 2009.

———. *Report of Hon. Theodore Roosevelt Made to the United States Civil Service Commission, upon a Visit to Certain Indian Reservations and Indian Schools in South Dakota, Nebraska, and Kansas.* Philadelphia: Indian Rights Association, 1893.

———. "Second Annual Message to Congress." December 2, 1902. Published online by Gerhard Peters and John T. Woolley, *The American Presidency Project.* http:// www.presidency.ucsb.edu/ws/?pid=29543.

———. *The Wilderness Hunter.* New York: Review of Reviews, 1893. http://archive .org/details/wilderneshunt02roosrich.

Russell, Charles Edward. *The Greatest Trust in the World,.* New York: Ridgway-Thayer, 1905.

Salmon, D. E. *Report on the Beef Supply of the United States and the Export Trade in Animal and Meat Products.* US Department of Agriculture, Bureau of Animal Industry, Special Bulletin (advance sheets from annual report, 1889). Washington, DC: US Government Printing Office, 1890.

———. "Texas Fever a Matter of National Importance." *American Veterinary Review* 6 (1882): 293–96.

Senate Select Committee to Examine into the Conditions of the Sioux and Crow Indians. *Testimony Taken by a Select Committee of the Senate Concerning the Condition of the Indian Tribes in the Territories of Montana and Dakota under Resolution of the Senate of March 2, 1883.* Report No. 48-283. Washington, DC: US Government Printing Office, 1884.

Shaw, James C. *North from Texas.* College Station, TX: Texas A&M University Press, 1996.

Sinclair, Upton. *The Jungle.* Mineola, NY: Dover, 2001. First published New York: Doubleday, Page, 1906.

Snow, Edwin Miller. *Report upon the Convention of Cattle Commissioners, Held at Springfield, Illinois, December 1, 1868, and upon the Texas Cattle Disease.* Providence, RI: Providence Press, 1869. http://archive.org/details/reportuponconven00snow.

"Southern Ice Exchange." *Ice and Refrigeration* 13, no. 2 (August 1897): 117.

Stuart, Granville. *Forty Years on the Frontier as Seen in the Journals and Reminiscences of Granville Stuart, Gold-Miner, Trader, Merchant, Rancher and Politician.* Lincoln, NE: University of Nebraska Press, 2004.

Sturgis, Thomas. *Common Sense View of the Sioux War with True Method of Treatment, as Opposed to Both the Exterminative and the Sentimental Policy.* Cheyenne, WY: Leader Steam Book and Job Printing House, 1877.

————. *The Ute War of 1879: Why the Indian Bureau Should Be Transferred from the Department of the Interior to the Department of War.* Cheyenne, WY: Leader Steam Book and Job Printing House, 1879.

Taylor, Joe F., ed. "The Indian Campaign on the Staked Plains, 1874–1875: Military Correspondence from War Department, Adjutant General's Office, File 2815–1874." *Panhandle-Plains Historical Review* 34–35 (1961): 1–382.

Trunk Line Executive Committee. *Report upon the Relative Cost of Transporting Live Stock and Dressed Beef.* New York: Russell Brothers Printers, 1883.

UK House of Commons, Environment, Food, and Rural Affairs Committee. *Food Contamination.* London: Stationery Office, 2013.

US Bureau of Corporations. *Report of the Commissioner of Corporations on the Beef Industry.* Washington, DC: US Government Printing Office, 1905.

US Commissioner of Patents. *Annual Report of the Commissioner of Patents.* Vol. 2. Washington, DC: US Government Printing Office, 1868.

US Congress and Senate Committee on Indian Affairs. *Testimony Taken by the Committee on Indian Affairs of the Senate in Relation to Leases of Lands in the Indian Territory and Other Reservations under Resolutions of the Senate of December 3, 1884.* Washington, DC: US Government Printing Office, 1885. http://catalog.hathitrust.org/api/volumes/oclc/13530731.html.

US Congress, Senate, and Select Committee on the Transportation and Sale of Meat Products. *Testimony Taken by the Select Committee of the United States Senate on the Transportation and Sale of Meat Products.* Washington, DC: US Government Printing Office, 1890.

US War Department. *Food Furnished by Subsistence Department to Troops in the Field.* Volume 1. Document No. 56-270. Washington, DC: Government Printing Office, 1900.

Von Richthofen, Walter. *Cattle-Raising on the Plains of North America.* New York: D. Appleton, 1885. http://archive.org/details/GR_3499.

Walker, Francis Amasa. *The Indian Question.* Boston, MA: J. R. Osgood, 1874.

Wilcox, Estelle Woods. *Buckeye Cookery and Practical Housekeeping.* Minneapolis: Buckeye, 1877.

Newspapers and Journals

Aberdeen Daily News (1887–89)
Aberdeen Weekly News (1885)
Bismarck Daily Tribune (1888)
Breeder's Gazette (1883–86)
Chicago Daily Tribune (1883)

Cleveland Plain Dealer (1885)

Columbus Daily Inquirer (1886)

Cosmopolitan (1906)

Critic-Record (1888)

Daily Inter-Ocean (1886)

Detroit Free Press (1883)

Economist (1883–88)

Frank Leslie's Illustrated Newspaper (1869)

Good Housekeeping (1890)

Grand Forks Daily Herald (1885)

Hours at Home (1869)

Idaho Statesman (1895)

Independent (1899)

Kalamazoo Gazette (1885–1909)

Las Vegas Daily Gazette (1883)

Littell's Living Age (1870)

Manufacturer and Builder (1888)

Manufacturers' and Farmers' Journal (1869)

Morning Olympian (1897)

New York Herald (1883)

New York Times (1873–1927)

Philadelphia Inquirer (1893–1900)

Refrigerating Engineering (1933)

Salt Lake Telegram (1915)

St. Albans Messenger (1870)

Sun (1895)

Washington Post (1898–2015)

Western Recorder (1884)

Secondary Sources

Ahmad, Diana L. *Success Depends on the Animals: Emigrants, Livestock, and Wild Animals on the Overland Trails, 1840–1869.* Reno, NV: University of Nevada Press, 2016.

Ajmone-Marsan, Paolo, José Fernando Garcia, and Johannes A. Lenstra. "On the Origin of Cattle: How Aurochs Became Cattle and Colonized the World." *Evolutionary Anthropology: Issues, News, and Reviews* 19, no. 4 (2010): 148–57.

Allen, Ruth Alice. *Chapters in the History of Organized Labor in Texas.* Austin, TX: University of Texas Press, 1941.

Allred, Jeff. "The Needle and the Damage Done: John Avery Lomax and the Guises of Collecting." *Arizona Quarterly* 58, no. 3 (2002): 83–107.

Anderson, Gary Clayton. *The Conquest of Texas: Ethnic Cleansing in the Promised Land, 1820–1875*. Norman, OK: University of Oklahoma Press, 2005.

———. *Ethnic Cleansing and the Indian: The Crime that Should Haunt America*. Norman, OK: University of Oklahoma Press, 2014.

Anderson, Virginia DeJohn. *Creatures of Empire: How Domestic Animals Transformed Early America*. Oxford: Oxford University Press, 2004.

Andreas, Carol. *Meatpackers and Beef Barons: Company Town in a Global Economy*. Niwot, CO: University Press of Colorado, 1994.

Andrews, Thomas G. *Killing for Coal: America's Deadliest Labor War*. Cambridge, MA: Harvard University Press, 2010.

Athearn, Robert G. "General Sherman and the Western Railroads." *Pacific Historical Review* 24, no. 1 (1955): 39–48.

Atherton, Lewis Eldon. *The Pioneer Merchant in Mid-America*. New York: Da Capo, 1969.

———. "The Services of the Frontier Merchant." *Mississippi Valley Historical Review* 24, no. 2 (1937): 153–70.

Bahre, Conrad J., and Marlyn L. Shelton. "Rangeland Destruction: Cattle and Drought in Southeastern Arizona at the Turn of the Century." *Journal of the Southwest* 38, no. 1 (1996): 1–22.

Baics, Gergely. *Feeding Gotham: The Political Economy and Geography of Food in New York, 1790–1860*. Princeton, NJ: Princeton University Press, 2016.

Barca, Stefania. "Laboring the Earth: Transnational Reflections on the Environmental History of Work." *Environmental History* 19, no. 1 (2014): 3–27.

Barnes, Will Croft. *The Story of the Range*. Washington, DC: US Government Printing Office, 1926.

Barrett, James R. *Work and Community in the Jungle: Chicago's Packinghouse Workers, 1894–1922*. Urbana, IL: University of Illinois Press, 1987.

Beckert, Sven. *Empire of Cotton: A Global History*. New York: Knopf, 2014.

Bederman, Gail. *Manliness and Civilization: A Cultural History of Gender and Race in the United States, 1880–1917*. Chicago: University of Chicago Press, 1995.

Beja-Pereira, Albano, David Caramelli, Carles Lalueza-Fox, Cristiano Vernesi, Nuno Ferrand, Antonella Casoli, Felix Goyache, Luis J. Royo, Serena Conti, and Martina Lari. "The Origin of European Cattle: Evidence from Modern and Ancient DNA." *Proceedings of the National Academy of Sciences of the USA* 103, no. 21 (2006): 8113–18.

Belgrad, Daniel. "'Power's Larger Meaning': The Johnson County War as Political Violence in an Environmental Context." *Western Historical Quarterly* 33, no. 2 (2002): 159–77.

Blackhawk, Ned. *Violence over the Land: Indians and Empires in the Early West*. Cambridge, MA: Harvard University Press, 2006.

Blake, Kevin S. "Zane Grey and Images of the American West." *Geographi* 85, no. 2 (1995): 202–16.

Blevins, Winfred. *Dictionary of the American West*. New York: Facts on Fi

Bourdieu, Pierre. *Distinction: A Social Critique of the Judgement of Taste.* C MA: Harvard University Press, 1984.

Bowden, Martyn J. "The Great American Desert in the American Mind: riography of a Geographical Notion." In *Geographies of the Mind: E torical Geosophy*, edited by David Lowenthal and Martyn Bowden, York: Oxford University Press, 1976.

Boyd, William. "Making Meat: Science, Technology, and American Pou tion." *Technology and Culture* 42, no. 4 (2001): 631–64.

Brayer, Herbert O. "The Influence of British Capital on the Western I Industry." *Journal of Economic History* 9, no. S1 (1949): 85–98.

Brown, Kate, and Thomas Klubock. "Environment and Labor: Introd national Labor and Working-Class History* 85 (2014): 4–9.

Bushnell, Charles Joseph. "The Social Problem at the Chicago Stoc dissertation, University of Chicago, 1902.

Carter, Nancy Carol. "U.S. Federal Indian Policy: An Essay and Anno raphy." *Legal Reference Services Quarterly* 30, no. 3 (2011): 210–30.

Chalfant, William Y. *Hancock's War: Conflict on the Southern Plains.* University of Oklahoma Press, 2014.

Chandler, Alfred D. *The Visible Hand: The Managerial Revolution in An* Cambridge, MA: Belknap, 1977.

Chavez, Ernesto. *The U.S. War with Mexico: A Brief History with L* York: Bedford/St. Martin's, 2007.

Clark, Christopher. "The Agrarian Context." In *Capitalism Takes Com Transformation of Nineteenth-Century America*, edited by Mic Gary J. Kornblith, 13–37. Chicago: University Of Chicago Press

Clayton, Lawrence, Jim Hoy, and Jerald Underwood. *Vaqueros, Co aroos*. Austin, TX: University of Texas Press, 2001.

Clemen, Rudolf Alexander. *The American Livestock and Meat Ind* Ronald, 1923.

———. "Cattle Trails as a Factor in the Development of Livestock N *of Farm Economics* 8, no. 4 (1926): 427–42.

Coclanis, Peter A. "Urbs in Horto." *Reviews in American History* 20, 1

Collingham, E. M. *Imperial Bodies: The Physical Experience of the* New York: Polity, 2001.

Commons, John R. "Labor Conditions in Meat Packing and the Recent Strike." *Quarterly Journal of Economics* 19, no. 1 (1904): 1–32.

Condra, Alli, and Emily Broad Leib. *Cottage Food Laws in the United States.* Boston, MA: Harvard Food Law and Policy Clinic, Harvard Law School, 2013.

Conger, Roger N. "Fencing in McLennan County, Texas." *Southwestern Historical Quarterly* 59, no. 2 (1955): 215–21.

Cothran, Boyd. *Remembering the Modoc War: Redemptive Violence and the Making of American Innocence.* Chapel Hill, NC: University of North Carolina Press, 2014.

Cowan, Ruth. *More Work for Mother: The Ironies of Household Technology from the Open Hearth to the Microwave.* New York: Basic Books, 1983.

Cronon, William. *Changes in the Land.* New York: Hill and Wang, 1983.

———. *Nature's Metropolis: Chicago and the Great West.* New York: W. W. Norton, 1992.

Cruse, J. Brett. *Battles of the Red River War: Archeological Perspectives on the Indian Campaign of 1874.* College Station, TX: Texas A&M University Press, 2008.

Cushman, Gregory T. *Guano and the Opening of the Pacific World: A Global Ecological History.* New York: Cambridge University Press, 2013.

Dale, Edward Everett. *The Range Cattle Industry.* Norman, OK: University of Oklahoma Press, 1930.

Dary, David. *Cowboy Culture: A Saga of Five Centuries.* Lawrence, KS: University Press of Kansas, 1989.

DeLay, Brian. *War of a Thousand Deserts: Indian Raids and the U.S.-Mexican War.* New Haven, CT: Yale University Press, 2009.

Diner, Hasia R. *Hungering for America: Italian, Irish, and Jewish Foodways in the Age of Migration.* Cambridge, MA: Harvard University Press, 2001.

Dobak, William A. "Killing the Canadian Buffalo, 1821–1881." *Western Historical Quarterly* 27, no. 1 (1996): 33–52.

Dykstra, Robert R. *The Cattle Towns.* New York: Knopf, 1968.

———. "Overdosing on Dodge City." *Western Historical Quarterly* 27, no. 4 (1996): 505–14.

———. "Quantifying the Wild West: The Problematic Statistics of Frontier Violence." *Western Historical Quarterly* 40, no. 3 (2009): 321–47.

English, Linda. *By All Accounts: General Stores and Community Life in Texas and Indian Territory.* Vol. 6. Norman, OK: University of Oklahoma Press, 2013.

Filene, Benjamin. "'Our Singing Country': John and Alan Lomax, Leadbelly, and the Construction of an American Past." *American Quarterly* 43, no. 4 (1991): 602–24.

Fink, Deborah. *Cutting into the Meatpacking Line: Workers and Change in the Rural Midwest.* Chapel Hill, NC: University of North Carolina Press, 1998.

Flores, Dan. "Bison Ecology and Bison Diplomacy: The Southern Plains from 1800 to 1850." *Journal of American History* 78, no. 2 (1991): 465–85.

Ford, Henry, with Samuel Crowther. *My Life and Work.* Garden City, NY: Doubleday, Page, 1922.

Freedman, Paul. "Women and Restaurants in the Nineteenth-Century United States." *Journal of Social History* 48, no. 1 (2014): 1–19.

Fullilove, Courtney. "The Price of Bread: The New York City Flour Riot and the Paradox of Capitalist Food Systems." *Radical History Review* 2014, no. 118 (2014): 15–41.

Gabaccia, Donna R. *We Are What We Eat: Ethnic Food and the Making of Americans.* Cambridge, MA: Harvard University Press, 2000.

Galenson, David. "Cattle Trailing in the Nineteenth Century: A Reply." *Journal of Economic History* 35, no. 2 (1975): 461–66.

Gard, Wayne. *The Chisholm Trail.* Norman, OK: University of Oklahoma Press, 1979.

———. "The Fence-Cutters." *Southwestern Historical Quarterly* 51, no. 1 (1947): 1–15.

Giedion, Sigfried. *Mechanization Takes Command: A Contribution to Anonymous History.* New York: Norton, 1969.

Giesen, James C. *Boll Weevil Blues: Cotton, Myth, and Power in the American South.* Chicago: University of Chicago Press, 2011.

Gisolfi, Monica. *The Takeover: Chicken Farming and the Roots of American Agribusiness.* Athens, GA: University of Georgia Press, 2017.

Glasrud, Bruce A., and Michael N. Searles. *Black Cowboys in the American West: On the Range, on the Stage, behind the Badge.* Norman, OK: University of Oklahoma Press, 2016.

Govindrajan, Radhika. *Animal Intimacies.* Chicago: University of Chicago Press, 2018.

Green, James. *Death in the Haymarket.* New York: Pantheon, 2006.

Greene, Jerome A. *Battles and Skirmishes of the Great Sioux War, 1876–1877: The Military View.* Norman, OK: University of Oklahoma Press, 1996.

———. *Lakota and Cheyenne: Indian Views of the Great Sioux War, 1876–1877.* Norman, OK: University of Oklahoma Press, 2000.

Gressley, Gene M. *Bankers and Cattlemen.* New York: Knopf, 1966.

———. "Teschemacher and deBillier Cattle Company: A Study of Eastern Capital on the Frontier." *Business History Review* 33, no. 2 (1959): 121–37.

Grua, David W. *Surviving Wounded Knee: The Lakotas and the Politics of Memory.* Oxford: Oxford University Press, 2016.

Hagan, William T. "Kiowas, Comanches, and Cattlemen, 1867–1906: A Case Study of the Failure of U.S. Reservation Policy." *Pacific Historical Review* 40, no. 3 (1971): 333–55.

——. "Private Property, the Indian's Door to Civilization." *Ethnohistory* 3, no. 2 (1956): 126–37.

Haley, Andrew P. *Turning the Tables: Restaurants and the Rise of the American Middle Class, 1880–1920*. Chapel Hill, NC: University of North Carolina Press, 2011.

Haley, James Evetts. "Texas Fever and the Winchester Quarantine." *Panhandle-Plains Historical Review* 8 (1935): 37–53.

Haley, James L. *The Buffalo War: The History of the Red River Indians Uprising of 1874*. Norman, OK: University of Oklahoma Press, 1976.

Hämäläinen, Pekka. *The Comanche Empire*. New Haven, CT: Yale University Press, 2009.

——. "The Western Comanche Trade Center: Rethinking the Plains Indian Trade System." *Western Historical Quarterly* 29, no. 4 (1998): 485–513.

Hamilton, Shane. "Agribusiness, the Family Farm, and the Politics of Technological Determinism in the Post–World War II United States." *Technology and Culture* 55, no. 3 (2014): 560–90.

——. *Trucking Country: The Road to America's Wal-Mart Economy*. Princeton, NJ: Princeton University Press, 2008.

Hanner, John. "Government Response to the Buffalo Hide Trade, 1871–1883." *Journal of Law and Economics* 24, no. 2 (1981): 239–71.

Hanson, Simon Gabriel. *Argentine Meat and the British Market: Chapters in the History of the Argentine Meat Industry*. Stanford, CA: Stanford University Press, 1938.

Hartog, Hendrik. "Pigs and Positivism." *Wisconsin Law Review* 1985, no. 4 (1985): 899–935.

Hauter, Wenonah. *Foodopoly: The Battle over the Future of Food and Farming in America*. New York: New Press, 2012.

Havins, T. R. "Texas Fever." *Southwestern Historical Quarterly* 52, no. 2 (1948): 147–62.

Hazlett, O. James. "Chaos and Conspiracy: The Kansas City Livestock Trade." *Kansas History* 15, no. 2 (1992): 126–44.

Henlein, Paul Charles. *Cattle Kingdom in the Ohio Valley, 1783–1860*. Lexington, KY: University of Kentucky Press, 1959.

Hoganson, Kristin. "Meat in the Middle: Converging Borderlands in the U.S. Midwest, 1865–1900." *Journal of American History* 98, no. 4 (2012): 1025–51.

Hornbeck, Richard. "Barbed Wire: Property Rights and Agricultural Development." *Quarterly Journal of Economics* 125, no. 2 (2010): 767–810.

Horowitz, Roger. *Negro and White, Unite and Fight!: A Social History of Industrial Unionism in Meatpacking, 1930–90*. Champaign, IL: University of Illinois Press, 1997.

——. *Putting Meat on the American Table: Taste, Technology, Transformation*. Baltimore, MD: Johns Hopkins University Press, 2005.

Howe, Daniel Walker. *What Hath God Wrought: The Transformation of America, 1815–1848*. Oxford History of the United States. Oxford: Oxford University Press, 2008.

Hyman, Paula E. "Immigrant Women and Consumer Protest: The New York City Kosher Meat Boycott of 1902," *American Jewish History* 70, no. 1 (1980): 91–105.

Igler, David. *Industrial Cowboys Miller and Lux and the Transformation of the Far West, 1850–1920*. Berkeley, CA: University of California Press, 2001.

Isenberg, Andrew C. *The Destruction of the Bison: An Environmental History, 1750–1920*. Cambridge, UK: Cambridge University Press, 2001.

Iverson, Peter. *When Indians Became Cowboys: Native Peoples and Cattle Ranching in the American West*. Norman, OK: University of Oklahoma Press, 1997.

Jablow, Joseph. *The Cheyenne in Plains Indian Trade Relations, 1795–1840*. Lincoln, NE: University of Nebraska Press, 1950.

Jacoby, Karl. *Crimes against Nature: Squatters, Poachers, Thieves, and the Hidden History of American Conservation*. Berkeley, CA: University of California Press, 2001.

Jager, Ronald B. "The Chisholm Trail's Mountain of Words." *Southwestern Historical Quarterly* 71, no. 1 (1967): 61–68.

Johnson, Walter. *River of Dark Dreams: Slavery and Empire in the Cotton Kingdom*. Cambridge, MA: Belknap, 2013.

Jordan, Terry G. *North American Cattle-Ranching Frontiers: Origins, Diffusion, and Differentiation*. Albuquerque: University of New Mexico Press, 2000.

Jørgensen, Dolly. "Running Amuck? Urban Swine Management in Late Medieval England." *Agricultural History* 87, no. 4 (2013): 429–51.

Kahneman, Daniel. *Thinking, Fast and Slow*. London: Penguin, 2012.

Kelman, Ari. *A Misplaced Massacre: Struggling over the Memory of Sand Creek*. Cambridge, MA: Harvard University Press, 2015.

Kurlansky, Mark. *The Food of a Younger Land: A Portrait of American Food—before the National Highway System, before Chain Restaurants, and before Frozen Food, When the Nation's Food Was Seasonal, Regional, and Traditional—from the Lost WPA Files*. New York: Riverhead Books, 2009.

Lause, Mark. *The Great Cowboy Strike: Bullets, Ballots and Class Conflicts in the American West*. London: Verso, 2018.

Law, Marc T., and Gary D. Libecap. "The Determinants of Progressive Era Reform: The Pure Food and Drugs Act of 1906." NBER no. 1094. Cambridge, MA: National Bureau of Economic Research, 2004.

LeCain, Timothy. *The Matter of History: How Things Create the Past*. New York: Cambridge University Press, 2017.

Lecompte, Janet. *Pueblo, Hardscrabble, Greenhorn: Society on the High Plains, 1832–1856*. Norman, OK: University of Oklahoma Press, 1978.

Leonard, Carol, and Isidore Walliman. "Prostitution and Changing Morality in the Frontier Cattle Towns of Kansas." *Kansas History* 2, no. 1 (1979): 34–53.

Leonard, Christopher. *The Meat Racket: The Secret Takeover of America's Food Business.* New York: Simon and Schuster, 2015.

Letwin, William. *Law and Economic Policy in America: The Evolution of the Sherman Antitrust Act.* Chicago: University of Chicago Press, 1956.

Levenstein, Harvey. *Revolution at the Table: The Transformation of the American Diet.* Berkeley, CA: University of California Press, 2003.

Libecap, Gary D. "The Rise of the Chicago Packers and the Origins of Meat Inspection and Antitrust." Working paper. National Bureau of Economic Research, September 1991. doi:10.3386/h0029.

Loftus, R. T., D. E. MacHugh, D. G. Bradley, P. M. Sharp, and P. Cunningham. "Evidence for Two Independent Domestications of Cattle." *Proceedings of the National Academy of Sciences of the USA* 91, no. 7 (1994): 2757–61.

Lomax, John A. "Half-Million Dollar Song: Origin of 'Home on the Range.'" *Southwest Review* 31, no. 1 (1945): 1–8.

Love, Clara M. "History of the Cattle Industry in the Southwest." *Southwestern Historical Quarterly* 19, no. 4 (1916): 370–99.

Lynn-Sherow, Bonnie. *Red Earth: Race and Agriculture in Oklahoma Territory* Lawrence, KS: University Press of Kansas, 2004.

Madley, Benjamin. *An American Genocide: The United States and the California Indian Catastrophe, 1846–1873.* New Haven, CT: Yale University Press, 2017.

———. "California's Yuki Indians: Defining Genocide in Native American History." *Western Historical Quarterly* 39, no. 3 (2008): 303–32.

Maret, Elizabeth. *Women of the Range: Women's Roles in the Texas Beef Cattle Industry.* College Station, TX: Texas A&M University Press, 1993.

Massey, Sara R. *Black Cowboys of Texas.* College Station, TX: Texas A&M University Press, 2000.

McCurdy, Charles W. "American Law and the Marketing Structure of the Large Corporation, 1875–1890." *Journal of Economic History* 38, no. 3 (1978): 631–49.

McFerrin, Randy, and Douglas Wills. "High Noon on the Western Range: A Property Rights Analysis of the Johnson County War." *Journal of Economic History* 67, no. 1 (2007): 69–92.

———. "Searching for the Big Die-off: An Event Study of 19th Century Cattle Markets." *Essays in Economic and Business History* 31 (2013): 33–52.

———. "Who Said the Ranges Were Overstocked?" Working paper, 2006.

McTavish, Emily Jane, Jared E. Decker, Robert D. Schnabel, Jeremy F. Taylor, and David M. Hillis. "New World Cattle Show Ancestry from Multiple Independent Domestication Events." *Proceedings of the National Academy of Sciences of the USA* 110, no. 15 (2013): E1398–406.

McWilliams, Mark. "Conspicuous Consumption: Howells, James, and the Gilded Age Restaurant." In *Culinary Aesthetics and Practices in Nineteenth-Century American Literature*, edited by Monika Elbert and Marie Drews, 35–52. New York: Palgrave Macmillan US, 2009.

Mechem, Kirke. "Home on the Range." *Kansas Historical Quarterly* 17, no. 4 (1949): 11–40.

Mellars, Paul. "Fire Ecology, Animal Populations and Man: A Study of Some Ecological Relationships in Prehistory." *Proceedings of the Prehistoric Society* 42 (1976): 15–45.

Miller, Darlis A. "Civilians and Military Supply in the Southwest." *Journal of Arizona History* 23, no. 2 (1982): 115–38.

Mitchell, John E., and Richard H. Hart. "Winter of 1886–87: The Death Knell of Open Range." *Rangelands* 9, no. 1 (1987): 3–8.

Mookerjee, R. N. "Muckraking and Fame: *The Jungle*," in *Modern Critical Interpretations: Upton Sinclair's "The Jungle,"* ed. Harold Bloom, 69–88. New York: Chelsea House, 2001.

Moore, Jacqueline M. *Cow Boys and Cattle Men: Class and Masculinities on the Texas Frontier, 1865–1900*. New York: New York University Press, 2010.

Moore, Jason W. *Capitalism in the Web of Life: Ecology and the Accumulation of Capital*. New York: Verso, 2015.

———. "The Modern World-System as Environmental History? Ecology and the Rise of Capitalism." *Theory and Society* 32, no. 3 (2003): 307–77.

Morris, Ralph C. "The Notion of a Great American Desert East of the Rockies." *Mississippi Valley Historical Review* 13, no. 2 (1926): 190–200.

Mullen, Patrick B. "The Dilemma of Representation in Folklore Studies: The Case of Henry Truvillion and John Lomax." *Journal of Folklore Research* 37, no. 2/3 (2000): 155–74.

National Bureau of Economic Research. "Wholesale Price of Cattle for Chicago, IL." *FRED*, Federal Reserve Bank of St. Louis, Economic Data. Updated August 16, 2012. https://fred.stlouisfed.org/series/M04007US16980M287NNBR.

Nibert, David A. *Animal Oppression and Human Violence: Domesecration, Capitalism, and Global Conflict*. New York: Columbia University Press, 2013.

Olmstead, Alan L., and Paul W. Rohde. *Arresting Contagion: Science, Policy, and Conflicts over Animal Disease Control*. Cambridge, MA: Harvard University Press, 2015.

Olson, K. C. "Regulation of the Livestock Trade." *Rangelands* 23, no. 5 (2001): 17–21.

Osgood, Ernest Staples. *The Day of the Cattleman*. Minneapolis, MN: University of Minnesota Press, 1929.

Ostler, Jeffrey. *The Plains Sioux and U.S. Colonialism from Lewis and Clark to Wounded Knee*. Cambridge, UK: Cambridge University Press, 2004.

Pachirat, Timothy. *Every Twelve Seconds: Industrialized Slaughter and the Politics of Sight*. New Haven, CT: Yale University Press, 2013.

Pacyga, Dominic A. *Slaughterhouse: Chicago's Union Stock Yard and the World It Made.* Chicago: University of Chicago Press, 2015.

Painter, Nell Irvin. *Standing at Armageddon: The United States, 1877–1919.* New York: W. W. Norton, 1987.

Pate, J'Nell L. *America's Historic Stockyards: Livestock Hotels.* Fort Worth, TX: Texas Christian University Press, 2005.

Paxson, Frederic L. "Review of *The American Livestock and Meat Industry* by Rudolf Alexander Clemen." *American Historical Review* 29, no. 2 (1924): 359–61.

Paxson, Heather. *The Life of Cheese: Crafting Food and Value in America.* Berkeley, CA: University of California Press, 2012.

Peck, Gunther. "The Nature of Labor: Fault Lines and Common Ground in Environmental and Labor History." *Environmental History* 11, no. 2 (2006): 212–38.

Perren, Richard. *Taste, Trade and Technology: The Development of the International Meat Industry since 1840.* Aldershot, UK: Ashgate, 2006.

Pollan, Michael. *The Omnivore's Dilemma: A Natural History of Four Meals.* New York: Penguin, 2006.

Porterfield, Nolan. *Last Cavalier: The Life and Times of John A. Lomax, 1867–1948.* Urbana, IL: University of Illinois Press, 2001.

Prucha, Francis Paul. *The Great Father: The United States Government and the American Indians.* Lincoln, NE: University of Nebraska Press, 1984.

Pyne, Stephen. *Fire: A Brief History.* Seattle: University of Washington Press, 2001.

———. *Fire in America: A Cultural History of Wildland and Rural Fire.* Seattle: University of Washington Press, 1997.

Raish, Carol, and Alice M. McSweeney. *Economic, Social, and Cultural Aspects of Livestock Ranching on Española and Canjilon Ranger Districts of the Santa Fe and Carson National Forests: A Pilot Study.* Fort Collins, CO: US Department of Agriculture Publications Division, 2003.

Rand, Jacki Thompson. *Kiowa Humanity and the Invasion of the State.* Lincoln, NE: University of Nebraska Press, 2008.

Rees, Jonathan. *Refrigeration Nation: A History of Ice, Appliances, and Enterprise in America.* Baltimore, MD: Johns Hopkins University Press, 2013.

Reilly, Nancy Hopkins. *Georgia O'Keeffe, A Private Friendship, Part 1: "Walking the Sun Prairie Land."* Santa Fe NM: Sunstone, 2007.

Remus, Emily A. "Tippling Ladies and the Making of Consumer Culture: Gender and Public Space in Fin-de-Siècle Chicago." *Journal of American History* 101, no. 3 (2014): 751–77.

Richardson, Heather Cox. *West from Appomattox: The Reconstruction of America after the Civil War.* New Haven, CT: Yale University Press, 2008.

Rippy, J. Fred. "British Investments in Texas Lands and Livestock." *Southwestern Historical Quarterly* 58, no. 3 (1955): 331–41.

Rogers, Ben. *Beef and Liberty*. New York: Vintage, 2004.

Rosenberg, Charles E. "The Place of George M. Beard in Nineteenth-Century Psychiatry." *Bulletin of the History of Medicine* 36, no. 3 (1962): 245–59.

Rosenberg, Gabriel N. "A Race Suicide among the Hogs: The Biopolitics of Pork in the United States, 1865–1930." *American Quarterly* 68, no. 1 (2016): 49–73.

Rothschild, Emma. "Social Security and Laissez Faire in Eighteenth-Century Political Economy." *Population and Development Review* 21, no. 4 (1995): 711–44.

Sabol, Steven. "Comparing American and Russian Internal Colonization: The 'Touch of Civilisation' on the Sioux and Kazakhs." *Western Historical Quarterly* 43, no. 1 (2012): 29–51.

Sanderson, Nathan B. " 'We Were All Trespassers': George Edward Lemmon, Anglo-American Cattle Ranching, and the Great Sioux Reservation." *Agricultural History* 85, no. 1 (2011): 50–71.

Santlofer, Joy. *Food City: Four Centuries of Food-Making in New York*. New York: W. W. Norton, 2016.

Savage, William W. *The Cherokee Strip Live Stock Association: Federal Regulation and the Cattleman's Last Frontier*. Norman, OK: University of Oklahoma Press, 1990.

Sayre, Nathan F. *The Politics of Scale: A History of Rangeland Science*. Chicago: University of Chicago Press, 2017.

Sayre, Nathan F., and M. Fernandez-Gimenez. "The Genesis of Range Science, with Implications for Current Development Policies." *Rangelands in the New Millennium: Proceedings of the VIIth International Rangeland Congress, Durban, South Africa* 26 (2003): 1976–85.

Schlosser, Eric. *Fast Food Nation: The Dark Side of the All-American Meal*. Boston, MA: Mariner Books/Houghton Mifflin Harcourt, 2012.

Schmidt, James D. *Industrial Violence and the Legal Origins of Child Labor*. New York: Cambridge University Press, 2010.

Schultz, J. L. *Sociocultural Factors in Financial Management Strategies of Western Livestock Producers*. Washington, DC: US Department of Agriculture, 1970.

Schultz, Marvin. "Anatomy of a Buffalo Hunt: Hide Crews on the Conchos in Texas, 1874–1879." *Arizona and the West* 28, no. 2 (1986): 141–54.

Scott, James C. *Seeing like a State: How Certain Schemes to Improve the Human Condition Have Failed*. New Haven, CT: Yale University Press, 1999.

Sellers, Charles. *The Market Revolution: Jacksonian America 1815–1846*. Oxford: Oxford University Press, 1994.

Sheffy, Lester Fields. *The Francklyn Land & Cattle Company: A Panhandle Enterprise, 1882–1957*. Austin, TX: University of Texas Press, 1963.

Sherow, James Earl. *The Chisholm Trail: Joseph McCoy's Great Gamble*. Norman, OK: University of Oklahoma Press, 2018.

————. *The Grasslands of the United States: An Environmental History*. Santa Barbara, CA: ABC-CLIO, 2007.

————. "Workings of the Geodialectic: High Plains Indians and Their Horses in the Region of the Arkansas River Valley, 1800–1870." *Environmental History Review* 16, no. 2 (1992): 61–84.

Sim, David. "The Peace Policy of Ulysses S. Grant." *American Nineteenth Century History* 9, no. 3 (2008): 241–68.

Simpson, Peter K. "The Social Side of the Cattle Industry." *Agricultural History* 49, no. 1 (1975): 39–50.

Skaggs, Jimmy M. *The Cattle-Trailing Industry: Between Supply and Demand, 1866–1890*. Norman, OK: University of Oklahoma Press, 1991.

————. *Prime Cut: Livestock Raising and Meatpacking in the United States, 1607–1983*. College Station, TX: Texas A&M University Press, 1986.

Skogen, Larry C. *Indian Depredation Claims, 1796–1920*. Norman, OK: University of Oklahoma Press, 1996.

Slotkin, Richard. *The Fatal Environment: The Myth of the Frontier in the Age of Industrialization, 1800–1890*. Norman, OK: University of Oklahoma Press, 1998.

————. *Regeneration through Violence: The Mythology of the American Frontier, 1600–1860*. Norman, OK: University of Oklahoma Press, 2000.

Slowik, Michael. "Capturing the American Past: The Cowboy Song and the Archive." *Journal of American Culture* 35, no. 3 (2012): 207–18.

Sluyter, Andrew. *Black Ranching Frontiers: African Cattle Herders of the Atlantic World, 1500–1900*. New Haven, CT: Yale University Press, 2012.

Smalley, Andrea L. *Wild by Nature*. Baltimore, MD: Johns Hopkins University Press, 2017.

Smith, Adam. *The Wealth of Nations*. Edited by Edwin Cannan. New York: Modern Library, 1994.

Smits, David D. "The Frontier Army and the Destruction of the Buffalo: 1865–1883." *Western Historical Quarterly* 25, no. 3 (1994): 313–38.

Soluri, John. *Banana Cultures: Agriculture, Consumption, and Environmental Change in Honduras and the United States*. Austin, TX: University of Texas Press, 2005.

Specht, Joshua. " 'For the Future in the Distance': Cattle Trailing, Social Conflict, and the Development of Ellsworth, Kansas." *Kansas History: A Journal of the Southern Plains* 40, no. 2 (2017): 104–19.

————. "The Rise, Fall, and Rebirth of the Texas Longhorn: An Evolutionary History." *Environmental History* 21, no. 2 (2016): 343–63.

Streeter, F. B. "Ellsworth as a Texas Cattle Market." *Kansas Historical Quarterly* 4, no. 4 (1935): 388–98.

Strom, Claire. *Making Catfish Bait out of Government Boys: The Fight against Cattle Ticks and the Transformation of the Yeoman South*. Athens, GA: University of Georgia Press, 2010.

———. "Texas Fever and the Dispossession of the Southern Yeoman Farmer." *Journal of Southern History* 66, no. 1 (2000): 49–74.

Taylor, M. Scott. "Buffalo Hunt: International Trade and the Virtual Extinction of the North American Bison." *American Economic Review* 101, no. 7 (2011): 3162–95.

Thompson, E. P. "The Moral Economy of the English Crowd in the Eighteenth Century." *Past and Present* 50 (1971): 76–136.

Todd, Matthew Ryan. "Now May Be Heard a Discouraging Word." MA thesis, University of Saskatchewan, 2009.

Tsing, Anna. "Supply Chains and the Human Condition." *Rethinking Marxism* 21, no. 2 (2009): 148–76.

Unrau, William E. *White Man's Wicked Water: The Alcohol Trade and Prohibition in Indian Country, 1802–1892*. Lawrence, KS: University Press of Kansas, 1996.

Vester, Katharina. "Regime Change: Gender, Class, and the Invention of Dieting in Post-Bellum America." *Journal of Social History* 44, no. 1 (2010): 39–70.

———. *A Taste of Power: Food and American Identities*. Oakland, CA: University of California Press, 2015.

Vitebsky, Piers. *The Reindeer People: Living with Animals and Spirits in Siberia*. Boston, MA: Houghton Mifflin Harcourt, 2005.

Wade, Louise Carroll. *Chicago's Pride: The Stockyards, Packingtown, and Environs in the Nineteenth Century*. Urbana, IL: University of Illinois Press, 1987.

———. "Hell Hath No Fury like a General Scorned: Nelson A. Miles, the Pullman Strike, and the Beef Scandal of 1898." *Illinois Historical Journal* 79, no. 3 (1986): 162–84.

Walker, Don D. *Clio's Cowboys: Studies in the Historiography of the Cattle Trade*. Lincoln, NE: University of Nebraska Press, 1981.

Walsh, Margaret. *The Rise of the Midwestern Meat Packing Industry*. Lexington, KY: University Press of Kentucky, 1982.

Warren, Wilson J. *Tied to the Great Packing Machine: The Midwest and Meatpacking*. Iowa City: University of Iowa Press, 2006.

Webb, Walter Prescott. *The Great Plains*. Lincoln, NE: University of Nebraska Press, 1981.

West, Elliott. *The Contested Plains: Indians, Goldseekers, and the Rush to Colorado*. Lawrence, KS: University Press of Kansas, 1998.

———. *The Way to the West: Essays on the Central Plains*. Albuquerque NM: University of New Mexico Press, 1995.

West, G. Derek. "The Battle of Adobe Walls (1874)." *Panhandle-Plains Historical Review* 36 (1963): 1–36.

Wheeler, David L. "The Blizzard of 1886 and Its Effect on the Range Cattle Industry in the Southern Plains." *Southwestern Historical Quarterly* 94, no. 3 (1991): 415–34.

White, John H. Jr. *The Great Yellow Fleet : A History of American Railroad Refrigerator Cars*. San Marino, CA: Golden West Books, 1986.

——. "Riding in Style: Palace Cars for the Cattle Trade." *Technology and Culture* 31, no. 2 (1990): 265–70.

White, Richard. "Information, Markets, and Corruption: Transcontinental Railroads in the Gilded Age." *Journal of American History* 90, no. 1 (2003): 19–43.

——. *"It's Your Misfortune and None of My Own": A New History of the American West*. Norman, OK: University of Oklahoma Press, 1991.

——. *Railroaded: The Transcontinentals and the Making of Modern America*. New York: W. W. Norton, 2011.

——. *The Roots of Dependency: Subsistence, Environment, and Social Change among the Choctaws, Pawnees, and Navajos*. Lincoln, NE: University of Nebraska Press, 1988.

Wilcox, Robert W. *Cattle in the Backlands: Mato Grosso and the Evolution of Ranching in the Brazilian Tropics*. Austin, TX: University of Texas Press, 2017.

Wilson, Bee. *Swindled: The Dark History of Food Fraud, from Poisoned Candy to Counterfeit Coffee*. Princeton, NJ: Princeton University Press, 2008.

Wise, Michael D. *Producing Predators: Wolves, Work, and Conquest in the Northern Rockies*. Lincoln, NE: University of Nebraska Press, 2016.

Wolf, Robb. *The Paleo Solution: The Original Human Diet*. Las Vegas NV: Victory Belt, 2010.

Woods, Rebecca J. H. *The Herds Shot Round the World: Native Breeds and the British Empire, 1800–1900*. Chapel Hill, NC: University of North Carolina Press, 2017.

Wooster, Robert. *Frontier Crossroads: Fort Davis and the West*. College Station, TX: Texas A&M University Press, 2005.

Worcester, Donald E. *The Chisholm Trail: High Road of the Cattle Kingdom*. Lincoln, NE: University of Nebraska Press, 1980.

Yeager, Mary. *Competition and Regulation: The Development of Oligopoly in the Meat Packing Industry*. Greenwich, CT: JAI Press, 1981.

Yeager Kujovich, Mary. "The Refrigerator Car and the Growth of the American Dressed Beef Industry." *Business History Review* 44, no. 4 (1970): 460–82.

Young, James Harvey. "The Pig that Fell into the Privy: Upton Sinclair's *The Jungle* and the Meat Inspection Amendments of 1906." *Bulletin of the History of Medicine* 59, no. 4 (1985): 467–80.

Zeide, Anna. *Canned: The Rise and Fall of Consumer Confidence in the American Food Industry*. Oakland, CA: University of California Press, 2018.

INDEX

A NOTE ON THE TYPE

This book has been composed in Arno, an Old-style serif typeface in the classic Venetian tradition, designed by Robert Slimbach at Adobe.